INQUIRY
AND
EDUCATION

SUNY series, The Philosophy of Education

Philip L. Smith, editor

INQUIRY
AND
EDUCATION

John Dewey and
the Quest for Democracy

JAMES SCOTT JOHNSTON

STATE UNIVERSITY OF NEW YORK PRESS

Published by
State University of New York Press, Albany

For information, address State University of New York Press,
194 Washington Avenue, Suite 305, Albany, NY 12210–2384

Production by Dana Foote
Marketing by Michael Campochiaro

Library of Congress Cataloging-in-Publication Data

Johnston, James Scott.
    Inquiry and education : John Dewey and the quest for democracy / James Scott
Johnston.
        p.   cm. — (SUNY series in philosophy of education)
    Includes bibliographical references and index.
    ISBN 0–7914–6723–6 (hardcover : alk. paper) — ISBN 0–7914–6724–4
(pbk. : alk. paper)   1. Dewey, John, 1859–1952.   2. Education—Philosophy.
I. Title. II. Series.
LB875.D5J65   2006
370′.1—dc22
                                                                2005020657

ISBN-13: 978-0-7914-6723-7 (hardcover : alk. paper)
ISBN-13: 978-0-7914-6724-4 (pbk. : alk. paper)

10 9 8 7 6 5 4 3 2 1

CONTENTS

PREFACE

This work combines Dewey's insights on science, scientific method, and experience with his equal insights on community, democracy, and education. The aim here is to read Dewey anew and to develop from his varied interests and topics, an orderly overview of how it is that these can all fit together and function to solve "the problems of men." Central to this task is the reinstatement of education in the discussion of Dewey's aims and notions of growth, community, and democracy: an institution that Dewey, at one point in his career claimed was coeval with philosophy.

Sadly, most philosophers that discuss Dewey do so with attention to his logical, epistemological, scientific, experiential, or democratic writings but neglect his educational writings. There are of course, exceptions to this. Recently, Raymond Boisvert has written an admirable little volume on understanding Dewey's thought, and Dewey's role in and with education receives an entire chapter. But these exceptions not only prove the rule, they fall far short of actually making a case for how education is to be integrated into Dewey's overall thinking and, particularly, his logical and epistemological, concerns. To my knowledge, this is the first book of its kind to weave education more or less seamlessly into the fabric of Dewey's overall thought.

As well, there is an abundant and ever-growing stock of research on Dewey by educators and philosophers of education that is rarely consulted by philosophers writing on Dewey. This is a mistake. Many of these researchers provide helpful insight into Dewey's thoughts on education. This book brings both philosophers and educators together: leading scholars on Dewey from both fields are abundantly represented here.

This book begins not with what Dewey said; rather with what his critics and supporters have said. I have written the book this way to begin with those points and issues on which Dewey seems weakest. The task is then to evaluate the claims of the critics and supporters and to see what can be made of Dewey's statements in light of these. The point here is to neither criticize nor apologize: it is rather to see what Dewey can and cannot be charged with, and if charged, what can be done to respond to the charges. A central claim that I make throughout the book is that reading Dewey with his thinking on each of inquiry, logic, science, experience, society, and politics as part of a larger point and purpose, requires us to conceive of linkages between each of these, and forces us to consider the import of education as the means to make these points and purposes happen.

The book is admittedly difficult. It does presuppose familiarity with Dewey, and particularly, his most famous texts (*Democracy and Education, Experience and Nature, Art as Experience, The Quest for Certainty*). However, a good primer, such as Raymond Boisvert's, will also do the job handily. This book is primarily for educators familiar with Dewey who want to see a treatment of education in accord with other of Dewey's main themes, as well as philosophers, social theorists, historians, and others interested in Dewey who wish to see Dewey's thinking on education treated as an integral part of Dewey's overall thoughts on various philosophic and political concerns. As well, those who want a good synopsis of Dewey's criticisms—both past and present—and the responses to these will also find much of interest here. Those that are uninterested in the debates, particularly the past debates on Dewey's work, may skip those sections in the chapters that deal with these without penalty. Finally, those that wish to see Dewey's various thoughts on logic, epistemology, metaphysics, society, and politics treated integrally; as linked together in such a fashion that they form a coherent (though not coherentist) philosophic approach to "the problems of men," will also be interested in this work.

ACKNOWLEDGMENTS

I thank the following individuals for their patience and assistance in what has proven to be a long and sometimes perilous journey through the thicket of dissertation development, drafts, reviews, more drafts, and finally, publication. To Walter Feinberg, Ralph Page, Nicolas Burbules, Jeanne Connell, and Larry Hickman. These individuals served on my dissertation committee and in so doing, helped me get this project off on the right footing. To Tim Simpson, who was helpful in reading initial drafts; to the reviewers of the manuscript at the State University of New York Press for their comments and concerns; to Lisa Chesnel at the State University of New York Press, who worked patiently with me while awaiting the manuscript's acceptance, to Kay Butler, copyeditor for the State University of New York Press, who had the onerous task of editing the manuscript, and to Phil Smith of Ohio State University, who encouraged me to submit the manuscript in the first place.

To those people closest to me; Carol, my loving wife, who always said that I could do it, Frank, my wonderful son, who patiently put up with me working when I could have (and probably should have) spent my time with him. And to Charlotte, my friend; you have no idea how wonderful an inspiration you are!

Finally, I wish to dedicate this book to the memory of my father, Lawrence James Johnston, who passed away October 1999. He is remembered.

I
INTRODUCTION

When it is understood that philosophic thinking is caught up in
the actual course of events, having the office of guiding them
towards a prosperous issue, problems will abundantly present
themselves. Philosophy will not solve these problems; philosophy
is vision, imagination, reflection—and these functions, apart from
action, modify and hence resolve nothing . . . Philosophy recovers
itself when it ceases to be a device for dealing with the problems of
philosophers and becomes a method, cultivated by philosophers,
for dealing with the problems of men.
> —John Dewey, "The Need for a Recovery of Philosophy"

The Problems with Inquiry

Forty years ago, the eminent Dewey scholars S. Morris Eames and Elizabeth
Ramsden Eames wrote of a long-held concern among critics: either inquiry
must profess to be rigorously scientific, which means that it must embrace the
view that objects exist external to the experience of them, or it must profess to
be thoroughly experiential, which means that all truth and all assertion must
take place within the realm of the mental. Eames and Eames note that this is
the most pressing criticism of Dewey's pragmatic theory of knowledge and of
experience, and the one that demands the utmost attention. Eames and Eames
put the contention this way:

> Dewey's critics seem to have placed his theory of inquiry between the
> horns of several dilemmas. With respect to the situation within which
> inquiry takes place, Dewey must choose between atomistic pluralism of
> unconnected individual situations and holistic unity. With respect to the
> doubtful or indeterminate situation and the satisfying or determinate
> situation, Dewey must choose between subjective idealism or dualistic
> realism. With respect to his treatment of propositions, the choice is be-
> tween extreme rationalism or extreme empiricism. With respect to war-
> ranted assertibility, the alternatives are an idealism in which truth is de-

I

termined within inquiry or a realistic view of truth as conformity to external fact. (Eames and Eames 1962, 326)

Eames and Eames claim that Dewey sees a way out of this impasse and that way is to,

> develop a theory of perception that even his sympathetic critics have had difficulty interpreting. . . . Dewey writes of the construction of common sense and science from the materials of the immediate qualities of experience . . . [but] Again his critics see Dewey as facing a dilemma: if the object . . . causes the perception of it, Dewey is a realist with respect to his theory of perception and must say what the object really is. However, if he refuses this alternative and emphasizes that the kind of object is determined by the needs of inquiry, he has a phenomenalist view of perception. (Eames and Eames 1962, 327–328)[1]

Eames and Eames characterize the dilemma of Dewey having to choose between an inquiry that serves to mirror an external world existing outside of experience, and an inquiry that constructs objects by relating the products of an immediate experience within one. He cannot, the critics claim, have both. Indeed, it is not too bold to say that this, or one or another variant of it, has been a chief criticism of Dewey's theory of inquiry throughout the past century. The variant of this criticism that I will discuss concerns Dewey's relationship to science, and specifically to scientific method/s (what I shall henceforth gather under the umbrella term "scientific inquiry").

It is fashionable to criticize John Dewey for paying too much attention to science and to the hope of a scientific solution to human concerns. Equally, it has become fashionable to defend Dewey by pointing out instances in his work where science is clearly subordinated to other concerns, notably those of experience and art. When critics complain of Dewey's overappreciation for all things scientific, they most often have in mind his supposed allegiance to the methods of science. When supporters complain of the overattention given to the place of science in Dewey's texts, they often respond by singing his anti-scientific praises. These praises are often to the tune of his rhetoric on the primordial nature of experience. The common fear is that viewing inquiry as scientific denies a strong place for imagination, curiosity, and emotion while promoting a techno-rational or means-end, instrumental approach to human problems. The consequences of this, both critics and supporters argue, is that ways of experiencing and of knowing beyond the scientific are denigrated, and experts fascinated with the power of science and scientific inquiry will blindly follow the technological, organizational, and managerial fruits of these, with catastrophic costs for democracy. The solution is to stress the immediacy and qualities had, of an experience that, as immediate, is temporally and ontologically prior to inquiry. But there are, equally, critics who have trouble with the subordination of science and inquiry to experience. For the turn to experience as primordial is evidence, critics say, of a reemergence of metaphysics that Dewey takes pains elsewhere to eschew.

The debate arising out of these criticisms has powerful implications for Dewey's related notions of growth, community, democracy, and education. In fine, if there is confusion or disagreement regarding whether inquiry, as Dewey has conceived of it, does not or should not operate along the lines of science, and inquiry is central to these above aims, are these aims of Dewey's also confused? And if, as Dewey claims, democracy must consist not only of democratic ends but democratic means to these, and inquiry is rigidly scientific and impermeable to changes in the wants and needs of the people as many of his critics suggest, then how can it be said that inquiry is the democratic means to a democratic end? On the other hand, if Dewey is shown to have a nonscientific theory of inquiry, and this is in the service of the having of an experience, does this obviate the problem of rigidity and impermeability? Or does it simply introduce a new one: to wit, an inquiry that is toothless because in the service of the satisfaction of an experience at once arbitrary and capricious: an experience of little aid to social concerns? And if either of these scenarios are the case, how can Dewey's notions of growth, community, democracy, and education, which seem to be predicated upon the flexibility of inquirers to attend to shared problems and solutions, endure? And why, then, should we bother with Dewey? These are the concerns that I claim must be dealt with.

No doubt, Dewey speaks a great deal about inquiry. Indeed, hardly an article or a book penned by Dewey lacks some reference to it. Critics and supporters agree: inquiry is central to Dewey. But with critics and supporters, much time is spent debating just what the model of inquiry is supposed to be. This assumes to a large degree that Dewey's statements on what might be the point, purpose, and ground (if there is one) of inquiry are of a piece with one another. But this would be a hasty conclusion. Given the fact that Dewey spoke at length about inquiry, can the assumption be made that Dewey treats inquiry to a rigorous examination and that the finally emerging product is smooth, polished, precise, and free from contradiction? To judge by the volume of secondary literature devoted to the topic, particularly the literature in education, and to judge from some of Dewey's own statements on the topic, the answer seems to be no.

There seems an uncertainty as to what Dewey means by inquiry, what characteristics are to be included in his notion of inquiry, and what, after all, the aim and purpose of inquiry is to be. Part of the problem may stem from Dewey's own hand. He has been described as a difficult writer. His prose is considered awkward and, indeed, turgid. He is said to be exceedingly redundant in the use of premises and conclusions to support an argument. Robert Westbrook has said of Dewey's text *Experience and Nature* that "some of this opposition [to Dewey's arguments] was the fault of Dewey's prose . . . his language was loose, his definitions slippery, and his arguments often elusive" (Westbrook 1991, 341). A very recent commentator complains that the "dense prose" of this work renders it as "incomplete" and "forbiddingly convoluted," and, believing Dewey's own recognition of this state of affairs, he well understands why the author would, in 1949, remark in a new (unpublished) introduction that if he had to do it over again, he would drop the term "experience" and replace it with "culture" (Dalton 2002, 125).

Perhaps one of the reasons interpreters have such a hard time with Dewey is that Dewey's approach to problems is often to attack them from a variety of angles. Often the context determines the tenor of the argument. If Dewey happens to be writing of physical science or logic in a text, then a scientific or logical solution to the problems at hand is often stressed: likewise with experience, education, and society, in those texts stressing these topics. And when inquiry is invoked or applied, it is an inquiry closely bound to the context of which it is spoken.

This leads the reader into some trouble. Though it may seem eminently reasonable to argue for a particular view of, or application for, science in the context of one text, when this view or application is transposed to another text and context, it seems to function in an awkward or misleading manner. More specifically, Dewey's statements on inquiry with regard to science do not always mesh well with his statements with regard to inquiry in experience and art. Supporters of Dewey, faced with a set of seemingly inconsistent statements, sometimes "choose" a view of inquiry. Often this is to the detriment of another view. Choosing one view over another often solves the critics' or scholars' particular concern, but opens up yet other concerns for those disinclined to that view.[2] Though it is unreasonable to expect all to agree on what Dewey meant by inquiry, it is reasonable to expect that Dewey meant that it was to be, for example, strongly scientific.

What is one to make of all this? I will examine what others have said and will develop and support my own arguments in the following chapters. For now, I will limit myself to a few preliminary observations. One fast and dirty way to come down on the side of inquiry as scientific or not is to lift passages out of Dewey's many works such that the reader cannot gauge the context from the passages and cannot, therefore, make an adequate estimation of the argument. What these passages are and what they claim will be taken up in the following chapters. It should be obvious, though, that this approach to the matter at hand will not do. One is required to go back to the texts and contexts from which the statements are pulled and, after having examined these, only then make an argument as to the purported inconsistencies.

I claim that going back to the texts and contexts from which the arguments arise will provide a response to thwart one criticism of Dewey: the charge that Dewey is of two minds about the aims, purposes, and functions of, inquiry. But this only scratches the surface: those critics and supporters that argue for Dewey as being pro- or con inquiry as scientific and inquiry—whether scientific or experience based—will remain unsatisfied. Of course, scholars do choose sides and claim that one view of inquiry does prevail over another, with certain consequences for science, logic, experience, art, and education in tow. But this cannot mean that these are imperiled thereby. To get to the root of these claims, I shall have to examine various philosophers' and educators' criticisms in close detail.

There are scholars who think of inquiry as found in the natural sciences as the model for all talk of Dewey's inquiry. These scholars often treat Dewey's talk of inquiry in relation to epistemological and logical issues, such as learning theory and the claims to knowledge. And often, these scholars read Dewey (sometimes unwittingly) scientistically or positivistically. To read Dewey scientistically is to claim that he meant for all inquiry to mimic scientific methodology—the sort practiced in high school science classrooms and university research laboratories. In a slightly weaker version, this mimicry might mean a fundamental, though not exhaustive, role for scientific methodology to play in contexts beyond science. This latter version is what Richard Bernstein calls the "positivistic temper" (Bernstein 1992, 330).

To read Dewey positivistically is to read Dewey's inquiry as endorsing the following characteristics:

1) Naturalism: the view that good (natural and social) science embodies the scientific method common to the physical sciences. Scientific method among the various sciences is thoroughgoing in terms of its content and its stages.

2) Operationalism: the view that all theoretical terms must be specified by the operations that measure them.

3) Behaviorism: only explanations that are based on directly observable factors are scientifically adequate.

4) Prediction and Inference: the use of statistics to explore predictability among phenomenal relationships.

5) Logical reductivism: a penchant for logical explanation as opposed to historical, social, or cultural understandings of phenomenon. In cases of strong positivism all empirically observable phenomena are reducible to logico-mathematical propositions. (Kinkaid 1998, 559)

To say a thinker is positivistic or that she endorses one or more of the above positions is often a high insult in present-day academic scholarship. Much of the scorn can be attributed to the fall from academic grace of *logical* positivism after World War II. Succinctly put, logical positivism requires the empirical verifiability of all experimental results and the logical necessity of the propositions involved, together with communicability of results through a realistic language following from logical propositions (Shlick in Ayer, 1950) (Reichenbach in Feigl and Brodbeck, 1953). This most extreme version of positivism drew scorn because it overemphasized the importance of logic and the verifiability of phenomenon, and underemphasized the effect of context and researcher effect. Werner Heisenberg, Albert Einstein, and others criticized this species of positivism from the side of the physical sciences, while Wilfred Sellars, W. V. O. Quine, and Ludwig Wittgenstein did so from the side of philosophy. As well, there was a reaction against positivism in the human sciences, largely mounted from within the disciplines of sociology and psychology, to the effect that it licensed behaviorism and, ultimately, domination and control of peoples through manipulation of rewards and punishments.

The charges that the critics level at Dewey's supposed positivism or scientism are in some measure the charges that Dewey succumbs to one or another variant of what has come to be, with the benefit of Hegelian and postanalytic hindsight, epistemological foundationalism. Some of these charges devolve into species of Quine's two dogmas of either epistemic reductivism or an analytic/synthetic distinction. Other charges devolve into Dewey maintaining a belief in the ultimate translatability of (ostensibly) synonymous terms, or of Sellars's "myth of the given," or of Wittgenstein's polemics against representationalism.[3] To say that Dewey succumbs to one or another of these is to say that Dewey's talk of inquiry is premised on a foundation. What this foundation might be depends in part, of course, on the specific dogma or myth said to be present; but in general, it is that which is precisely *not* subject to change, interpretation, further investigation, and inquiry. In other words, it is the immutable and certain, whether it be an empirical given such as a quale or a primitive, a logical one such as a perfectly translingual and/or translatable term, or a set of fixed logical steps to the solution of problems.

Some examples are in order. To say that Dewey is a foundationalist along the lines that Quine might think is to say that Dewey, in one place or another of his logical theory, privileges a distinction between analytic propositions or statements and synthetic ones. I will come back to this in more detail in chapter 2, but for now I want to simply say that if Dewey were to suggest that there are, residing somewhere in his logic, statements to the effect that all definitions that point to the same logical object or term are meaning-synonymous and, thus, universal (Quine would say, analytic), then he would be not only guilty of making a distinction where a distinction is not found, but of turning to a foundation. Likewise, if he were to suggest that logical objects had some direct or one-to-one correspondence with an object immediately beheld, he would be guilty of reductionism to observables. This reductionism is of course premised on the copy or picture theory of knowledge, wherein to say something is logical is simply to say that it contains the same features as the object immediately beheld. This of course, was a central criticism of Wittgenstein's *Philosophical Investigations* and much of linguistic philosophy after this.

Many current Dewey scholars disagree with those who view Dewey as either positivistic or scientistic, and in doing so, point toward statements in Dewey that challenge this reading of inquiry. Rather than inquiry as wedded to the concerns of science and what they see as its offspring—technology—inquiry, according to these scholars, serves as the means to foment what Dewey has called the "generic traits of existence." Science, if it is a concern at all, is a subordinate one. What really concerns inquiry, they argue, is the satisfaction of one's experiences. As such, these scholars often treat Dewey's talk of inquiry in relation to experiential and aesthetic concerns. The argument is that inquiry is, for Dewey, beholden to experience. As the goal for experience and for social institutions is read as consisting of the manifestation of or assistance toward the having of satisfying traits or qualities of existence (such as symmetry, continuity, coming-to-be and passing-away, rhythm, regularity, and relation), inquiry works to achieve, through the order and control of the environment, a maximum of these traits. The point is to get to the sort of experience in which all generic traits of existence are at a maximum: what Dewey in *Art as Experience* calls an aesthetic, consummatory experience.

For these critics and sympathizers of Dewey, inquiry functions as a means to (re) produce further and more satisfying experiences. The way inquiry (and its avatars, reflection, cognition, thought, and meaning) works in relation to experience is to relate the qualities of experiences had to each other. More accurately, it orders objects gained through the transaction of person and environment such that these have meaning. In this way habits are developed: organic complexes of transactional "products" that serve, when made routine, as a ready means to increase the likelihood and satisfaction of the generic traits of existence. This suggests that a two-level, or stage theory of experience and inquiry is in operation: the first being immediate experience—the qualities immediately had in an experience undergone—the second being relation, cognition, thought, meanings; in fine, inquiry. In this way, inquiry emerges as supervenient on immediate experiences, and the qualities of an experience had the *fons et origo* of inquiry.

This view obviously has problems of its own to contend with. For example, if we think of the criticisms of Wilfred Sellars in his characterization of what counts as the given in traditional accounts of empiricism, what these Dewey scholars put forth as an alternative reading to the positivistic comes dangerously close to Sellars's notion of the myth of the given. The idea that there are quales, qualities, traits, immediate wholes, or some roughly synonymous "having" existing in and responsible for, all experiences, may well be to say that there are "givens" that exist as foundations for further knowledge or as postulates to fill in the gaps in knowledge. Sellars, of course, rejects these givens as question-begging claims for a foundation that cannot be known. I will have more to say about this criticism of immediate experience in chapter 3.

What seem to get lost in this debate are the *aims* of inquiry. What I mean is that inquiry as Dewey himself puts it, its claims to knowledge and its attention to aesthetic and experiential concerns notwithstanding, is about the capacity to solve "the problems of men." For Dewey, these are problems at once personal, interpersonal, community, and society-wide. Inquiry, for Dewey, is a tool that is brought to bear on the problems at hand such that individual growth and community relations can flourish. The task is nicely stated by Dewey in *Democracy and Education*, wherein he argues that the ultimate achievement of inquiry is its function as a tool to foster increasingly democratic living (Dewey [1916] 1984, 83).

In the zeal to pinpoint the supposed model of inquiry, scholars sometimes lose sight of this purpose: to serve in the investigation and solution to the problems of men. Dewey himself sometimes makes this an easy task. As I maintain, Dewey's many statements on inquiry seem not always to fit easily together. The tendency to have Dewey come down on the side of science, or the side of experience, for example, is but one consequence of this unhappy state of affairs. As I have said, critics, often paying attention to one set of statements over another, conclude that Dewey is either too scientistic or not scientistic enough. Inquiry becomes a contested turf, one on which the rights of ownership of Dewey is fought. This contest, I argue, is the end result of a fruitless hunt for a supposed model, a model that would ostensibly reveal, once and for all, the function, point, and purpose of inquiry.

I believe that Dewey scholarship needs to rethink this very debate. I believe that the hunt for *the* model of inquiry, a model that once and for all captures the traits, tempers, tools, and techniques that are inclusive of inquiry, is a vain pursuit and ought to be given up. This is so not because I believe that there is not a point and purpose to inquiry: far from it. Rather, I argue that, as a result of searching for a model of inquiry, scholars are in fact missing that point and purpose. To be precise, I believe that the clue to the discovery of the point and purpose of inquiry is to be found in its interconnectedness with the situations in which it is used, and in its capacity to serve Dewey's educational and philosophical aims; that is, growth, community, and democracy. And further, I believe that epistemological, logical, experiential, and aesthetic concerns, though not by themselves inclusive of inquiry, are all deserving of important places in inquiry, inasmuch as I believe that without attention to these concerns, we (as a community) cannot achieve what it is we desire. I call this trait of sensitivity to the contexts in which inquiry is used, "context bound" and the ability of inquiry to adjust itself accordingly, "self-correction." My aim in this work is to read Dewey as having suggested that inquiry has just these traits and that it is of a piece not only with other traits of inquiry but with the larger aims of an education for democratic living. To say so is not only to say that Dewey's theory of inquiry exists without foundations, but it is to say that "empirical knowledge, like its sophisticated extension, science, is rational, not because it has a foundation but because it is a self-correcting enterprise which can put any claim in jeopardy, though not all at once" (Sellars [1956] 1997, 79).

Not only is inquiry to be read as (though not exhausted by) context bound and self-correcting, the linkages between it and Dewey's other aims must be displayed. If inquiry is seen as detached from these, or as rigid and slavish in its relationship to science or to experience, its worth to these aims will be imperiled, and these aims, torn from the soil by which they receive sustenance, will wither and die. Dewey spoke often of his commitment to experience and to growth. As voluminous as his statements on inquiry and science are, they are matched by his statements on experience and growth. Often the connection between inquiry, on the one hand, and experience and growth (for Dewey, as I shall show, made growth the *terminus ad quem* of an experience) is blurred owing to the context that Dewey is writing in, whether scientific or experiential. But this is not to suggest that the connection is somehow weak. Inquiry must presuppose experience and growth, as the increase in the fund of *meaningful*, as well as satisfying, experiences.[4]

Growth in turn requires community; a conjoint association of peoples bound together by shared experiences and common problems, to flourish. Community, the notion that Dewey uses to capture this association, presupposes for its very vitality the ability of the peoples therein to come to agreement on a topic of mutual concern. This agreement, Dewey claims, can only be had voluntarily, and not on the outcome of authoritarian means. The one way left for this to come about is through shared inquiry. It is through shared inquiry that problems can be identified, methods to their solution proffered, and results evaluated that are acceptable to all involved. But the ability for the community to engage in inquiry presupposes the presence of the skills, habits, and attitudes of inquiry.

Community in turn insists upon education: a means for the development of inquiry by the child, and a community in which shared experiences, leading to shared investigations of and solutions to the problems of men can occur. Education in the formal sense—that is, schooling—is the best means, Dewey argues, for the mass of children to learn the attitudes, habits, and skills of inquiry. As such, education, particularly of the formal variety, becomes a central concern in any attempt to expand the capacity of the populace to experience, share, inquire into, and work to resolve problems of living.

Finally, I argue that democracy, as the formalization of institutions through communicative and legislative means, cements this community. I construe democracy for the purposes of my project as the legitimation of the means to inquire. Perhaps this is the most controversial point, particularly as several Dewey scholars insist that democracy is built into the having of an experience.[5] I have more to say about this in chapter 5, though I will say at this point that I do not think my focus on one facet of democracy is at all reductive, as long as it is borne in mind that this is for the purposes of capturing the exquisite linkage between community means, as formalized, and Dewey's other aims. For all of inquiry, growth, community, and democracy work together: this notion is best captured by the notion of *boundedness*, in which each derives from, and leads to, the other.

Conceiving of inquiry as context bound, self-correcting, and in a close relationship with growth, community, and democracy is, I claim, the best way to avoid the mutually contradictory readings of Dewey as scientistic or positivistic, on the one hand, and what I will henceforth call "aestheticized" on the other. It functions equally to preserve what I believe is inquiry's chief task— the necessary means to the realization of growth, community, and democracy. But this concern can seem to some to be merely of scholarly interest. There is equally a practical side, an educational side, to this conception. I claim that if inquiry is to work toward a solution to the problems of men, not only must it keep close to the aims of growth, community, and democracy, but that this has a strong bearing on the point and purpose of inquiry as used in our schools. This is a point that is often overlooked by Dewey scholars—particularly in the discipline of philosophy—in their various attempts at synthesizing Dewey for the purposes of a unified outlook. Too many introductions and treatises on Dewey's philosophy have been written that treat education as an appendage to Dewey's overall thought; a nice attachment, but superfluous to the functioning of his philosophic or social thinking. As Dewey spent much time and labor on education so, I suggest, should Dewey scholars; and the fact that this is seldom done with the exception of those writing in the field of education betokens a sad ignorance of what is a central concern for Dewey, to wit: the "how" of fostering the habits of inquiry. For education is the means by which inquiry is developed, and therefore one cannot talk of growth, community, or democracy without education at once being invoked. Inquiry that is detached from education will not only not accomplish these aims but may emerge, through its misuse or bastardization in educational institutions, as serving the interests of those inclined to less-than-savory aims, with tragic consequences for our democracy. Clearly, if we as a community are serious about the fostering of these aims, we cannot afford to support an inquiry that is at odds with these aims. This effort is put forth as a contribution to the conversation of how inquiry is to be best utilized in our communities and educational institutions.

Overview

Each chapter is split into four parts. In part 1 of chapter 2, I begin with the debate on the nature of inquiry. I turn to some of Dewey's early critics: philosophers and educators that conceive of Dewey's theory of inquiry as overly scientistic or positivistic, and on this basis, question the feasibility of Dewey's entire project. After this, I turn to some of Dewey's early supporters: philosophers and educators that believe his theory of inquiry can be defended from the critics' charges. If the reader feels somewhat overwhelmed by the various names and disputes discussed in these first sections of each chapter, he or she may omit this section without penalty of confusion with respect to what follows. In part 2, I turn to contemporary critics and apologists of Dewey's theory of inquiry. I demonstrate that many of the criticisms from the early and middle twentieth century have not disappeared: variants of one or another of these continue to surface. I demonstrate that apologists cannot, without further work, defend the position of inquiry as beholden to science. In part 3, I begin to provide some context to this debate by detailing what seems to critics to be ambiguous statements that Dewey himself makes concerning the subject. I claim that it is not enough to take these passages at face value, for these are passages that do seem to be in disagreement with each other. I then examine Dewey's statements on inquiry very closely, paying particular attention to the works *How We Think*, *The Quest for Certainty*, and *Logic: The Theory of Inquiry*, as well as other texts and articles. In part 4, I reread Dewey's theory of inquiry as strongly supporting the traits of context-boundedness and self-correction.[6] I provide what seem to me to be instances of similarity between contemporary epistemological thinking, as outlined in Michael Williams's *Problems of Knowledge*, and Dewey's theory of inquiry.

Chapter 3 deals with the relation of inquiry to Dewey's talk of experience. In part 1, I look at specific early criticisms and apologies of Dewey's talk of experience. In part 2, I do the same with respect to Dewey's contemporary critics and apologists. In these sections, I look at the possibility of reconceiving inquiry along the lines of Dewey sympathizers; that is, as an experiential endeavor. I turn to critics of this reading—philosophers and educators who suggest that a different set of problems emerges when one reads Dewey as privileging an inquiry that is chiefly experiential or, what I shall call in this chapter aesthetic, as opposed to scientistic or positivistic. I also turn to proponents of this reading and lay out their arguments for why it is that conceiving of inquiry as experiential is superior to other conceptions. I conclude that the arguments for the view that inquiry is an experiential affair are, as put by Dewey's sympathizers, unsatisfactory. In part 3, I claim and defend the position that the way out of this impasse is to link the conclusion of the previous chapter—that Dewey should be read as advocating the traits of context-boundedness and self-correction—with Dewey's greatest aim for experience: growth. I concentrate heavily on Dewey's experiential texts in this section: notably *Experience and Nature* and *Art as Experience*, as well as other texts and articles. I discuss growth fully in part 4 and define it as the continuous augmentation of the fund of one's (satisfying) experience and meanings. I look again at Michael Williams's *Problems of Knowledge* and discuss how Dewey anticipates solutions to prevailing problems in the theory of knowledge.

I turn to the question of inquiry and one of Dewey's other chief aims, community, in chapter 4. I turn to early critics and supporters of Dewey in part 1: philosophers and educators that have taken the thinker to task for supposedly advocating a rationalized, bureaucratic, and expert society, in the service of corporate interests, and the attendant consequences this has for education, as well as early sympathizers of Dewey: those that have responded positively to Dewey's theories of society and democracy. In part 2, I turn to contemporary critics and supporters of Dewey that have engaged in the same debates. I argue that, even in defending Dewey, these supporters see problems inherent in Dewey's response to the critics' concerns. I conclude that, rather than being dismissive of these concerns as some Dewey scholars have been, these be taken seriously. I argue that, as it stands, the issue remains begged, and further work remains to be done to see the way for Dewey to escape the charges. In part 3, I turn to Dewey. As in chapters 2 and 3, I look at statements of Dewey's that give critics pause: statements that seem to support the claim that inquiry of a strongly scientific sort is the way to alleviating social concerns. I then present statements that run counter to these. Again, I suggest that these statements by themselves cannot address the quandaries arising from this state of affairs. I then address the concerns of the critics, and in so doing, argue that, if Dewey is to be read as not promoting these interests, then linking his notion of community tightly with inquiry and with education and growth is the best way out of this impasse. I make this argument with attention to Dewey's "social" texts, notably *The Public and Its Problems, Individualism, Old and New, Theory of Valuation*, and *Freedom and Culture*, as well as other texts and articles. In part 4, I finish with a discussion of what the implications of rereading Dewey's notion of community in this are for education theory, and I address at length the importance of how inquiry, growth, and community are to be read for the practice of what Dewey considered the most important institution for the development of growth, of community, and of democracy: school. I turn to statements that Dewey makes tying inquiry to the shared concerns of growth, community and democracy: those that arise out of particular school and classroom settings. I also look closely at Dewey's laboratory for a democracy in miniature: the Laboratory School at the University of Chicago, 1896–1903. I believe that some of Dewey's strongest statements on the role and scope of inquiry are to be found here, in his discussion of the classrooms, subject matters, and pedagogical techniques of the Laboratory School.

In chapter 5, I turn to the question of inquiry and Dewey's conception of democracy. Part 1 deals with Dewey's early critics and supporters. With regard to the critics, I demonstrate how and why it is that they are suspicious of Dewey's theory of inquiry as leading the community and the schools toward a nondemocratic, even war-supporting state. I then turn to an early sympathizer of Dewey's—Sydney Hook—and see whether he is able to defend Dewey from these charges. I then turn in part 2 to contemporary critics and supporters of Dewey: those who see pragmatic theory as unhelpful at best and democratically dangerous at worst, and those that dismiss these charges as unfounded. I conclude that Dewey's notion of democracy needs work. In part 3, I begin with statements of Dewey's: in this case, statements Dewey makes regarding the Great War, America's involvement in it, and the role and scope of education therein. I show that when juxtaposed, some statements seem to be in disagreement with others. Indeed, Dewey seems to be of two minds regarding America's involvement and the subsequent role for education. Taking Dewey's critics seriously, I argue that conceiving of Dewey's notion of democracy as bound to his other aims of inquiry, growth, community, and democracy is the best defense against the critics' charges. Here, I concentrate heavily on Dewey's statements on democracy in *Democracy and Education* and articles on the Great War. I finish by responding to those critics who see the future of pragmatism as a nontheoretical enterprise and agree, in the main, with these. I challenge, however, the reading of inquiry as wholly theoretical and suggest that, even if pragmatism turned away from theorizing, inquiry would still have work to do. In part 4, I conclude by noting the consequences that this reading of democracy sets for education theory.

II
INQUIRY AND SCIENCE

Perhaps the most serious charges against Dewey concern his strong role for science in the quest for solutions to the problems of men. Some dispute or dismiss entirely the claims of inquiry as science. Richard Rorty is a telling example of the latter. Rorty has little patience with the view that Dewey was somehow positivistic or that Dewey embraced something like a "general method." Though Rorty admits Dewey's rhetoric concerning the capacity of science to solve "the problems of men" was strong, he nevertheless chides Dewey and Dewey scholars—whether for or against method—who make much of this. Rorty does not believe that method (or anything else) can get us closer to "the way things really are," or that it somehow stabilizes once and for all the flux of sensation. What Rorty is giving up when he claims that we cannot get closer to a thing's nature is the idea of the correspondence theory of truth (Rorty, *Truth and Progress*, 1998, 2). For Rorty, such thinking creeps into talk of method when method is made to be uniform or constant. Rorty argues that this talk of Dewey's betrays a quest for certainty, for objectivity. Rorty puts his claim this way:

> Granted that Dewey never stopped talking about "scientific method," I submit that he never had anything very useful to say about it. Those who think I am overstating my case here, should, I think, tell us what this thing called "method"—which is neither a set of rules nor a character trait nor a collection of techniques—is supposed to be. Unless some reasonably definite third element can be specified, and chapter and verse cited from Dewey showing that this is what he had in mind, I shall stick by my claim that Dewey could have said everything he needed to say if he dropped the term "scientific method." (Rorty in Saatkamp 1995, 94)[1]

This is a central motif in all of Rorty's writings, and it provides one of the clearest examples as to how it is that Dewey scholars and Rorty, all avowed pragmatists, can differ so greatly on an issue of mutual concern. I shall have much more to say about Rorty's particular reading of Dewey in further chapters, but for now the point I want to make is that this sentiment, though extreme in the case of Rorty, nevertheless underlies a great deal of current Dewey scholarship. Otherwise sympathetic readers of Dewey often conclude that Dewey did not really mean to stress so strongly the scientific import of inquiry, and they attempt to temper his rhetoric in their interpretations of him. For now, I wish to examine what critics and supporters have made of Dewey's strong claims of science as inquiry. There are many critics and supporters to choose from and, consequently, much redundancy. Many newer commentators repeat the concerns of past critics and supporters, and in many cases, the claims are otiose. Nevertheless, to provide clarity and context to these debates, it will do to spend some time examining past criticisms and supports of Dewey's theory of inquiry, if only to help us get a sense of the present ones. I shall begin with some past debates concerning Dewey's theory of inquiry. This is by no means an exhaustive undertaking; it is provided only to lend context to the present-day debates and to show that the concerns of these older debates are far from settled, and in fact, play a strong role in the current ones.

Part One:
A Short History of the Debate on Inquiry

The question of whether Dewey did or did not support a strong role for science and the scientific method in his theory of inquiry is an old one that begins with Dewey attempting to find his unique voice among the various and competing theories of knowledge extant at the turn of the twentieth century. As is well known, Dewey advocates a theory of logic known as instrumentalism, primarily in his work completed at the University of Chicago entitled *Studies in Logical Theory*. What is less well known is that Dewey was in close and sometimes heated dialogue with philosophers and psychologists adamantly opposed to what was (correctly) seen as the naturalization of inquiry. Early disputes concerned Dewey's allegiance to what John Shook has called "naïve realism": the view that there really are natural events, of which we become aware, and that these events are experienced directly, with no intermediaries or *tertia*, such as sense data or sense perceptions.[2] Characteristically, it was the idealists that had the most trouble with Dewey and served as the point of departure for Dewey's new thinking. In fact, a large section of *Studies in Logical Theory* was devoted to undermining the position of R. H. Lotze, the well-known idealist logician of the latter half of the nineteenth century.

As is also well known, Dewey supported an inquiry that was at once experimental: problem solving was what drove the processes and outcomes of inquiry. This engendered much criticism, particularly from self-described realists and positivists. Examples of those that were critical of Dewey's stance on inquiry were (most famously) Bertrand Russell (whom I shall consider more fully in the following chapter), Arthur Lovejoy, Morris Cohen, and Hans Reichenbach. But these were only representatives of a much larger number of scholars in philosophy, psychology, social science, and education who had difficulty either understanding or accepting Dewey's naturalization and experimentalization of scientific method. Indeed, by the time of Dewey's *Logic: The Theory of Inquiry* (1938), which was to bring together forty years of study on the topic to the intellectual and lay public, Dewey had assumed a certain degree of notoriety among traditional logicians: what Dewey was producing bore little resemblance to the symbolization of logic that became de rigeur in the nineteenth century. Shorn of any symbolic representation, Dewey's *Logic* looked nothing at all like a standard textbook in logic, let alone a treatise. Camps were drawn up: those opposed to Dewey, such as Russell, Reichenbach, and Cohen, claimed either that Dewey was incomprehensible or (more profoundly) that his *Logic* had serious flaws in argumentation owing to the diminution of universal or analytic propositions. Of course, Dewey had his sympathizers, notably Sydney Hook, Dewey's one-time student and lifelong friend; but equally his friend and later writing partner, Arthur Bentley; and Ernest Nagel, perhaps the best equipped of the pragmatist philosophers of science in Dewey's day.

By the time of Dewey's death (1952) the landscape of philosophy in America had changed. No longer was pragmatism seen as a viable or workable option. Indeed, from a pragmatist perspective, ground that had been gained by declaring many philosophical problems to be "pseudo-problems" had been lost. The turn to analytic philosophy and its close counterpart, the philosophy of language, not only displaced pragmatism but was critical of its seeming intellectual sloppiness. Morton White, a close friend and colleague of W. V. O. Quine, would criticize Dewey in the 1950s and 1960s over his alleged confusion of universals. Another analytically minded philosopher who dealt with educational issues, Israel Scheffler, mounted a strong critique of the consequences of Dewey's theory of inquiry for education, beginning the decade of Dewey's death. Nevertheless, Dewey had his stalwart supporters. Nagel, with certain reservations, continued to support a broadly pragmatic take on logic through to his death. Here I shall develop the thoughts of Morris Cohen, Morton White, and Israel Scheffler, all early critics of Dewey's *Logic*, as well as Ernest Nagel, an early supporter.

Morris Cohen, Morton White, and Israel Scheffler are good past representatives of the sort of criticism I have in mind. Cohen thinks that Dewey's exclusive focus on problems of a practical nature both obviates and demeans abstract and theoretical thought. White believes that Dewey's theory of inquiry betrays a distinction between "analytic" conceptions—those that are nonexperiential, fixed, and timeless—and "synthetic" conceptions—those that are experiential and temporal. In this scenario, Dewey is a closet rationalist because he reifies an element of inquiry such that it does not transform in problematic situations. Dewey comes to look a lot like the positivist A. J. Ayer, of whom I shall say more shortly. The second is that Dewey, because his notion of inquiry is experimental and historical, shares affinities with early self-proclaimed positivists who had a similar argument as to the complexion of method. Scheffler claims that Dewey gives short shrift to non-problem-solving ways of thinking and being. This leads Scheffler to conclude that Dewey separates theory and practice and reduces all thought to instrumental method.

Morris Cohen was a contemporary of Dewey and a philosopher and historian of science who advocated metaphysical realism—the view that objects outside of our experience exist irrespective of our interaction with them. Cohen has two main criticisms of Dewey's theory of inquiry. The first is that Dewey saddles scientific inquiry with altogether too much responsibility for the solution to human problems. Cohen argues that human problems are simply not amenable to inquiry in the way that the natural sciences are, and that Dewey is naïve to think so. The second is that Dewey's theory of inquiry leaves no room for abstraction, contemplation, and conception. This is to say that inasmuch as all knowledge is generated from, and responsive to, practical matters, there is little space for nonpractical judgments and thinking. Further, Cohen thinks that what the public wants of a philosopher is not philosophical solutions to practical problems, but rather an abstract and disinterested search for truth. To the extent that Dewey does not perform this service, Cohen argues, he degrades philosophy.[3]

Cohen's most vehement response to Dewey occurs in a Festschrift, entitled John Dewey: Philosopher of the Common Man, published on the occasion of Dewey's eightieth birthday. The history of antagonism between Cohen and Dewey has its roots in Dewey's earlier review of Cohen's, Reason and Nature: An Essay on the Meaning of Scientific Method. In his review, Dewey charges Cohen with a failure to define certain issues in psychology and the social sciences. Of this, Dewey states: "But philosophically, this work suffers, in my estimation, from failure clearly to define issues . . . this blurring is apparently due to the author's aversion to certain views opposed to his own, and to a somewhat intense moral conviction of the harm these views work" (Dewey [1931] 1985, 300). Cohen responds by defending his original claims and Dewey responds once again, to these. By 1940, when the Festschrift was published, Cohen was a well-known antagonist of Dewey's. Cohen claims that Dewey makes experience so broad as to be tautological: there is no place of contrast from which one could criticize it. Of Dewey's theory of inquiry, he states: "Taken literally, Dewey's attitude on this point . . . would condemn pure mathematics and all theoretic science that has not found and may never find any practical application, but also all music and fine art that has not been devoted to influencing the course of social events" (Cohen, 1940 in Dewey [1939–1941] 1988, 402). Cohen sees the reduction of theory to practicality as mischievous.

Morton White is particularly interested in the debates between the older pragmatist thinkers, represented by Dewey, and the newer, analytically minded thinkers, represented by W. V. O. Quine and Wilfred Sellars. For his part, he tends toward making critical judgments of the earlier pragmatists by bringing the newer techniques of postanalytic philosophy to bear upon them. One of these techniques is to examine philosophies for evidence of analytic/synthetic thinking: what Quine had labeled a dogma of empiricism. Analytic thinking, for Quine and White, consists of thinking that has recourse to a lawlike principle, conception, or proposition as its ground; whereas, synthetic thinking is thoroughly empirical, relying on conceptions and propositions corresponding to observation of phenomenal data. For example, on the account of analytic thinking, when the syllogism "All men are mortal: Socrates is a man; therefore, Socrates is mortal" is considered as logically correct, it is because the kinds "men" and "mortal" have meaning-synonymy. Man implies mortal (though mortal does not imply man). No meanings beyond the ones invoked in the syllogism are necessary for the syllogism's completion, and it is this property that defines a statement as analytic. The kinds "men" and "mortal" take on a lawlike significance. This is tantamount to saying that analytic statements do not require experience, such as sense perceptions or phenomena, for their being.[4] White claims he finds such thinking in Dewey.

Of Dewey's *Logic: The Theory of Inquiry*, White diagnoses

> a sharp distinction between what [Dewey] calls "ideational" and "existential" propositions. . . . When Dewey comes to apply his distinction between ideational and existential propositions, he moves in the direction of classical rationalism. In other words, he holds that laws of physics are what a positivist would call "analytic" and hence to be established by an examination of meanings. (White 1973, 143)

White's argument is that "Dewey, unable to deal sufficiently with the 'problem' of causality, is forced to find refuge for such laws as Newton's (of motion) by virtue of the fact that they are 'established by an examination of [synonymous] meanings'" (White 1973, 143). White thinks that because Dewey subscribes to the view of physical laws as established not by sense experience but rather through their meanings, that they are a priori (devoid of experience) and thus analytic. This is in contradistinction to the laws of logic and mathematics, which are, oddly enough for White, a posteriori (transformable and conditional on observation and/or operation), because Dewey labels them as "existential" and not "ideational."[5]

This has deeper ramifications. For it suggests that Dewey wants to reify what White claims is really an element of experience, through having physical laws lie outside of experience and not be specifiable by the operations that they (ostensibly) direct, thus betraying the experimental tenor of the *Logic*. White finds this reification present in the following passage of *Dewey's Logic*:

> Propositions . . . are of two main categories: (1) Existential, referring directly to actual conditions as determined by experimental observation, and (2) ideational or conceptual, consisting of interrelated meanings, which are non-existential in content in direct reference but which are applicable to existence through the operations they represent as possibilities. (Dewey [1938] 1986 in White 1973, 149)

Here, White argues, is a disturbing hypostatization of the analytic proposition. For if Dewey holds that ideational propositions are nonexperiential, he has then admitted an analytic proposition into a posteriori logic and heralded a sharp division between existential and non-existential principles. Analyticity for White is tantamount to rationalism and so White claims that Dewey is a "rationalist in the worst sense of that word, one who thinks that the laws of natural science are established by examining the relations between concepts alone" (White 1973, 150). In White's estimation, Dewey comes to look a lot like the rationalist and self-proclaimed positivist A. J. Ayer, who maintained a similar sentiment.[6]

Ayer's book *Language, Truth, and Logic* was published not two years before Dewey's *Logic*. The goal of this work was to provide a completely empirical argument for knowledge: a knowledge completely shorn of metaphysics. This, Ayer claimed, could only be done by dismantling the metaphysical argument for knowledge; that knowledge somehow has about it a transcendental component that serves as a ground:

> What is required is rather a criticism of the nature of the actual statements which comprise it. And this is the line of argument which we shall, in fact, pursue. For we shall maintain that no statement which refers to a "reality" transcending the limits of all possible sense-experience can possibly have any literal significance; from which it must follow that the labours of those who have striven to describe such a reality have all been devoted to the production of nonsense. (Ayer 1936, 16)

Ayer turns to verifiability as the decisive factor in assessing a statement's truthfulness.

The criticism which we use to test the genuineness of apparent state-ments of fact is the criterion of verifiability. We can say that a sentence is factually significant to any given person, if, and only if, he knows how to verify the proposition which it purports to express—that is, if he knows what observations would lead him, under certain conditions, to accept the proposition as being true, or reject it as being false. (Ayer 1936, 19)

Now Ayer does push beyond the claim that only in observation can the valid-ity of a statement be ascertained. For he does admit that there are universal truths, though these are empirical rather than transcendental; that is, they are internal to the statement proffered and in this way, tautological. And these truths are the truths of logic:

The principles of logic and mathematics are true universally simply be-cause we never allow them to be anything else. And the reason for this is that we cannot abandon them without contradicting ourselves, without sinning against the rules which govern the use of language, and so making our utterances self-stultifying. In other words, the truths of logic and mathematics are analytic propositions or tautologies. (Ayer 1936, 67)

And these tautologies, according to Ayer, are "true solely in virtue of the mean-ing of its constituent symbols, and cannot therefore be either confirmed or re-futed by any fact of experience" (Ayer, 1936, 16). White thinks that what analysis does for Ayer, it does as well for Dewey.

White draws out the consequences of Dewey's seemingly analytic/syn-thetic distinction. In so doing, he concludes that a failure occurs in Dewey's theory of logic and a fortiori his methodology. The failure is manifest not only at the level of the conception but at the level of operation: practice. Accord-ing to White, if a scientific method applied to the solution of practical, human problems must draw upon analytic conceptions, the method will no longer re-spond to these problems and science will fail in its quest. White believes that Dewey must say that moral knowledge, accrued through the use of scientific method, can result in only self-evident principles. Since the conception is it-self tautological and thereby self-appealing, the conception and not the exis-tential proposition or practice becomes the final court of appeal. This provokes in White the fear that Dewey falls back upon an ethics of lawlike principles. All of this portends a split in Dewey's logic: generic (synthetic) propositions are amenable to transformation; universal (analytic) ones are not. As a result, White declares Dewey's social use of inquiry a failure. With this unresolved dualism at the heart of Dewey's inquiry, the sort of moral knowledge that Dewey quests for simply cannot be found.

Similar sentiments are shared by Israel Scheffler. In many ways, Scheffler has the most acute and penetrating criticisms of Dewey's theory of inquiry. Scheffler resembles Dewey in some respects. Both figures disagree with the correspondence theory of truth; the view that our minds simply "hook" onto a piece of the world by and through pictorial representation of objects. Both figures think the divorce of facts from contexts lamentable. And both see the importance of intelligently directed inquiry as the means to an increasingly democratic public. But there are seeming differences between these two, particularly insofar as inquiry is concerned. Scheffler rather values abstract thinking for its own sake. Scheffler believes that, in addition to knowledge gained from certain contexts, there is also much to be gained from abstract theorizing. Also, Scheffler contends that science, if it is to be successful, must not only take into consideration the close relationship between the learner and the context in which she finds herself, but must also anticipate contexts with which she is not familiar and has not been exposed to. And finally, Scheffler believes that learning outstrips knowledge. Learning encompasses much more than does knowledge, and logical techniques, though necessary for knowledge, do not themselves participate in all learning. Imagination, curiosity, and emotion, to name but a few noncognitive concerns, are also paramount to what Scheffler considers learning. His philosophy resembles Whitehead's, inasmuch as it stresses process over act and whole over part. Scheffler, for example, argues: "To view past works—whether art or science, or architecture, or music, or literature, or mathematics, or history, or religion, or philosophy—as given and unique objects rather than incarnations of process is to close off the traditions of effort from which they emerged. It is to bring these traditions to a full stop" (Scheffler 1988, 77).

Scheffler is critical of Dewey's turn toward thinking as problem solving. He disputes this turn, noting that progress in the sciences does not grow out of contexts in which problems are identified. Of Dewey's problem-solving method, Scheffler argues that

> it holds at best for simple types of practical thinking and for technological applications, but it does not do justice to science as an autonomous theoretical endeavor. Scientific theories do not, generally, grow out of practical conflicts, nor do they, in themselves, serve to guide practical activities; they are embedded in complex intellectual structures linked only indirectly, and as wholes, to contexts of evidence and experiment. (Scheffler 1973, 130)

What is missing from Dewey's talk of problem solving as thinking, Scheffler concludes, is attention to the prior context of scientific formulation, of which the results are but a part. The activity that Dewey suggests as being begun by problem solving, Scheffler argues, is rather begun by problem finding, that is, the hunt for questions that arise out of prior scientific theory and not a problem at hand.

> Problems cannot be identified with difficulties of practice; the problems that organize scientific research arise in a context of prior theory and experimentation. Moreover, the life of science is not exhausted in resolving problems that arise without effort; the scientist's thought does not subside when his questions have been answered. Problem-finding is as important as problem-solving, and scientific thought of the greatest significance is expended in seeking, formulating and elaborating questions that have not yet intruded on practice. (Scheffler 1974, 252)

Scheffler is led to conclude that Dewey misses much in his equation of thinking with problem solving. Scheffler believes that Dewey means problem solving to be the very model of thinking and inquiry and, unhappy with Dewey's supposed claim, argues for thinking to encompass much more:

> Much of our thinking is problem-oriented, but much is not, growing out of free speculation, playfulness, curiosity, or out of the need to express, describe, or create. One can attempt to force all these varieties into a common abstract framework, but the advantages of doing so would need to be so evident as to override the cost in artificiality and generality. I do not think the problem-theory is adequate in this respect; even if it were, we should need to provide, in education, a concrete and realistic awareness of the special features differentiating science from history, art from mathematics, poetry from legal reasoning, philology from philosophy. We should, in other words, need to transmit the several traditions of thought as we now possess them, rather than simply filtering them through an abstract philosophical schema of thinking as problem-solving. (Scheffler 1973, 253)[7]

Scheffler argues that the answer to the "problem" of problem solving, the alleged collapse of all learning and inquiry into a single model, is to separate theory from practice. What we have then is two inquiries, theoretical and practical. Practical inquiry is said to be inquiry applied to specific problems. Theoretical inquiry, though, is inquiry in the service of itself. And this is the self of philosophy and of science.

> To argue . . . that thought is not generally to be conceived as a response to practical difficulty and that theoretical inquiry involves critical dis-

tance and autonomous development does not, after all, imply that practical application is to be shunned. . . . The root assumption that the scope
of schooling is fixed by the limits of thought must itself be rejected as the
source of much mischief. (Scheffler 1974, 133)

What drives this (Aristotelian?) division of theory and practice is Scheffler's
concern regarding the state of education under a problem-solving model.
Scheffler fears that, should the schools adopt wholesale a problem-solving
model of learning, application will intrude upon, and overtake, theoretical inquiry, and the theoretical inquiry will be neglected.[8] Scheffler admits the importance of scientific inquiry as a model of learning. But he disputes that problems are to, or ought to, drive inquiry. Rather inquiry is to be driven by its own
range of problems and then, after coming to grips with these, settle down to
the business of being applicable to social concerns. So, to Scheffler again, "indeed, application is the ultimate end to which inquiry is a means, and, from
the standpoint of society, the school must thus be viewed as an instrument for
the realization of its goals" (Scheffler 1974, 152).

Before I proceed to discuss views apologetic of Dewey's theory of inquiry,
it will do to summarize the various criticisms of Dewey thus far:

1) Dewey pays little or no heed in his theory of inquiry to pure mathematics or pure science (Cohen).
2) Dewey's theory of inquiry conceals an analytic/synthetic distinction,
   and as such, is rationalistic and positivistic (White).
3) Dewey's theory of inquiry is reductivist, and leaves little room for
   other ways of knowing, such as imagination, curiosity, and emotion
   (Scheffler).

I shall turn to a sympathizer of reading Dewey as having a strong role for
science to play in inquiry. The philosopher who best encapsulates the view that
Dewey's theory of inquiry is strongly scientific and that this is a good thing, is
Ernest Nagel. After a brief treatment of other contemporaries of Nagel sympathetic to this reading of inquiry, I shall focus on Nagel.

Almost no sympathizers today claim Dewey was a logical positivist.
Nevertheless, there are those who, with Ernest Nagel, claim Dewey advocated
a strong place for scientific inquiry in any context—including that of education. Though it may fairly be assumed that this is not by itself a logical positivistic pronouncement, yet it does raise the question of whether Dewey is positivistic in another way, if positivism is (taken together with scientism) to mean
the advocacy of the necessity for inquiry of a scientific sort to be present in
physical, social, intellectual, or educational concerns. One may well ask, then,
whether Dewey does not have at least a positivistic or scientistic temperament.

What is claimed in saying that science is the model of inquiry is that it is "the ideal of inquiry as implied in the fundamental postulate of scientific activity" (Kaufmann 1950, 224). This statement from Felix Kaufmann, who contributed an essay to Sidney Hook's 1950 symposium in celebration of Dewey's ninetieth birthday, sums up well what these interpreters are getting at. And what scientific activity does is develop standards of criticism that can be brought to bear on problems at hand. These standards are found throughout inquiries in all contexts. So to Kaufmann again, "the various systems of rules have a common formal structure. Such terms as 'knowledge,' 'method,' 'problem,' 'explanation,' 'probability,' 'induction' are supposed to be significant for any domain and any stage of inquiry; and they have to be clearly defined" (Kaufmann 1950, 227). Scientific inquiry, on this take is "not 'just another part' of . . . [Dewey's] philosophy, but rather is the very fiber which weaves the parts into a well-patterned whole" (Rosenthal [1981] in Tiles 1992, 155). Such claims have led critics to think that Dewey's theory of inquiry is scientistic.

A central feature of the program of these readers of Dewey has been to downplay the charges that Dewey is somehow beholden to a thoroughgoing operationalism; that all statements and terms must submit to some form of measurement. Of course, we find this concern with critics of Dewey. But we also find it with certain of Dewey's sympathizers. The project for these readers of Dewey becomes one of carefully chastising Dewey for not paying enough attention to certain problems in his account of knowledge while at the same time acknowledging his fine contribution to the state of the philosophy of science. Anthony Quinton who, in an edited volume on Dewey's thought by R. S. Peters, argues against what he perceives as Dewey's position that "at some stage of inquiry the inquirer must be a spectator, however questioning and actively experimental or manipulative he may be at other stages. The object must be left room to do its part" (Quinton in Peters 1971, 14). The conclusion seems to be that inquiry must somehow be exempt from the reconstruction that inquiry necessitates of its problematic situation.

It is in the above spirit that Ernest Nagel cautiously pushes Dewey to acknowledge the difficulties created by his thoroughgoing operationalism. Nagel was a student of Morris Cohen's at Columbia and did his dissertation in 1930 under Cohen's direction. Cohen was very critical of Dewey. But one must not get the impression that because Cohen was Nagel's advisor, therefore Nagel set his project in opposition to Dewey's. In point of fact, it is rather the opposite. Nagel wrote a very "Deweyan" dissertation entitled *On the Logic of Measurement*. Nagel advances two central and Deweyan theses in this work. The first is that

the distinction between those characters of the world measurable [mathematical symbols], has served to produce a metaphysical chasm between a supposedly ontological order of relations and a subjective domain of qualities, or between a realm of essence intuitively clear and knowable and a realm of matter reached only by an animal impulse, rationally justifiable. (Nagel 1930, 1)

The second is that "the study of any theory of physics, as well as the observation that physics has a history, demonstrates the fact that the theoretical structure of any science is not an immediately apprehended aspect of the world revealed in sense perception" (Nagel 1930, 57). Nagel clung to these two tenets throughout his long career.

Notwithstanding Nagel's avowed antimetaphysics, he maintains that the logic of inquiry holds an esteemed place in all contexts in which inquiry is present. And this is his reading of Dewey as well. In commenting upon Dewey's experimental version of inquiry, he states: "For the laws of logic are so unique in that they turn up in every conceivable inquiry, and in that no alternative postulates have every been successfully applied; one suspects, therefore, that they represent factors invariant in *every* subject-matter" (Nagel [1930] in Dewey [1929–1930] 1984, 457). So put, Dewey's theory of science is considered for Nagel *the* method of inquiry found in all contexts in which controlled transformation of materials was attempted.

Despite Nagel's broad acceptance of Dewey's experimentalist take on logic, he is concerned with the same issue as is Morton White: Dewey's making of a distinction between generic propositions and universals in his *Logic: The Theory of Inquiry*. The problem for Nagel is that, though Dewey

> explicitly declares that universals formulate possible modes of acting, so that the execution of the operation prescribed by the proposition also tests its force and relevance for solving the problems at hand . . . [nevertheless] no analytic proposition, in the contemporary sense, would be tested in the way frequently proposed by Professor Dewey for his universals. (Nagel [1939] 1954, 146)

The question becomes Is Dewey faithful to his original standpoint: that of propositions as "helping to prepare existential material in order to identify it for the sake of other operations to be performed " (Nagel [1939] 1954, 145)?

Nagel concludes that the distinction between generic and universal propositions is not a sharp one. But then Nagel locates within Dewey's talk of universals two sorts of propositions. The first is exemplified by physics (Newton's laws of motion, for example), the second by mathematics (arithmetic, geometry). Of the first, and in contradistinction to White, Nagel claims this as synthetic. For these universals arise out of, and enter back into, empirical ma-

terial. Of the second, though, Nagel puts forth the claim that certain propositions just are analytic:

> But the propositions of mathematics differ radically from those just men-
> tioned. They are analytic [having meaning-synonymy], and though also
> instrumental in inquiry are instrumental in a different way. For their
> function is to make transitions in discourse, to facilitate calculations of
> various sorts, rather than to direct the analysis of empirical material or
> to formulate possible modes of action. The recognition of these distinc-
> tions seems to me fundamental for an adequate theory of inquiry; but
> while Professor Dewey does not overlook them, his discussions of them
> and of related topics do not constitute the most enlightening portions of
> his treatise. (Nagel [1939] 1954, 147)

The upshot of all of this is (though he does not say so) to suggest that, for
Nagel, Dewey ought to have treated analytic propositions in a manner similar to Ayer: that propositions have meaning-synonymy. For Nagel, Dewey's
theory of inquiry is not so much defended from the charges of analyticity as
tacitly endorsed as analytic, with the proviso that Dewey ought to have pushed
further and declared universal propositions to be what they are: statements of
identity.

Part Two:
The Present-Day Debate on Inquiry

There is affinity between the old and the new criticisms and supports of Dewey.
The question of whether Dewey was scientistic or positivistic has not gone
away, despite repeated attempts by apologists of Dewey's theory of inquiry to
claim otherwise. Many of these criticisms and supports build on older ones.
Here, I shall look in detail at a number of different contributions to the debate
on just this topic. I shall again begin with criticisms of Dewey and proceed to
apologies. What is central in this examination is the degree to which the present criticisms build upon past ones, and how successfully the apologies fend off
these concerns. As I shall show, the supports of Dewey largely fail in their efforts, and the criticisms, many of them having a long pedigree, stand fast. I
choose two representative critical examples here. One, from H. O. Mounce,
suggests that Dewey is positivistic and that this positivism is Comtean and can
be teased out of Dewey's writing.

A good example of present criticism built upon a past one is found in the
Wittgenstein scholar and pragmatism critic H. O. Mounce's reading of Dewey.

Mounce's reading is heavily indebted to the critic Morris Cohen, who we visited in the prior section. Now Mounce sanctions Cohen's suspicion of Dewey's desire to have philosophy's role be that which contributes to the alleviation of human problems. Mounce's first move is to link Dewey closely with nineteenth-century positivism. Of Dewey's essay "The Need for a Recovery of Philosophy," Mounce sees a view expressed that had become "familiar during the course of the nineteenth century" (Mounce 1997, 144). This view was that of Auguste Comte, an early positivist. Mounce draws two conclusions from this linkage of Dewey with Comte. The first is that, for each thinker, "inquiry finds the correct method, which consists in ignoring a priori notions and confining itself to phenomena, to the world as it appears to the senses. . . . It progresses, for example, by splitting into specialisms, which follow their own way. . . . The result is that much scientific knowledge is devoid of human significance" (Mounce 1997, 145). What ties Comte and Dewey together is said to be their faith in naturalism, the view that explanations of natural phenomena do not require recourse to extranatural premises, and phenomenalism, a turn towards the immediacy of experience as the domain from and upon which reflection occurs. These are thoroughgoing empiricist philosophies that eschew supernatural metaphysics and claim the methods of the sciences to be of value to moral concerns.

With Comte's threefold development of philosophical method from religion to metaphysics and to science in mind, Mounce traces what he sees as a similar development in Dewey's genetic model of philosophical method. He quotes Dewey as follows: "Savage man recalled yesterday's struggle with an animal not in order to study in a scientific way the qualities of an animal or for the sake of calculating how better to fight to-morrow, but to escape from the tedium of to-day by regaining the thrill of yesterday" (Dewey [1920] 1982, 80 in Mounce 1997, 146). Mounce considers the development of myth and ritual as similar to Comte's religious stage of method. Mounce as well finds Comte's metaphysical stage of method in Dewey's talk of the Greek philosophers.

> The growth of positive knowledge and of the critical, inquiring spirit undermined those in their old form. . . . [What was to be done?] Develop a method of rational investigation and proof which should place the essential elements of traditional belief upon an unshakeable basis; develop a method of thought and knowledge which while purifying tradition should preserve its moral and social values unimpaired . (Dewey [1920] 1982, 89–90 in Mounce 1997, 147)

Dewey is said to find in the metaphysical stage an "element of insincerity" (Dewey [1920] 1982, 91 in Mounce 1997, 148). This is so because metaphysical principles are said to be taken for higher social and political values, leading to the reification of existing customs. Dewey's solution to the problems of the meta-physical stage is to expose the stages' origins. This, claims Mounce, is similar to Comte's exposure of the metaphysical stages. Mounce quotes Dewey's favorable estimation of the genetic (historical/developmental) method from the text.

> Common frankness requires that it be stated that this account of the origin of philosophies claiming to deal with absolute Beings in a systematic way has been given with malice prepense. It seems to me that this genetic method of approach is a more effective way of undermining this type of philosophic theorizing than any attempt at logical refutation would be. (Dewey [1920] 1982, 93 in Mounce 1997, 148)

Mounce then draws the (correct) conclusion that, since Dewey fully endorses the genetic method, and (wrongly, as I shall show) that the genetic method was staged in a manner similar to Comte's characterization of positivistic method, therefore Dewey's method is positivistic.

As with philosophers, educators too have taken sides in the debate over whether Dewey was or was not scientistic, positivistic, or held out for a strong role for science to play in inquiring into social concerns.

D. C. (Denis Charles) Phillips is a champion of the view that inquiry is to be construed as scientific. In a Deweyan spirit, Phillips notes of educational research that

> it is important to note that although natural scientists might be solely interested in behaviors (in their professional role) and in the laws or theories that can explain or predict them, the social scientist and educational researcher are rarely interested in mere physico-chemical changes. . . . What is of special concern to them are the actions performed by students, parents, teachers, administrators, policy makers, and others, as well as the sociocultural contexts that provide the framework of meanings and goals and purposes and values in which these actions are located. (Phillips and Burbules 2000, 70)

What is being claimed is that natural behaviors and social actions are explained in terms of their respective subject matters. But this does not a fortiori mean that the research methods utilized in coming to an explanation are therefore different. In fact, the opposite is the case.

Phillips is harsh with those who claim that the social sciences (or literature) cannot be approached with experimentalist methodologies:

> It is always possible, out of the masses of material available, to select *some* items that apparently support a given interpretation, and thus the fact

that the account is apparently supported by some evidence does not count for much. . . . What serves as more genuine support is that no evidence can be found to disprove the account that is being given; it is up to the person giving the interpretation to convince the rest of us that such negative evidence has been sought vigorously. (Phillips and Burbules 2000, 80)

Thus, what is in question in any context is the validity of the argument put forth. And this is always testable. All of this leads Phillips to conclude that "There is nothing unscientific about an educational researcher studying human actions . . . and seeking to understand the reasons, beliefs, motives, purposes, and so forth, that lead individuals to act the way they do in educational and other social settings" (Phillips and Burbules 2000, 82).

In many ways, Phillips's talk of experimentalism resembles Dewey's seemingly "strong" talk of science. This leads Phillips to consider himself (most of the time) a fellow traveler with Dewey. But Phillips is quite critical of Dewey in his earlier writings. In *Holistic Thought in Social Science*, Phillips emphasizes the weaknesses of psychological holism (the claim that a stimulus or environment and organism form a circle, not a reflex arc) of which Dewey is said to be a leading proponent. Of holism in general and Dewey in particular, it is said that the distinctive methods of "historical inquiry" and "inductive inquiry" are collapsed (Phillips 1976, 107). What this means is that Dewey, projecting continuity and interconnection in a variety of contexts (the reflex arc, habit, evolution, experience), has no place for a viewpoint outside of the circle of interpretation that he constructs. All of this is to say that Dewey's "holism" was tautological, circular, because all-embracing. One cannot claim a causal point of reference in a circle.[9] Phillips finishes his look at Dewey by intimating that Dewey was a "positivistic organicist" (Phillips 1976, 112).

Phillips gradually comes to view Dewey in a positive light. In his 1987 work *Philosophy, Science and Social Inquiry*, on speaking of the abandonment of the "spectator view of knowledge," Phillips claims: "Popper held much the same view; and earlier still John Dewey realized that perception was not 'neutral' but that knowledge and intelligence operated so as to influence it " (Phillips 1987, 9). Speaking of those who recognize the difficulties inherent in running the methodologies of the natural and social sciences together, Phillips states:

Some in this very same camp, however, recognize that this is a difficult road to take, and they opt instead for an "easier road" to naturalism— they, too, hold that there is no epistemological difference between the natural and the social sciences, but (critically) they hold a "softer" view of the nature of science, a view influenced by the "new philosophy of sci-

ence." They can cite Popper as an ally. . . . It is also reasonable to construe John Dewey as being in this camp; he regarded scientific thinking
as effective thinking, and because effective thinking can occur in all sorts
of realms, all realms are potentially scientific. (Phillips 1987, 81)

Phillips claims that both Popper and Dewey share this sentiment: all contexts
are potentially scientific and what makes them actually scientific is the use of
science to make causal and relational claims.

At the beginning of this section, I stated that almost no one would claim
Dewey a logical positivist. H. O. Mounce, as the reader may recall, does insist
that Dewey resembles to a great degree, a different positivist: Auguste Comte.
Mounce is not the only one. Phillips, too, sees this connection.

> The nineteenth-century French philosopher Auguste Comte had an el-
> evated respect for science, and he believed the scientific method could
> be applied to human affairs, including the study of morals. The sciences,
> he argued, focus upon observable, objectively determinable phenomena.
> He regarded all sciences as being related, and as forming a sequence that
> has developed historically from mathematics, through astronomy, the
> physical and then the biological sciences to sociology. . . . The later sci-
> ences grew out of the earlier ones but were not reducible to them. Her-
> bert Spencer, John Stuart Mill, Ernest Mach, the logical positivists, and
> John Dewey, all had certain affinities with Comte. (Phillips 1987, 38)

Phillips hardens his rhetoric further on:

> Comte would be pleased. Some, like Dewey, regard scientific inquiry as
> normal everyday inquiry writ large, so that finding a solution to a prob-
> lem in quantum mechanics is in principle no different from solving a
> moral problem or from solving how to get to a pressing appointment on
> the other side of town. Comte would be delighted. (Phillips 1987, 42)

On what grounds can Phillips make the claim that Dewey and Comte demonstrate affinities? Phillips finds three shared criteria. The first is operationalism;
the view that all theoretical terms must be specified by the operations that measure them. The second is behaviorism; the claim that only explanations that
are based on directly observable factors are scientifically adequate. The third is
empiricism; the claim that our concepts are based (at least in part) upon experience (Phillips 1987, 40–41). All of this is not to say that Phillips is critical
of Dewey. Phillips has something rather different in mind. He is at pains to
show that both Dewey *and* the logical positivists are heirs to Comte's positivism, and that Dewey has affinities with the logical positivists as well. As

Phillips puts it, "All this is significant because some folk in education and the social sciences who revel in the fact that logical positivism is a dead deal are very fond of Dewey" (Phillips 1987, 39).

I now turn to present-day apologies of Dewey's theory of inquiry. Characteristically enough, many of Dewey's present-day supporters of the notion that inquiry is scientific and that this way of viewing inquiry is correct, are educators. When educators debate the merits of scientific inquiry, they do so with an eye to practical concerns and consequences. It is not simply the case that they dispassionately argue for one side or another. In the case of those who hold that scientific inquiry has a strong (transcontextual) role to play in any human activity, they often do so because they are attempting to find the best characterization of learning and the best methods of teaching. As such, they turn to science and scientific inquiry to help them in their quest. The invocation of Dewey is important because it lends not only academic weight to the arguments, but provides them with a seemingly sturdy method with which they can begin to construct their own hypotheses on learning and teaching.

A central motif of educators espousing Dewey's strong talk of science is the desire to see inquiry as *the* model of problem solving. Here is the point, nicely made:

> Could we not argue that Dewey is being circular in deciding what the scientific method is? For he plans to determine what the scientific method is by examining how actual scientific investigations are conducted, having already told us that a scientific endeavor is one that follows the scientific method. Not quite. What saves the day for Dewey is that he has identified the scientific method—inquiry—in a much broader context as general problem-solving material activity. What he simply does is observe the pattern of inquiry wherever it occurs and declare that to be the scientific method. (Bhattacharaya 1976, 119)

Another important motif is the strong place of scientific inquiry in the solution of social problems. Inquiry is to be the one sure way to both solve the problems of men and to carry out increasingly democratic living. In this way, science extends to moral, intellectual, social, and educational problem solving. Scientific inquiry is invoked in the cause of democracy: Science, inasmuch as it involves experimentalism in the service of democratic aims and ideals, can be called, ex hypothesi, democratic. Leonard Waks nicely conveys this sentiment. "Scientific democracy is not an end-in-view for Dewey, but a philosophical ideal" (Waks 1998, 19). And further, "The scientific conception of democracy was the pattern through which ran the axis of Dewey's experimentalist project" (Waks 1998, 19).

Of course, many interpreters of Dewey do not share Waks's enthusiasm regarding scientific inquiry. They particularly do not like what they see as a naturalistic fallacy: to wit, the conflation of descriptive science with normative concerns. Waks is characteristically unsympathetic to these charges. "It is problematic to lay claim to the Deweyan heritage while downplaying his idea of 'science,' or excusing it as an accident of his proscientific age, or even rejecting it" (Waks 1998, 2). And where more experiential and aesthetic interpreters (as I shall further discuss) point to Dewey's experiential texts for validation of the argument that science is properly subordinate to art, Waks claims "a new emphasis on the relation between science and art (a new way of speaking about his perennial concern, continuity between reflective delay and free flowing experience)" (Waks 1998, 2ff). The suggestion here is that art and science are at the very least, equals.

Christine McCarthy holds a view similar to Waks. She claims that

> examination of the consequences of human belief and action allow the recognition of such patterns as may exist, leading us to the recognition of general principles of moral action. Such empirically identified principles can serve, just as general principles in other sciences serve, to guide future practice successfully toward desired goals. (McCarthy 1996, 27)

McCarthy's research interests in critical thinking and constructivist approaches to learning and teaching ethics have led her to proclaim a strong role for science in Dewey's theories of knowledge and value. In her early research, she focuses heavily on the question of whether critical thinking is justified rationally or instrumentally. Her first foray into this debate consists of a critique of Harvey Siegel's notion of critical thinking as premised on justified true belief. In place of justified true belief, McCarthy argues that we should rather premise critical thinking upon the instrumentalist account of warrant offered by pragmatism in general and John Dewey in particular. Critical thinking is best viewed as an episodic activity that is helpful to solve specific moral problems (McCarthy 1993, 67). Critical thinking as a pragmatic endeavor is carried forward in further essays on probabilistic thinking and moral decisions (e.g., McCarthy 1993).

It is with her *Philosophy of Education 1996* essay entitled "When You Know It, and I know It, What Is It We Know? Pragmatic Realism and the Epistemologically Absolute" that McCarthy qualifies her reading of pragmatism. Whereas McCarthy, in her earlier work, was content to invoke pragmatism as a general method for ascertaining epistemological warrant, she here restricts this invocation. It is not pragmatism writ large that is beneficial for constructing moral knowledge, rather a variant of it. And this variant is what she heretofore labels "pragmatic realism." As she puts it, "Meanings, the objects of knowledge, like objects themselves, are objective, independent things to be discovered, not subjective belief-dependent things to be made. And hence knowledge, the apprehension of meaning (however limited and partial that apprehension might be) is similarly an objective, belief-independent sort of thing" (McCarthy 1996, 25).

For McCarthy, pragmatic realism is premised on there being "real, mind-independent things/events [that] are complexes of qualities" (McCarthy 1996, 25). It is the existence of these antecedents that allows the actor to make claims about a set of circumstances in question. Drawing upon both Dewey and C. S. Peirce, McCarthy claims that it is doubt, arising from a particular problem, that initiates the investigation, and it is the failure to find a cause for doubt that leads to a "reason to believe (tentatively) that no such cause for doubt actually exists" (McCarthy 1996, 26). From this, McCarthy advances the normative conclusion that "for the aim, always, is to actively seek out those experiences that might lead to Doubt, so that, after strong testing, one might judge a belief, so far, to have 'passed'. (McCarthy 1996, 28).

McCarthy's investment in mind—independent things/events leads her to a criticism of what she considers "subjectivist" readings of constructivist pedagogy. She is particularly keen to deny for Dewey a role in these readings. Her targets are interpreters of Dewey's experiential texts, most notably Jim Garrison. Drawing upon her earlier essay on pragmatic realism, McCarthy claims:

> What makes the world "objective" in Dewey's sense is not a putative isolation of the world from human experience. It is simply the fact that the world, the sets of interactive thing/events in which it consists, are [sic] not products of the human mind. The thesis that there is an objective reality about which we learn and come to know is central to the pragmatic ontological realism of Dewey. (McCarthy 2000, 220)

How does McCarthy justify this claim? She argues that Dewey held a "correspondence theory of truth," and that this meant "for a proposition to be *true* it must *correspond* to some 'relevant occurrence.' . . . So a proposition [p] is true if and only if it has a particular relation, namely 'correspondence,' to certain 'existential consequences' (McCarthy 2000, 223). Presumably this 'relevant occurrence' is just the existential thing/event that McCarthy proposes can safeguard Dewey from a thoroughgoing subjectivist constructivism.

It is just the premise that there are objectively occurring things and events, which allows McCarthy to posit a strong role for scientific method in the construction of normative claims. Normative judgments can be as objectively real as descriptive judgments because the consequences of human beliefs are as objective as any other traits of experience.

Moral knowledge is said to be in no essential way different from scientific knowledge. Indeed, moral knowledge is scientific knowledge if it is carried out in a scientific manner.

> In Dewey's view, moral knowledge is no more problematic than is any knowledge; "moral" knowledge is simply that knowledge which is useful in certain sorts of problems, in this case, moral problems. Moral knowledge is thus not knowledge belonging to some isolated realm of transcendental truths. Nor is moral knowledge in any way isolated from, nor even different than, our other knowledge, in other words, from knowledge *simpliciter*. Indeed, we have, in all knowledge, a knowledge that is potentially, "moral knowledge." (McCarthy 1999, 342)

McCarthy's argument that moral knowledge is scientific knowledge and that scientific inquiry can bring it about is premised upon two previous claims. The first is that there are real existences and events independent of human cognition. The second is that these existences and events lead to occurrences, kinds, and consequences in our interactions with them. Once these two premises are put forth, McCarthy is able to argue, with quotations from Dewey's *Theory of Moral Life* (the middle section of the second edition of *Ethics*), that

> we begin a moral inquiry, as any other, with an examination of particular occurrences. We do not end with the particular, however, because "problems for the most part fall into certain recurrent kinds . . . [so that] there are general principles which . . . operate in an empirically regulative way in given cases." These general principles will emerge as the result of continued investigation, given three conditions: first, the investigation(s) would have to be continued, extended in time and space; second, the possibility of locating such generalizations would have to be recognized; and third, the ongoing investigations would have to be matters of open public discourse, widely and thoroughly joined. (McCarthy 1999, 245)

McCarthy sums up her position on the need for scientific method in the realm of ethics by suggesting (in a question-begging manner) that without ethics of a scientific sort we are imperiled. This is so because we no longer have recourse to the real and the true. The obvious implication is that only by making ethics a scientific enterprise can ethics be saved from subjectivism and its (infamous) corollary, relativism. So to McCarthy once again:

> Unfortunately, once scientific inquiry is segregated from the realm of ethics, we are shortly forced to admit that the "standards" to which we

perforce resort, themselves, have no warrant. . . . What is missing in this
picture of nonscientific ethics is some objective method of inquiry that
would allow warranted conclusions as to the real better value, better standard, better belief. The problem is that this picture-ethics sans scientific
empirical inquiry [suggests] "there is no question of false and true, of *real*
and seeming, only of stronger and weaker." And this "puts an end to all
attempt at consistency and organization" in moral theory—a consequence that could scarcely be worse. (McCarthy 1999, 346. Italics mine)

No doubt McCarthy, Waks, and others mean well when they argue science and scientific method as the paradigm case of inquiry. Unfortunately, their
considered responses do not so much absolve Dewey of the critics' complaints
as beg these criticisms, and in the case of Phillips, prove them correct. On this
reading of inquiry, science is the model that all investigation and experimentation should (must?) follow. It is the sure method of alleviating technological,
social, political, and ethical ills. It is premised upon an objective, external
world. And it welcomes (for Phillips at least) the label "positivist." There is
nothing in these thinkers' writings that can be shown to defend Dewey against
the claims that he advocates a reduction of all inquiry in all contexts and situations, to that of the scientific model; that he privileges the analytic/synthetic
distinction; that he subordinates imagination, curiosity, and emotion. Not only
are present-day criticisms not undermined, but older criticisms, those that have
their genesis in debates occurring in the distant past, also stand fast. Questions
of Dewey's allegiance to scientism, to positivism, to the denigration of abstract
thinking, to imagination and curiosity, remain as cogent today as they did over
fifty years ago. It seems as though conceiving science as the model of inquiry
creates more problems for Dewey than it solves.

A great deal of the problem, I claim, arises not only through the invocation of context-free passages, but also through the hunt for a *context-free model
of inquiry*. For these sympathetic readers of Dewey, that model is of course science. Science and the particular techniques that scientists use in coming to
explain natural phenomena becomes, for these readers, the way for inquiry undertaken in all contexts and for all problems. There is no room for the possibility of nonscientific techniques in this reading, because ex hypothesi, all
techniques are scientific. When this is claimed, and the further claim that the
best way to proceed in inquiry is to emulate what the scientists are doing, the
solution to all of the problems of men becomes a scientific one.

Now I shall make a strong claim. This is that inquiry should be read as
context bound and self-correcting. By this, I mean that inquiry, far from consisting of a rigid set of formulae or steps, is to be thought of as protean: it is to
be flexible enough to mold itself according to the context in which it is used.

Further, inquiry ought not to be construed as a general method, if by general method a fixed formula, algorithm, or stage theory is meant. Rather, inquiry is to be thought of as a set of methods, of techniques, of habits, as well as attitudes and tempers that have arisen historically through experimentation. Seeing inquiry in this way obviates the charges of positivism or scientism on the part of Dewey. I turn to support this reading of Dewey.

Part Three:
Rereading Inquiry

In the previous section, I concluded that the various attempts by past and present-day apologists to shield the thinker from the charges laid to him fall short. This is, I claim, because these apologists read inquiry as a scientific, monistic enterprise. The problem with the singular, monist reading is that inquiry is reduced to a model of stages, techniques, or formulae that are applied in every context. Those critics who think Dewey overly scientistic will not be swayed by sympathizers who claim a strong place for science in all contexts. What is required is to read out of Dewey the strong claims to science as having preeminence in every doing and undergoing. In what follows, I put forth my thesis. This is that inquiry should be thought of as not only context bound but self-correcting, self-adjusting. For if inquiry is self-correcting then it follows that it can vary with time, with context, and with its capacity to proffer workable solutions to problems.

I proceed in this section to take up the criticisms of Dewey's theory of inquiry: criticisms that support the reading of Dewey as positivistic or scientistic. The concerns are as follows:

1) Dewey pays little or no heed in his theory of inquiry to pure mathematics or pure science (Cohen).
2) Dewey's theory of inquiry conceals an analytic/synthetic distinction and, as such, is rationalistic and positivistic (White).
3) Dewey's theory of inquiry is reductivist and leaves little room for other ways of knowing, such as imagination, curiosity, and emotion (Scheffler).
4) Dewey's theory of inquiry is scientistic and positivistic, and in particular, bears a striking resemblance to Auguste Comte's version of positivism (Mounce).

To summarize: Dewey's theory of inquiry is scientistic and/or positivistic and has allegiances to Comte's positivism: Dewey's theory of inquiry betrays an analytic/synthetic distinction that undermines his desire to have a logic that is free from metaphysical commitments: Dewey's theory provides little room for imagination, curiosity, or emotion—all very important aspects of thinking.

I begin with the claim that Dewey was positivistic and/or scientistic owing chiefly to a shared set of methods with an earlier positivism best represented by Auguste Comte. This is the most telling of the claims and requires examination into Comte's system, in addition to an unpacking of Dewey's logical works. The middle claim will be treated next. This is the claim that Dewey maintains an analytic/synthetic distinction in his *Logic*. This will also require careful unpacking to overcome. The last claim—that of Dewey as having provided little room for other ways of knowing such as curiosity, imagination, and emotion—will be dealt with subsequent to this. But before I begin with the claims themselves, I wish to discuss the perils of the textual interpretation of Dewey and why I approach the criticisms in the manner that I do.

The Inconsistency of Dewey on Inquiry and Science

I first turn to several of Dewey's statements on inquiry and the role and scope of science, therein. As discussed in chapter 1, I believe that Dewey's inconsistency with respect to his statements on inquiry and science is at least partly responsible for the confusion over what Dewey means by inquiry, and what role science is to play in inquiring. To see that this is the case, I choose a few random passages of Dewey's; those that support and limit his allegedly strong role for the place of science in inquiry.

> Upon examination, each instance [of thinking] reveals more or less clearly, five logically distinct steps: (i) a felt difficulty; (ii) its location and definition; (iii) suggestion of possible solution; (iv) development by reasoning of the bearings of the suggestion; (v) further observation and experiment leading to its acceptance or rejection; that is, the conclusion of belief or disbelief. (Dewey [1910] 1978, 236–37)

> Logical order is not a form imposed upon what is known; it is the proper form of knowledge as perfected. (Dewey [1916] 1980, 227)

> [T]he value of any cognitive conclusion depends on the method by which it is reached, so that the perfecting of method, the perfecting of intelligence, is the thing of supreme value. (Dewey [1929] 1984, 160)

> The demand for reform of logic is the demand for a unified theory of inquiry through which the authentic pattern of experimental operational inquiry of science shall become available for regulation of the habitual

methods by which inquiries in the field of common sense are carried on. (Dewey [1938] 1986, 102)

These statements, pulled randomly from Dewey's varied texts, all seem to agree on the importance, indeed, necessity of, science as *the* method of inquiry. The first statement claims that inquiry has stages and that these stages are clear. The second, third, and fourth statements make the claim that inquiry is to be perfected through unification, and that perfecting and unification of inquiry will lend itself to the domain of common sense. But it is easy to find statements in Dewey calling for a hesitation, if not skepticism concerning the capacity of scientific inquiry to be the model of all inquiry. For example:

> Imposing an alleged uniform general method upon everybody breeds mediocrity in all but the very exceptional. And measuring originality by deviation from the mass breeds eccentricity in them. Thus we stifle the distinctive quality of the many, and save in rare instances . . . infect the rare geniuses with an unwholesome quality. (Dewey [1916] 1980, 180)

> The difference between physical and social inquiry does not reside in the presence or absence of an end-in-view, formulated in terms of possible consequences. It consists in the respective subject-matters of the purposes. The difference makes a great practical difference in the conduct of inquiry: a difference in the kind of operations to be performed in instituting the subject-matters that in their respective interactions will resolve a situation. (Dewey [1938] 1986, 496)

> What is needed is not the carrying over of procedures that have approved themselves in physical science, but *new* methods as adapted to *human* issues and problems, as methods already in scientific use have shown themselves to be in physical subject-matter. (Dewey [1949] 1989, 379)

These statements seem to counter the strong rhetoric of inquiry as science prevalent in the first set. The first statement claims that any general method (presumably a scientific method or otherwise) cannot be applied *tout court* to all without significant negative consequences for inquiry. The second statement insists that scientific inquiry differs from other "forms" of inquiry in that it and these have different subject matters that portend differing conduct. Finally, the third statement claims that new methods are required to solve distinctly human problems, and that the carrying-over of methods from (physical) science is unhelpful at best. Juxtaposing these myriad statements cannot but leave the reader in a state of confusion as to what the role is and should be for science and scientific methods, in inquiry.

What I am suggesting by juxtaposing these (and many other and similar statements can be invoked) is that turning to passages as these will not bring the issue to a satisfactory conclusion. One can easily cite passages in favor of Dewey's high regard for all things scientific and at the same time counter with statements suggesting his caution, if not his skepticism for the role and scope of science in inquiry. Unfortunately, there is a tendency in the scholarship of Dewey to do just this: to invoke passages out of context, *pro utilitate argumentum*, and not pause to consider how this practice might alter the import of his other statements. This has led both critics and sympathizers to come down on one side or another of the debate as to whether Dewey was or was not scientistic, positivistic, or of a positivistic temper. It seems clear to me that textual citations alone cannot negotiate this impasse, though they certainly can and do, something further needs to be done. And this, in my opinion, is the placing of inquiry firmly in the context of its avowed aims and purposes: its self-correction in the face of changing contexts and changing evidence.

The First Claim: Inquiry, Positivism, and Scientism

Perhaps the most incriminating concern raised by the critics is that of Dewey's alleged positivism or scientism.[10] On what grounds do the critics base their charges? H. O. Mounce and Denis Phillips see that in Dewey's *Reconstruction and Philosophy* an approach to the development of scientific method is shared (unwittingly) with Auguste Comte.[11] I develop this argument in more detail, noting exactly where Mounce draws from Dewey to buttress his claims.

At first glance, it would seem that Dewey, given as he is to naturalistic explanations of the growth of knowledge, counts himself (loosely) a positivist. In a 1902 contribution to the *Dictionary of Philosophy and Psychology*, Dewey writes that "the term [positivism] is used more loosely to denote any philosophy which agrees with that of Comte in limiting philosophy to the data and methods of the natural sciences—opposition to the a priori, and to speculation by any method peculiar to metaphysics" (Dewey [1903] 1976, 209). If positivism is to be taken as a naturalistic and therefore nonmetaphysical approach to knowledge, then it seems that Dewey would have to include himself in the definition. And it would seem, a fortiori, that Dewey could be saddled with the label of being Comtean. But the issue is not yet settled.

To rebut the claim that Dewey shared strong affinities with Comte requires an (brief) examination of Comte's major tenets. Now it is certainly correct that Comte did think that the history of human reason consisted of three stages. And Dewey, too, seems to argue for three stages of the growth of knowledge. This claim is not in contention. But what is in contention is the status accorded the growth of knowledge. Whereas the growth of knowledge is for Dewey a genetic, naturalistic (though not one that necessarily follows the method of the natural sciences), and experiential process, it is unclear if this is also the case for Comte. For example, Comte, in his *First Course of Philosophy*, says:

> In thus studying the total development of human intelligence in the diverse spheres of activity . . . I believe that I have discovered a great and *fundamental* law, which is accompanied by *fixed necessity* and which seems to me to be so solidly established on *rational proofs* furnished by knowledge of our [scientific] organization which arise as a result of our historical examination of the past. This law claims that each of our principle conceptions, each branch of our knowledge, passes successively through three different theoretical stages: the stage of theology, or the fictive stage; the stage of the metaphysical, or the abstract stage; and the stage of the scientific, or positivistic stage. In other words, our human spirit, through its own nature, successively uses in its growth, each of these philosophical models [méthods]. . . . Of these three philosophical approaches . . . the first is the necessary point of departure for any further human intellectual growth; the third is the definitive and settled state [état fixé et définitive] and the second is uniquely destined to serve the *final* transition. (Comte [1830] 1975, 21 italics mine)

There are (at least) two claims that Dewey would disagree with. The first is that the very development of the growth of knowledge from religious to scientific can be given lawlike status. Though this is an inductive conclusion, it nevertheless seems a mischievous statement coming from Comte: one supposedly critical of metaphysical pronouncements. This is a claim that Dewey would of course reject. Growth of knowledge may be naturalistic, but Dewey would argue that we do not have the sort of insight into the nature of growth to claim a universal law of it. Secondly, Dewey would have trouble with the notion that the scientific stage of the growth of knowledge is a settled affair. The practice of inquiry depends upon inquiry's ability to meet the needs of the particular problem undertaken. As such, it cannot proclaim itself as final in the sense that Comte wants. In fact, Dewey *did* criticize the Comtean method for concealing a nonnaturalistic metaphysics. Dewey's criticism of Comte's method (and its subsequent uptake by the logical positivists) comes late in his career. In the work coauthored with Arthur Bentley, entitled *Knowing and the Known*, Dewey states:

> Comte's "positive" method retained something from his "metaphysics," just as his "metaphysics" retained something from his "theological." He

substitutes "laws" for "forces," but gives them no extensive factual construction. "Logical Positivism" has anachronistically accepted this Comtean type of law, emptied it of what factuality it had, and further formalized it. (Dewey and Bentley [1949] 1989, 98)

Even if Dewey cannot without extreme qualification be labeled a Comtean positivist, he still seems saddled with the label of positivism *simpliciter*. Dewey's espousal of naturalism and of scientific methodology does, it seems, place him in the positivist camp. If one wants to extract Dewey from this camp, one must find another point of entry. But before this point of entry is accessed, it will do to dismantle one other obstruction impeding the way. And this is Dewey's reference to something called a "general method." This obstruction must be dismantled because undue and uncritical attention to Dewey's talk of a general method can make it seem as though this is the fixed, rigorous method of the natural (and physical) sciences that Comte maintains and that Dewey mentions as a central feature in his Encyclopedia article on positivism. Dewey's most famous general statement on inquiry comes from his *Logic*. Here, Dewey claims that "inquiry is the controlled or directed transformation of an indeterminate situation into one that is so determinate in its constituent distinctions and relations as to convert the elements of the original situation into a unified whole" (Dewey [1938] 1986, 108).[12] Three characteristics of method writ large are proffered here. The first is that inquiry involves control and transformation. What is transformed is an indeterminate (problematic) situation. And the result of the transformation is the conversion of a problematic state of affairs into a unified whole. Inquiry transforms a problematic situation into a nonproblematic one through the use of distinctions (analysis) and relations (synthesis) of data and meanings. Other characterizations of inquiry are more and less robust. For example, Dewey speaks of the general method of thinking in the first edition of *How We Think*:

> Upon examination, each instance [of thinking] reveals more or less clearly, five logically distinct steps: (i) a felt difficulty; (ii) its location and definition; (iii) suggestion of possible solution; (iv) development by reasoning of the bearings of the suggestion; (v) further observation and experiment leading to its acceptance or rejection; that is, the conclusion of belief or disbelief. (Dewey [1910] 1978, 236–237)

At another point in the *Logic*, Dewey says of the social sciences:

> Until social inquiry succeeds in establishing methods of observing, discriminating and arranging data that evoke and test correlated ideas, and until, on the other side, ideas formed and used are (1) employed as hy-

potheses, and are (2) of a form to direct and prescribe operations of an-alytic-synthetic determination of facts, social inquiry has no chance of satisfying the logical conditions for attainment of scientific status. (Dewey [1938] 1986, 485)

From *The Quest For Certainty*, Dewey claims:

The subject-matter which had been taken as satisfying the demands of knowledge, as the material with which to frame solutions, became some-thing which set *problems*. . . . The differences between the earth, the re-gion of the planets, and the heavenly ether, instead of supplying ultimate principles which could be used to mark off and classify things, were some-thing to be explained and to bring under identical principles. . . . Mod-ern experimental science is an art of control. (Dewey [1929] 1984, 80)

From *Democracy and Education*, Dewey proclaims:

Such matters as knowledge of the past, of current technique, of materi-als, of the ways in which one's own best results are assured, supply the material for what may be called *general* method. There exists a cumula-tive body of fairly stable methods for reaching results, a body authorized by past experience and by intellectual analysis, which an individual ig-nores at his peril. (Dewey [1916] 1980, 177)

Finally, from (again) *The Quest for Certainty*, Dewey claims:

The scientific attitude may almost be defined as that which is capable of enjoying the doubtful; method is, in one respect, a technique for making a productive use of doubt by converting it into operations of definite in-quiry. (Dewey [1929] 1984, 182)

One can easily become bewildered by the many and varied ingredients of method. For example, in the first passage, Dewey suggests that thinking as method, *uberhaupt*, has five stages that begin with a problem and lead through to a satisfying conclusion. Though he would admit that the stages do not have to occur in order and that, in some instances, not all of the stages are required for a conclusion, he would (here) nevertheless require that inquiry begin with a felt difficulty and end with a conclusive belief. The second passage suggests that hypothesis formation is very important in inquiry and that "operations of analytic and synthetic determinations of fact" are at least important for the physical and social varieties of inquiry. The third passage suggests that inquiry is akin to experimentation and that the goal of inquiry is control of facts. The fourth passage suggests a much broader view of inquiry. Here, past knowledge and techniques are brought into the fold. And finally, the fifth passage suggests that attitudes and the enjoyment of the doubtful are important. What is one to make of this?

There are two paths one can take. One can emphasize, in the spirit of the first edition of How We Think, that inquiry has stages and in these stages, specific tasks are accomplished, and specific tools utilized.[13] Or, one could emphasize, in the spirit of Democracy and Education or The Quest for Certainty, that many different tools are brought to bear on a problematic situation and that any general manifestation of inquiry is, as a result, very broad. Before I argue which of these readings better solves the concern at hand, I want to turn to some further sentiments of Dewey's on the place of scientific method in relation to other methods. Doing so will provide me recourse to an answer to this dilemma.

In some passages of Dewey's, it does seem as if scientific method is granted preeminence. Most of these occur, curiously enough, not in his logical or scientific texts, but (as stated in chapter 1) his social ones. But little specific is said about the nature, or ingredients, of scientific method. For this, one must turn to Dewey's logical and scientific texts. But when one does, one is faced with the paradox of a less than preeminent role and scope for scientific method. As early as Studies in Logical Theory, Dewey claims that "there is no difference of kind between the methods of science and those of the plain man. The difference is the greater control by science of the statement of the problem, and of the selection and use of relevant material, both sensible and conceptual" (Dewey [1903] 1976, 305). In The Quest for Certainty, Dewey, speaking of physical inquiry, claims that "it would be misinterpreted if it were taken to mean that science is the only valid kind of knowledge; it is just an intensified form of knowing in which are written large the essential characters of any knowing" (Dewey [1929] 1984, 200). In the Logic, Dewey states: "In what is called common sense, the problem is that of some use-enjoyment. In science, the generic problem is promotion of controlled inquiry" (Dewey [1938] 1986, 496). And further:

> The difference between physical and social inquiry does not reside in the presence or absence of an end-in-view, formulated of possible consequences. It consists in the respective subject-matters of the purposes. The difference makes a great practical difference in the conduct of inquiry: a difference in the kind of operations to be performed in instituting the subject-matters that in their interactions will resolve a situation. (Dewey [1938] 1986, 496)

In these passages, Dewey is claiming that there is no difference in kind between physical, social, and common sense versions of inquiry. The differences are in the greater control that scientific inquiry exerts, and the subject matter that scientific, as opposed to other sorts of inquiry, engages. What does this have to do with the dilemma of the construal of general method of inquiry as either broad or narrow, preeminent or not? I claim that these passages suggest two good arguments as to why anything like a general method ought to be construed as broad rather than narrow, and not preeminent in relation to specific methods.

My first claim is that, if inquiry is to be seen as narrow, an argument as to how inquiry is to remain general in the face of differing problems and contexts must be proffered. For if general inquiry is to be construed as a set of fixed and invariable stages, as some supporters say, then it must be argued that in *any* context or for *any* set of problems, inquiry must act in the same manner. But consider the differences between a philosopher pondering the question of the interpretation of a particular passage in a particular text written by a particular thinker, as opposed to a teacher working closely with a student on the reproducibility of a physics experiment. In the first case, the observable material undertaken in problem solving is minimal: in the second, it can presumably be thought that much material is required to demonstrate the application of a physical law. Further, different activities are required to operationalize inquiry and test its results. In the first case, operationalization will involve nonobservable changes in the material. No doubt, something "new" will be produced. But the work involved is at the level of ideational propositions (conceptions) rather than generic propositions. In the second case, observable changes are tested for. And generic propositions (mathematical laws) are brought to bear on the relevance of these changes. The point is that even if the manner in which one reflects is similar in these cases, the material reflected upon, the propositions utilized, and the manner in which inquiry is operationalized are markedly different. A narrow definition of general method, such as that suggested by Dewey's talk of the reflective enterprise in his five-stage description of the activity in the first edition of *How We Think* (though later relaxed by Dewey in the second edition), cannot be held as the *fons et origo* of inquiry without being of little service to varied problems. This is so because such a narrow definition does not and cannot exhaust how one is to inquire, what tools one is to use in inquiring, and what inquiry is to count for in varied problem-solving activities.[14] As such, this reflective exercise can only be said to be markedly incomplete. Though such common elements of method may be found in any and all experiences, this cannot be said to exhaust all of the inquiring activity undergone in problem solving. Such common elements cannot be both the necessary *and* sufficient condition of inquiry. The only recourse one has to avoiding this dilemma is to construe inquiry in the broad sense that Dewey gives: as a cluster of specific methods, together with past experiences and attitudes (what could be called the "experimentalist: temper) brought to bear on specific problems.

My second and related claim is that general inquiry cannot be construed in a strictly scientific manner. Dewey seems to make this point plain in several of his works. What is at stake here is the feasibility of inquiry for its problem. Scientific inquiry, on Dewey's account in the *Logic*, privileges strongly control of factual material and the development of analysis and synthesis. Yet, it does not seem to be a task of inquiry in the settling of, for example, a problem of the commonsense variety, such as how to dodge a puddle so as to not get wet. Propositions about how to respond are no doubt (subconsciously?) invoked. Thus, it cannot be claimed that no inquiry is involved. Rather, there is no requirement for development of new propositions in situations such as this. Of course, one can speculate that multiple encounters with puddles and the consequences of wading into them led to propositions being formed. But once formed, they function more or less automatically. Knowledge involved in avoiding a puddle is generally nonexperimental: it does not require the construction of novel propositions, conceptions, or ideas to conclude a solution; nor does it require testing of possible solutions, unless something about the situation warrants further investigation, owing to a failure (existential or imagined) of response. It is a case of the conclusions of prior inquiries invoked in an existentially similar situation. In short, it is the use of habituated inquiry.

I am now in a position to bring these results to bear on the question of Dewey and positivism and scientism. Positivism and scientism assume that scientific method is the best method for solving the problems of men. And though Dewey often thought just this way, particularly (as I have demonstrated) in certain of his social texts, he nevertheless did not think this way in his logical and scientific works. He clearly is at pains to distance himself from the idea that scientific method is somehow the preeminent method or that scientific method contains some ingredient not found in other methods that therefore occasion its supremacy. I urge that it be said of scientific method that it is to be brought to bear on problems that occasion the sort of inquiry, of rigorous hypothesis testing, ordering, and control, that would be of benefit in coming to a solution to these problems. To the extent that scientific solutions to the problems of men are of benefit, scientific method is to have a place. But to the extent that solutions occasioned in settings other than those of the physical or natural sciences are required, or that scientific solutions would not fit the bill, scientific method would not be occasioned. This is not to claim that other methods are nonexperimental; rather that what is to count as a method being "scientific" is the aims that are set for inquiry and the context in which it is used. Scientific method thus exists as a *variant* or (even better) *variants* of inquiry, highly technical and controlling variants, to help in the search for the solutions to the problems of men, but they are not the only variants.[15] Within the panoply of methods, attitudes, and tempers that coalesce to form inquiry, it is but one of many, as I shall show with the aid of Dewey's supporters, in the following chapter. Inasmuch as positivism and scientism carve out a much stronger role for method, I claim that Dewey cannot be labeled positivistic or scientistic.

The Second Claim: Inquiry and the Analytic/Synthetic Distinction

The second concern of the critics is the distinction between universal conceptions (analytic statements) and generic propositions (synthetic statements). The criticism is that if analytic statements are allowed into Dewey's logical theory, then they become the *fons et origo* of all inquiry. Inquiry can proceed no further than self-evident identity ('A=A') statements. The effect of this is to halt inquiry at the level of the concept: because conceptions are said to be analytic, they cannot transform themselves, or be transformed. They become unresponsive to the situations in and through which they operate. They are, in all essentials, fixed kinds. This is Morton White's claim of a contradiction on the part of Dewey. Recall that White draws from this statement of Dewey's to support his contention.

> Propositions . . . are of two main categories: (1) Existential, referring directly to actual conditions as determined by experimental observation and (2) ideational or conceptual, consisting of interrelated meanings which are non-existential in content to direct reference but which are applicable to existence through the operations they represent as possibilities. (Dewey [1938] 1986 in White 1973, 149)

There is a taken-for-grantedness of the meaning-synonymy of the terms, existential with synthetic, and ideational/conceptual with analytic. This taken-for-grantedness, however, is problematic, as I shall show. I shall argue that the very meanings that are considered proof of the a priori nature of physical laws are themselves premised on the ability of generic propositions (those of classes and kinds) to order existential data and are thus operationalized in this process. Though concepts may be at one remove from these experiences, they nevertheless are connected, through their capacity to be operationalized to them. Further, physical laws can exist only as tools and, insofar as they produce other meaningful experiences, have their status as concepts confirmed. But these cannot be considered a priori if this is to be taken as prior to, or independent of, experience. That is, these cannot be analytic laws in the sense that White makes of them: self-justifying, fixed, and timeless ideas. In contrast to the received meaning of analytic (the meaning given by White), this term for Dewey denotes the capacity of certain propositions to provide for discrimination and distinction, *simpliciter*.

I begin with statements that Dewey makes in his two editions of *How We Think*. In the first edition, Dewey tells us of analytic and synthetic statements that "every judgment is analytic in so far as it involves discernment, discrimination, marking off the trivial from the important, the irrelevant from what points to a conclusion; and it is synthetic in so far as it leaves the mind with an inclusive situation within which the selected facts are placed" (Dewey [1910] 1978, 269). In the second edition of *How We Think*, Dewey claims:

> Through judging, confused data are cleared up, and seemingly incoherent and disconnected facts are brought together. The clearing up is *analysis*. The bringing together is *synthesis*. . . . If the element thus selected clears up what is otherwise obscure in the new experience, if it settles what is uncertain, it thereby gains in positiveness and definiteness of meaning. (Dewey [1932] 1986, 216)

Taken together, these statements strongly suggest that what Dewey means by analytic and synthetic is not the inherent quality of a statement or proposition (a priori vs. a posteriori; categorical vs. empirical), rather an activity within an experience, of sorting out and bringing together. Analytic and synthetic, for Dewey, are terms denoting a function, not a quality or a form. The meaning-synonymy granted to these respective terms is quite dubious.

Nevertheless Dewey, it is true, does distinguish between existential (generic) propositions and ideal (conceptual or categorical) propositions. Generic propositions are said to be "propositions about kinds and classes" (Dewey [1938] 1986, 253). Ideal or conceptual propositions, by contrast, are said to work exclusively in the realm of logic. Dewey puts it this way:

> In science, there are many propositions in which the clause introduced by "if" is known to be contrary to conditions set by existential circumstances; that is, to be such that they cannot be existentially satisfied, as "If a particle at rest is acted upon by a single moving particle, then," etc. In such propositions, *if* and *when* designate a connection of conceptual subject-matters, not of existential or temporo-spatial subject-matters. (Dewey [1938] 1986, 254)

Dewey tells us that the failure of much modern logic lies in its tendency to collapse conceptual propositions into existential ones, or, as Dewey puts it, "that propositions about kinds [generic propositions] are ultimately of the same logical dimension as are *if-then* propositions" (Dewey [1938] 1986, 255). Dewey puts the problem of physical laws as fixed and timeless, this way:

> [In the received view] fixed, unquestioned rules determine the recognized kinds, while kinds are so fixed by the rules that they do not serve to test and modify the ruling conceptions but are taken rather to exemplify and

support the rules. At best, inquiry is confined to determining whether or not given objects have the traits that bring them under the scope of a given standardized conception—as still happens to a large extent in popular "judgments" in morals and politics. (Dewey [1938] 1986, 264)

Here, the central concern—the concern that some aspect of inquiry may become reified —is occasioned. But this is just the scourge of prior logical thinking that Dewey wishes to do away with. And Dewey's response is to make clear the operational nature of even so-called analytic statements.[16] When he does this, Dewey invokes a line of thought that has its origins in an earlier essay, "The Logic of Judgments of Practice." Here, Dewey claims:

We may frame at least a hypothesis that all judgments of fact have reference to a determination of courses of action to be tried and to the discovery of means for their realization. In the sense already explained, all categorical propositions would be hypothetical, and their truth would coincide with their tested consequences effected by intelligent action. (Dewey [1915] 1985, 22)

In the *Logic,* Dewey provides a more robust version of this claim. He provides us the famous example of what is known as a *modus ponens:* All men are mortal; Socrates is a man; therefore, Socrates is mortal. The point Dewey makes is that the class of individuals of the kind "men" requires involvement with specific and existential individuals. The kind "men" applies to all individuals within that kind. The first propositions mentioned, generic propositions, are rooted in existential matters. The second, conceptual or ideational propositions, are not rooted in existential matters and indeed, are said be universal, confirming as they do both the actual and the possible. Yet, they are said to be hypothetical, and contingent upon the consequences of thought. What to make of this?

Universal propositions are "formulations of possible ways or modes of acting or operating" (Dewey [1938] 1986, 263). The universal relation is stated as a conjunction between an antecedent "if" clause, and a consequent "then" clause. What are ordered in this relationship are kinds and classes. That is to say, given a generic proposition of a kind or class (say, of men), the universal proposition, the if-then clause, serves to control and direct these. For example, one might say, "if Socrates is a man, and all men are mortal, then Socrates is mortal." The universal if-then proposition serves to distinguish and order the general propositions; that is, the kind "men" and "mortal." It is on the basis of there being an if-then clause that the kind and class of men and mortals can be maintained. As Dewey puts it, universal propositions "serve[s] to direct the operations by means of which existential material is selectively discriminated and related (ordered) so that it functions as the ground for warranted inferential conclusions" (Dewey [1938] 1986, 269).[17] In this way, universal propositions are functional: they "prescribe the conditions to be satisfied by existential material, so that if singular it is determined to be one of a specified kind, or if a kind, it is included in and/or is inclusive of certain other specified kinds" (Dewey [1938] 1986, 271). The example Dewey himself gives of a universal proposition is that if anything is a material body, it thus attracts other material bodies directly as its mass and indirectly as the square of the distance. This proposition expresses the condition of being a material body and the further conditions that any observed material body must satisfy to be labeled as 'material:' the kind 'material' and 'bodies' are the generic propositions that are ordered by the 'if-then' clause.

Universal conceptions also serve as boundary concepts: that is, they limit the tendency of kinds and classes to become fixed and unquestioned. Universal conceptions function to standardize conceptions in every occasion that generic propositions occur, such that generic propositions do not become reified. "No grounded generic propositions can be formed save as they are the products of the performance of operations indicated as possible by universal propositions" (Dewey [1938] 1986, 274).[18] The outcome of reification—the taking of kinds and classes for fixed, metaphysical entities is the overriding concern that the separation of the generic from the conceptual is to address.[19]

The conclusion to draw from this is that, though generic and universal propositions are distinct in terms of their (logical) forms, they are not distinct in terms of their larger function, which is to direct the course of existential data. They are distinct in terms of their smaller functions, which are directed by the contexts they serve; and it is the contexts which they each serve that determine the logical form of the propositions. This is nowhere more evident than in what counts as proof for a universal conception. Commenting on the supposed impossibility of a universal conception being applicable to existential material, Dewey tells us that

> no amount of reasoning can do more than develop a universal proposition; it cannot, of itself, determine matters-of-fact. Only operational application can effect the latter determination. On the other hand, existential data cannot of themselves *prove* a universal. They can *suggest* it. But proof is affected by (1) the formulation of the idea suggested in a hypothetical proposition, and (2) by the transformation of data into a unified situation through execution of the operations presented by the hypothetical as a rule of action. (Dewey [1938] 1986, 276)

A close reading of this passage suggests that, although universal conceptions are not applicable to existential material (data) they nevertheless at least indirectly rely for their very proof upon the outcome of the transformation of the data by generic propositions into kinds and classes. The usefulness of universal conceptions in directing existential operations through the ordering of generic propositions, which in turn categorize traits of experience, is the driving force of their being. Further, their proof lies in their capacity to accomplish the unification of data. Put another way, it is the fact of their being tools to order and determine generic propositions which do classify and categorize existential traits and events according to classes and kinds, that serves as the raison d'etre of a universal conception. It is through the operationalization of universal propositions that they are tested and found acceptable. The characterization of universal propositions as analytic, if analytic is taken to mean nonexperiential; rationalistic; fixed and timeless, or self-identical, is untenable in the face of the operationalization of conceptions.

The Third Claim: Inquiry as Denigrating Emotion, Imagination, and Curiosity

The claim that little room in Dewey's inquiry is left for emotion, imagination, and curiosity is the concern of Israel Scheffler. Here, a passage of Dewey's *Democracy and Education* is invoked to support the claim: "The aim of education . . . is first and foremost to develop critical methods of thought." This leaves out much thinking that is not problem-oriented; thinking that is playful, curious, emotive, and imaginative (Scheffler 1974, 244). In support of this, a passage from *Democracy and Education* is quoted.

> Study is effectual in the degree in which the pupil realizes the place of the . . . truth he is dealing with in carrying to fruition activities in which he is concerned. This connection of an object and a topic with the promotion of an activity having a purpose is the first and the last word of a genuine theory of interest in education. (Dewey [1916] 1980, 135 in Scheffler 1974, 244)

This is a rather weak passage to cite if one wants to claim that Dewey somehow denigrated curiosity, imagination, and emotion in the turn to a problembased notion of inquiry. It should not prove difficult to counter this criticism. As an educational text of Dewey's is quoted, I shall do the same, restricting myself in this instance to Dewey's second edition of *How We Think*.

It is quite right to consider Dewey's theory of inquiry a problem-solving, operationalist one. Claims of inquiry as operationalized are abundant in the Dewey corpus. To choose but one example from *How We Think*:

> Simple or complicated, relating to what to do in a practical predicament or what to infer in a scientific or philosophic problem, there will always

be the two sides: the conditions to be accounted for, dealt with, and the ideas that are plans for dealing with them or are suppositions for interpreting and explaining the phenomena. (Dewey [1933] 1986, 199)

But the problem-solving nature and operationalization of inquiry cannot be a justification for the claim that emotion, imagination, and curiosity have a subordinate place in problem solving. In fact, they play a very large role, though not indicated as such in this particular passage. But the claim that there are other ways of knowing than that of problem solving and that only these involve emotion, imagination, and curiosity as apart from problem solving, is foreign to Dewey. Dewey does not make room for other ways of knowing: what he does is make room for many variants of *one* knowing, if knowing is to be coeval with thinking. Emotion, imagination, and curiosity are necessary, though identifiable, participants in this thinking and the presence, absence, and quality of one or more of these will have an incalculable impact on subsequent thought. But they are not coeval with thinking or knowing.

In the same paragraph as the quote above, Dewey makes the case for the importance of nonlogical ideas in the activity of thinking:

Many ideas are of great value as material of poetry, fiction, or the drama, but not as the stuff of knowledge. However, ideas may be of intellectual use to a penetrating mind even when they do not find any immediate reference to actuality, provided they stay in the mind for use when new facts come to light. (Dewey [1933] 1986, 199)

The implication seems clear: nonlogical ideas are not nonintellectual by virtue of their being nonlogical. Rather, nonlogical ideas are such until they become intellectual through the (further) activity of being brought to bear on novel facts. Thus, there is no idea that comes stamped with the label or form "intellectual." Now imagination is said to be a sort of testing of ideas in thought (Dewey [1933] 1986, 193). It has its counterpart in testing an imagined act overtly. Ideas, first tested in thought, are then attempted *in vivo*. What is being tested for is consistency: consistency of one's inferences and consistency between thoughts as imagined and as fact. Note that the operationalizing character of inquiry is not confined to the passage of idea from thought to fact. Rather, it is operationalized at the level of the testing of ideas, which is imagination, and at the level of fact, which is "experimental corroboration" (Dewey [1933] 1986, 205).

Emotion, too, plays a very important role in thinking. For Dewey, emotion denotes the quality of an experience. Further, it is an immediate quality: one does not cognize an emotion. An emotion is rather had. There is a sort of primacy granted to emotion on Dewey's reading of its role in inquiry. Emotion is said to rouse the thinker to reflection and reflection is then brought to bear on the problem at hand. "But in every case where reflective activity ensues, there is a process of *intellectualizing* what at first is merely an *emotional* quality of the whole situation. This conversion is effected by noting more definitely the conditions that constitute the trouble and cause the stoppage of action" (Dewey [1933] 1986, 202).

The issue of curiosity and inquiry is also dealt with in *How We Think*. Here Dewey develops a genetic reading of curiosity: curiosity begins as a "vital overflow, an expression of abundant organic energy" (Dewey [1933] 1986, 142), which is augmented "under the influence of social stimuli" (Dewey [1933] 1986, 142), and finally "rises above the organic and the social level and becomes intellectual in the degree in which it is transformed into interest in finding out for oneself the answers to questions that are aroused by contact with persons and things" (Dewey [1933] 1986, 143). Far from being denigrated in Dewey's reading of inquiry, curiosity emerges as a vital participant. For curiosity, as interest, is a necessary occasion for the undertaking of any inquiry into any matter. It is the spark that ignites the fuel of reflective activity. As such, it (and emotion and imagination) exists within and as part of, an inquiry.

Part Four:
Inquiry as Self-Correcting

Several characteristics of inquiry can be sifted from the previous discussions. First of all, inquiry, far from being a monolithic technique or instrument that is brought to bear equally on all problems, is a broad set of techniques, tempers, and traits. Some of these techniques are situational: they vary according to, and are driven by, the problems undertaken. Thus, inquiry of a scientific bent has different techniques to offer than does inquiry of a commonsense bent. As well, personal tempers and attitudes play a role. If this is so, then inquiry comes to be more personalized than hitherto estimated. And because of the differing situations in which inquiry is used, and the personal traits and characteristics of the inquirer, I claim that no two inquiries will be exactly alike. Against Dewey's critics, inquiry does not privilege analytic statements over synthetic ones. As well, inquiry is not Comtean, or positivistic. Inquiry does not denigrate imagination, curiosity, or emotion either. But to make this position strong, to counter the charge that I am merely reading those passages that fit my claims, more must be done. I must construct a cohesive reading of inquiry; one that lends context to the claims I proffer.

One aspect of inquiry that has received only cursory attention thus far is that of continuity. As Dewey demonstrates in his *Reconstruction and Philosophy*, (philosophical) inquiry is a developing process. It gets further and further refined as the consequences that emanate from the problems to which it is put, are favorable. In that text, inquiry is said to build on itself. But the theme of continuity is itself a continuous one. Dewey puts this sentiment nicely in his *Logic:*

> Just as the validity of a proposition in discourse, or of conceptual material generally, cannot be determined short of the consequences to which its functional use gives rise, so the sufficient warrant of a judgment as a claimant to knowledge . . . cannot be determined apart from connection with a widening circle of consequences. (Dewey [1938] 1986, 484)

All inquiry, and a fortiori, all logical forms, "arise within the operation of inquiry and are concerned with control of inquiry so that it may yield warranted assertions" (Dewey [1938] 1986, 11). These operations in turn "involve both material and instrumentalities, including in the latter tools and techniques. The more material and instrumentalities are shaped in advance with a view to their operating in conjunction with each other as means to consequences, the better the operations performed are controlled" (Dewey [1938] 1986, 23). All tools and techniques are functional: that is, they serve as instruments that are accorded status based upon their ability to produce desirable consequences. Of mathematical laws, for example, Dewey claims, "It is, accordingly, impossible to give descriptive value to the mathematical conceptions and propositions. They have instrumental and functional status" (Dewey [1938] 1986, 472).

Operationalizing inquiry places constraints on the tools of inquiry. For example, conceptions and propositions are said to derive their status not from their purely logical nature, rather from their ability to effect a satisfying conclusion to (a set of) problems. This does not minimize the capacity for these propositions and conceptions to work across a variety of distinct problems; but it does suggest that, if new problems emerge that cannot be managed with these, new propositions and conceptions must be constructed. The obvious example of this is the laws of motions' inability to deal with the discoveries of subatomic, subparticulate matter. Further, conceptions and propositions are, as Dewey says, intermediate judgments: they operate as tools to effect the transformation of a problematic situation to a satisfactory resolution. They do not stand alone if standing alone is taken to mean that they are of no further use in the solution to real problems. These uses can range from the macro (social problems) to the micro (mathematical problems that indirectly terminate in the advances of particle physics, etc.).

Most problems require only a habitualized form of knowledge. Habitualized knowledges are those that have been built up as a result of past experiences, trial and error, and shared, social knowledge. As Dewey puts it:

> Because commonsense problems and inquiries have to do with the interactions into which living creatures enter in connection with envi-

roning conditions in order to establish objects of use and enjoyment, the symbols employed are those which have been determined in the habitual culture of a group. They form a system but the system is practical rather than intellectual. It is constituted by the traditions, occupations, techniques, interests, and established institutions of the group. (Dewey [1938] 1986, 118)

Here, little or no reflection into inquiry itself is required, as past inquiries are successful in resolving these problems. Habitualized knowledge is the conclusion of prior experimentation, brought to bear on a "commonsense" problem, but of itself having no need of reconstruction, as it is eminently equipped for the task at hand. It is only when novel problems are encountered, or unsatisfactory or half-satisfactory solutions to older problems are occasioned, that reconstruction of the habits of inquiry are required. At this point, inquiry becomes experimental. This reconstruction first takes place at the level of ideas, or conceptions and propositions, and concerns what Scheffler considers the imaginative. What is at stake is the introduction of new meanings: unsolved problems or new ones force the construction of new relations at the level of conception and this requires that meanings themselves are re-related in such a way that new meanings can emerge.

> In scientific inquiry, then, meanings are related to one another on the grounds of their character as meanings, freed from direct reference to the concerns of a limited group. Their intellectual abstractness is a product of this liberation, just as the "concrete" is practically identified by directness of connection with environmental interaction. (Dewey [1938] 1986, 119)

The point here is that any of the aspects of inquiry are potentially reconstructed when a problem goes unsolved by earlier methods, or a novel problem emerges from the reconsideration of a situation. Conceptions and propositions are in no way exempt from reformulation simply because they relate to each other and not to direct, occasioning concerns. Responses to these concerns, already habitualized, are dependent upon the satisfaction gained from the response. When that satisfaction is jeopardized or put into question, the conceptions and propositions themselves come under scrutiny. Of course, this scrutiny is only indirectly related to the concern-at-hand; it is directly related to the meaning arising out of the problem of failed satisfaction. Nevertheless, scrutiny does occur. All of this is to suggest that inquiry, when faced with a problem that cannot be resolved satisfactorily, transforms itself directly, through its response to the environment or context in which it is used, and indirectly, through its concepts and propositions. This transformation of inquiry potentially transforms every ingredient, stage, tool, and technique. The transformation can go all the way down. It implicates continuity in all of its linkages.

I urge that inquiry be described in much the same manner that Dewey emphasizes habit and behavior in his article on "The Reflex Arc Concept in Psychology."[20] In this likening, a felt but seemingly unsolvable problem triggers investigation not only of the problem, but of inquiry. New ideas are proffered; new universal propositions formed; new relations entertained. The new relations are tested in vivo, in the context of the problematic situation. The satisfaction arising as a result of the solution leads to general, existential propositions for acting that, if performed frequently, become habitualized. These habitualized, routine propositions are then pressed into service for further like problems, and, if the problem remains unsolved, this necessitates a reinvestigation of inquiry, leading (again) to the formation of new propositions.[21]

Dewey has called this "the self-developing or self-correcting nature of scientific inquiry" (Dewey [1938] 1986, 483). The context in which this statement arises is that of what counts as a validity claim:

> Just as the validity of a proposition in discourse, or of conceptual material generally, cannot be determined short of the consequences to which its functional use gives rise, so the sufficient warrant of a judgment as a claimant to knowledge (in its eulogistic sense) cannot be determined apart from connection with a widening circle of consequences. An inquiry in a given special field appeals to the experiences of the community of his fellow workers for confirmation and correction of his results. (Dewey [1938] 1986, 483–84)

Dewey here ties the notion of self-correction to the consequences out of which inquiry arises, and to which it is to help direct, as well as the experiences of one's "community of fellow workers" that serve to confirm the results. The metaphor that best captures this sense of what counts as validity is that of an inextricable linkage of consequences and community, from which inquiry arises, is directed, and is confirmed.

I alluded in the introduction to a number of postanalytic thinkers that have debunked the common "myths" of an empiricism premised on foundations. These are thinkers that are suspicious and/or hostile to fact/norm, analytic/synthetic, and form/matter distinctions. I would like to return to these latter-day views and see how Dewey's notion of self-correction accords. I shall follow Michael Williams's *Problems of Knowledge* in doing so.

To begin with, Williams, in summarizing the state of epistemology (or perhaps "postepistemology" would be a better characterization), notes that the fact/value distinction common to much of nineteenth- and twentieth-century positivism and early analytic thinking is nowadays untenable:

Knowing is not just a factual state or condition but a particular *norma-tive status*. Such statuses are related to appropriate factual states: winning depends on crossing the line before any other competitor. But they also depend on meeting certain norms or standards which define, not what you do do, but what you *must* or *ought* to do. To characterize someone's claim as expressing or not expressing knowledge is to pass judgment on it. Epistemic judgments are thus a particular kind of *value-judgement* [sic]. It is far from obvious that investigations with such a strongly normative component can be fully "naturalized." (Williams 2001,11)[22]

Williams goes on to say, "Philosophers who advocate a naturalistic approach to epistemology sometimes intend only to reject the high apriorism mandated by the idea of epistemology as first philosophy. If this is naturalism—and it certainly is part of what Quine and Rorty have in mind—then I have no objections to it. My quarrel is not with this methodological naturalism but with the reductive naturalism that aspires to account for knowledge in wholly natural-scientific terms" (Williams 2001, 251). This claim fits nicely with Dewey's claim that inquiry sets its own expectations of the anticipated result: to claim that judgments are value-judgments is to claim that that which is judged is judged according to some end, goal, or standard. It is to say that the inquirer has a stake in the methods and outcomes of the inquiry. The converse is to have fully "naturalized" judgments: those that are entirely descriptive. What makes this a dubious enterprise is the difficulty separating out what is descriptive from what is normative; what is a fact from what is a value. Further, it places almost the entire emphasis of inquiry on the procedure rather than the standards or norms that guide the inquiry. Dewey would claim that, far from inquiry functioning along the lines of a fact/value dichotomy it is both fact *and* value all the way down. What seems clear is that, whatever sort of naturalist Dewey was, he was *not* a reductive naturalist.

Further, Williams discusses the importance of viewing knowledge as a context-driven affair: "The background presuppositions—often unspoken and sometimes even unrecognized—that guide non-demonstrative inference is, even when reasonably made, always defeasible (i.e., subject to correction), often highly so. The degrading of seemingly strong evidence is a result of the recontextualization that takes place when we identify and revise some presuppositions, either because we have run into trouble with our conclusions or acquired direct reasons for thinking that the presuppositions in question is false" (Williams 2001, 46). This idea of the indefeasibility of knowledge claims is worked out further by Williams: "There is an intuitively powerful idea here: that knowledge-yielding justifications should not be undermined by improvements in one's informational state. Our new suggestion, then, is that no one counts as knowing something if there exists a true body of evidence such that, if he were aware of it, his original justification would be undermined or 'defeated.' According to this 'indefeasibility' approach, knowledge requires justification that is indefeasible, proof against undermining by the acquisition of further true beliefs" (Williams 2001, 49).

Now this indefeasibility requirement; the requirement that knowledge is firm enough to counter challenges from further true beliefs, or the results of further inquiries, cannot, Williams claims, hold up. As Williams puts it: "Information that 'establishes the truth' of S's conclusion in one context may be seriously undermined by new evidence, even though that evidence may itself be undermined in turn. Or, even if we think that, when S's new information is misleading, his original evidence continues to establish the truth of his belief, his taking it to do so would be epistemologically irresponsible, so he would fail to know for that reason" (Williams 2001, 53).

Not only does the defeasibility thesis remove one of the cardinal problems of naturalist epistemology—the problem of the irreducibility of scientific facts—it allows for the possibility of knowledge that is justified, is true, and yet is itself subject to correction on the basis of new evidence, whatever that evidence might be.[23] This context-bound notion of knowledge is very similar to Dewey's (context-bound) notion of inquiry: in both cases knowledge is that which remains at the end of the day, and is subject to further correction should new evidence (perhaps garnered through new methods) come along. Given the insistence that Dewey's theory of inquiry be considered as self-correcting, there is this in common with Williams's similar claim for epistemology.

Williams also challenges the viability of an analytic/synthetic distinction. Williams agrees with Quine (and White) that "The notion of synonymy [of meaning] needed to explain the analytic/synthetic distinction is not the everyday notion of 'having the same meaning.' That notion is highly contextual and interest-relative. No one denies that for certain purposes . . . 'brother' can be treated as meaning 'male sibling.' But 'brother' stands in complex relations to other words: there are blood brothers, lay brothers, brothers in arms, and brothers under the skin. Prescinding from all purposes and interests, there is no way of deciding when words 'mean the same thing'" (Williams 2001, 112). Yet Williams also suggests that contextualists such as he also avoid the problems generated by the analytic/synthetic dichotomy because they do not distinguish between the foundational statuses of beliefs. Put simply, they do not accord one set of beliefs (call these second-order beliefs or beliefs about how our conceptions operate upon first-order beliefs) preeminence in comparison to another set of beliefs (call these first-order beliefs or beliefs about the world). Now this is just what White and Quine's charge against pragmatist logic was— that it introduced a foundationalist distinction between universal and generic beliefs. Williams has this to say about the matter: "The criteria of coherence— which embody 'second-order,' epistemic beliefs about what makes the beliefs in any system more likely to be true—function as the fixed points by reference to which first-order acceptance is regulated. These epistemic beliefs thus enjoy a *foundational status*. In so far as this status is assigned *a priori*, the coherence theory represents a rationalistic—'top down' as opposed to 'bottom up'—variant of foundationalism" (Williams 2001, 135). Here, Williams is eager to charge the coherence theory of knowledge—the theory that all beliefs must fit within a justified belief system, and that all singular justifications of beliefs depend on their fit with the total system—with a foundationalism of its own: that of granted preeminence to second-order beliefs or beliefs about how justification claims are made. I have shown how Dewey avoids just this trap in his own theory of inquiry. If I am correct about this, then, ceteris paribus, not only can Dewey's logic not be charged with this sort of foundationalism, he cannot be called a coherence theorist either.

Finally, Williams's characterization of "justified true belief" accords with Dewey's requirements for the objects or finished products, of an inquiry. Williams asserts that "because knowledge contrasts not just with ignorance but also with error, only true beliefs count as knowledge: I cannot *know* that the battle of Hastings was fought in 1056, since it wasn't. 'Know' is a success term, which means that we only attribute knowledge to another person when we are ourselves prepared to endorse the person's assertion or belief" (Williams 2001, 18). Of true belief, Williams says, "Because knowledge is a form of true belief, it is inconsistent to say that someone knows something that is false. However, this way of excluding error has nothing to do with being mistake-proof. All the 'factive' character of knowledge implies is that if you turn out to have been wrong, then you didn't really know: you just thought you did" (Williams 2001, 19). With all of this, Dewey is in accordance: not only does Dewey claim that falsities cannot "be" knowledge (as settled products of inquiry) owing to their incapacity to be instrumental or operative, Dewey would agree that knowledge is an honorific term. As well, Dewey's characterization of truth as assertible warrant is quite compatible with Williams's characterization of justified, true, and believable as allowing for mistakenness.

There are therefore good reasons to emphasize this self-correcting nature of inquiry.[24] First of all, it gets Dewey out of the "positivism" trap. Far from being an isolated, fixed method that is brought to bear on all contexts and problems, inquiry emerges as that capable of transformation, as the context requires. This renders it more sensitive, and ultimately more beneficial, to pressing human concerns. But another argument exists. This takes the form of a reductio ad absurdum. For suppose it is granted that inquiry is a fixed and stable set of stages or formulae brought to bear equally on all contexts and problems. The possibility that inquiry could recognize that it is unsuccessful in solving a particular problem would not occur unless at least some elements of inquiry were malleable. To not recognize self-limitations would occasion a failure of imagination and, thus, scientific progress: the very sort of thing Israel Scheffler bemoans. Further, inquiry would be unable to give a satisfactory account of how science (and philosophy) transformed through history. Presumably, positivism could (and does) say that the final formulation of method has been reached. Comte certainly maintained just this point. But this then assumes that all problems (scientific and social) can be solved with this final and fixed notion of inquiry. Not only is this is an extremely contentious conclusion, but this account of inquiry manifests a contradiction. Positivists claim that all phenomena, mental and environmental, are amenable to scientific inquiry. And this inquiry is experimental: it orders sequences of data through conscious manipulation of materials. But to say that method is fixed is to say that it cannot be considered among the phenomena studied. It exists somehow outside of the purview of itself. This not only implies a spectator theory of knowledge that Dewey discredits, but it equally implies that there is something that cannot be investigated by scientific inquiry. Such an admission is performatively self-contradictory.

Secondly, it provides Dewey with a strong response to the claim that his theory of inquiry denied a role for imagination. A self-correcting inquiry is responsive to the problems that it attempts to resolve. Failure of this resolve, the sense (Dewey would say "emotion") that the solution is not quite right does not fit or function well, necessitates some transformation of inquiry. This implies that new meanings are created from old: anticipation of possible responses to problems together with experimentation (whether conceptual, propositional, or material) of these responses occurs. Inasmuch as imagination connotes the re-relation of already built-up meanings for the purpose of creating new ones, imagination is present in the self-transformation of inquiry. And this imagination provides the onus for the person to engage in problem finding. As new possibilities open up by way of imagination, new relations are conceived and new problems occasioned. Problem finding and problem solving become linked in and through the use of the person's imagination.

Finally, emphasizing the self-corrective nature of inquiry obviates the criticism that inquiry is somehow premised on analytic statements. For, inasmuch as conceptions and propositions (statements) are themselves tested and reconstructed or abandoned according to their ability to satisfactorily solve problems (whether abstract or observable), they cannot be accorded a priori or fixed status. Propositions and conceptions are synthetic, as Quine re-argued some twenty years after Dewey: they depend on a problem-at-hand for their construction, testing, and maintenance. Though this problem may be abstract (as in mathematics) or material (as in physics), nevertheless, the propositions and conceptions proffered are beholden in some measure, to it.

III
INQUIRY, EXPERIENCE, AND GROWTH

The conclusion of the previous chapter is that inquiry ought to be thought of as context bound and self-correcting. Not only does this obviate a number of the criticisms of Dewey, it provides, as I shall demonstrate, a suitable means for linking closely Dewey's avowed aims of growth, community, and democracy. In this chapter, I turn to another way that Dewey has been read: a nonpositivistic, nonscientistic, and experiential way. Indeed, most Dewey scholars, both in philosophy and in education, read Dewey as making experience and not inquiry central. Though there is some variability as to what, in experience, counts as primary, there is nevertheless broad agreement that experience is the context from which inquiry develops and is beholden to. One might say that experience is a first-order state and inquiry a second, or alternatively on this read, experience is the base structure, and inquiry the superstructure. There are, however, problems with construing experience as primordial and inquiry as supervenient upon this. These concern the resultant metaphysical implications of conceiving experience in this way. In fine, if experience or one facet of it (as is usually the case with Dewey scholars) is made the *fons et origo* of inquiry, then Dewey's naturalistic, nondualistic, and nonanalytic account of experience is imperiled. Further, the question as to how inquiry can self-correct, tied as it is to the primitives of experience, is raised. If inquiry is unable to self-correct—to be responsive to the context in which it is used, the aims to which it is set, and the community of inquirers to which it conforms and is judged—it seems helpless in the face of the problems of men.

Part One:
A Short History of the Debate on Experience

As with inquiry, experience has been a central concern of Dewey's from the beginning of his career: Dewey's interest did not commence with the publication of *Experience and Nature*, though this is certainly the central text on the issue.

Despite changing his mind on what counts as an experience, Dewey never doubted that an experience was central to philosophy, to logic, to inquiry. It is a testament to Dewey's Hegelian roots that he conceived of experience as central (though at the time, absolute) to any philosophical discussion of knowledge, and continued to do so to the end. Nevertheless, Dewey's placing of experience front and center occasioned much criticism: first, by realists that claimed Dewey made experience absolute and tautological; second, and later in Dewey's career, several eminent critics came forward to dismiss Dewey's talk of experience, particularly, though not exclusively, as developed in *Experience and Nature*. Most notable among these were Bertrand Russell, George Santayana, and Morton White. Though Russell does not say so directly, his criticism of Dewey amounts to the charge of idealism: he had no place for objects, primitives, quales, outside of an experience; therefore all experience was reduced to a mental act. White and Santayana charged Dewey with drawing a strong distinction between immediate experience, on the one hand, and knowledge, on the other. The net effect of this was not only to create an unbridgeable gap between experience and knowledge, but more ominously given Dewey's antifoundationalist proclivities, to render knowledge dependent upon immediate experience.[1] As I shall show in an upcoming section, variants of these early criticisms remain to dog Dewey's talk of experience.

I shall begin here with Russell, White, and Santayana. Bertrand Russell is a polymath philosopher who is very critical of Dewey's theory of inquiry. Much of his disagreement with Dewey arises out of the differences in their respective metaphysics. For while Dewey was a naturalist Russell was a realist in the robust, ontological sense of the term. Russell maintained this basic position in one variant or another throughout his career. The distinction is nicely made in the following passage from *The Analysis of Matter*. "Whereas Dewey does not allow for elements outside of experience," Russell claims, "there is . . . no ground for the view that percepts cannot be physical events, or for supposing that they are never compresent with other physical events" (Russell 1955, 99).[2]

Russell led several incursions into the debate over the nature and function of inquiry.[3] The first of these was a review of Dewey's *Essays in Experimental Logic*. In this review, Russell charges that Dewey's theory

> is amazingly light-hearted in its assumption of knowledge as to causality. . . . His conception of signs and inference, his whole notion of knowledge as instrumental, depends throughout upon acceptance of the ordinary common-sense view of causation. . . . The point is not that this view must be false, but that, for instrumentalism, it must be *known* to be true. We must actually know particular causal laws. . . . [T]he very conception of an "instrument" is unintelligible otherwise. (Russell [1917] 1977, 242)

Here Russell claims Dewey advocates a position that is premised upon a commonsense notion of causation. Russell is led to conclude that instrumentalism finds itself in a quandary. Instrumentalism requires that, to claim that common sense counts as causality, one must go beyond common sense to know causal laws in themselves. Of course, access to this beyond is denied by the very requirement that causality be known as common sense. Thus, Dewey is forced into a corner. He either admits that causality is known by common sense, which limits the very validity of his claim, or he grants that common sense is not what counts as knowing causal laws, which places his instrumentalism in peril. Further on in the review, Russell charges Dewey with dismissing contemplative thought. This is as a result of his supposed turn toward inquiry in the service of practical affairs.

> Professor Dewey has nothing but contempt for the conception of knowledge as contemplation. He is full of that democratic philanthropy which makes him impatient of what seems to him a form of selfish idleness. . . . The habit of making everything subservient to practise is one which takes the color out of life, and removes most of the incentives to practise of a really noble mind. (Russell [1917] 1977, 246)

In a review of Dewey's *Logic: the Theory of Inquiry*, Russell takes aim at two of Dewey's specific claims. The first is that inquiry is holistic, borne out of experience that encompasses both inquirer and environment. The second concerns the social matrix in which Dewey argued that inquiry takes place. The first charge is that one cannot come to a descriptive statement of the world without first separating precepts from judgments. Russell is dismissive of Dewey because Dewey refuses to admit that there is a causal chain, beginning with a stimulus to a sense organ that thus forms the prerequisite for any possible judgment regarding the world. For Russell there are epistemological primitives, but for Dewey, there are only qualities to be had. This leads Russell to claim "I do not contend that the holistic world is logically impossible, but I do contend that it could not give rise to science or to any empirical knowledge" (Russell [1939] 1989, 142).[4] Russell then sets his sights on Dewey's supposed claim that the evaluation of any judgment hinges on the detection of "desired ends." What this means for Russell is that whatever ends one chooses are desirable and therefore the completion of a judgment is but a question of deciding on whether one's ends have been met to one's satisfaction. A species of hedonism is what Russell thinks he sees in Dewey's pragmatism.

> [For Dewey] instead of the objective biological test of success, we must adopt a subjective test: "success" means "achieving desired ends." But this

change in the definition of "success" weakens the position. When you see a man eating salt, you cannot tell whether he is acting on knowledge or error until you have ascertained whether he wishes to commit suicide. To ascertain this, you must discover whether the belief that he wishes to commit suicide will lead you to your own success. This involves an endless regress. (Russell [1939] 1989, 153)

In concluding that the completion of judgment hinges on one's achieving one's desired ends, Russell is then led to the concern that

> the pragmatist may say, in reply, that the success which is a test of truth is social, not individual: a belief is "true" when the success of the human race is helped by the existence of the belief. This, however, is hopelessly vague. What is "the success of the human race"? It is a concept for the politician, not for the logician. (Russell [1939] 1989, 153)

Russell, after stating his reservations regarding Dewey's inquiry, comes to the conclusion that "The pragmatist's position, if I am not mistaken, is a product of a limited skepticism supplemented by a surprising dogmatism. . . . [I]n spite of his skepticism, he is confident that he can know whether the consequences of entertaining a belief are as such to satisfy desire" (Russell [1939] 1989, 154). Russell's chief complaint of Dewey (beyond the familiar one of denigrating rationalistic logic) is that his theory of inquiry leaves little room for real, existential objects and situations.

With respect to experience, Morton White finds a dualism in Dewey's talk that he considers of consequence. This is the dualism of immediate experience over and against scientific knowledge:

> Dewey had no compunction about making a very sharp distinction between scientifically knowing that something is the case and having a direct, immediate experience of the kind that one has after one tastes sugar, smells a rose, scratches a diamond, or touches velvet. In fact, this is one of the fundamental distinctions in Dewey's entire philosophy, upon which he built not only his theory of physical knowledge but also his theory of value as well. (White 1972, 277)

The problem with this dualism is that it makes difficult the question of how a judgment can be good if it merely terminates in a satisfying experience. If satisfying is considered that which is merely desirable, then one may question how deliberate and scientific the judgment is.[5] On the other hand, if Dewey clings to the view that all judgment that can properly be called moral terminates in a "standard deliberate action" (White 1973, 280) that does not have as its cri-

terion desirability, then the question of what this action is based upon, immediately arises. A *regressus ad infinitum* is thereby occasioned, whereby one standard deliberate action is used to reinforce another. This leads to a charge that
Dewey cannot supply a scientific and nonevaluative action *and* maintain the
impossibility of questing for noncertainty.

Perhaps Dewey's most challenging early critic on the topic of experience
was George Santayana. Santayana reviewed Dewey's *Experience and Nature* for
the *Journal of Philosophy* of 1925. What was the central question for Santayana
concerned Dewey's allegiance to naturalism: for Santayana, either Dewey was
a naturalist, which meant that he could not have a metaphysics, or Dewey was a
metaphysician, which meant that he could not hold a position of naturalism.

For Santayana, all philosophers, whether conscious of it or not, developed and relied on foregrounds and backgrounds. Foregrounds were "positions
relative to some point of view" (Santayana in Dewey [1927–1928] 1984, 373).
Now a naturalist, for Santayana, could draw upon no foreground, for nature, as
Santayana claims, itself has no foreground; no point of view. And yet Santayana charges Dewey with "a dominance of the foreground." For Santayana,
Dewey was no naturalist; he was a metaphysician. And what Santayana
claimed led him to the conclusion that Dewey was a metaphysician was his talk
of "events." Dewey posited an experience in its immediacy that was, for Santayana, metaphysical. But Dewey cannot have it both ways. He either must
endorse the reading of experience as a metaphysical one, in which case naturalism must go by the wayside; or he must endorse naturalism, in which case
he cannot claim that only the immediate is the real. Santayana asks rhetorically: "Why could not Dewey have worked out his shrewd moral and intellectual economy within the frame of naturalism, which he knows is postulated by
practice, and so have brought clearness and space into the picture without in-
terposing any metaphysics? Because it is an axiom with him that nothing but
the immediate is real . . . the immediate is . . . any object—whether sensible or
intelligible makes no difference—found lying in its own specious medium; so
that immediatism is not so much subjective as closely attentive and mystically
objective" (Santayana in Dewey [1927—1928] 1984, 378—379).

This was not all. Santayana, in addition to concluding that Dewey privileges the foreground of experience, also charges the thinker with proffering an
"empty" experience: one that exists as mere form, awaiting its matter. For Santayana, this matter was "convention," "the social world" (Santayana in Dewey
[1927–1928] 1984, 376). In Santayana's estimation, the social world, 'the present,' was a flimsy substitute for a real world filled with natural comings and go-
ings. This "half-hearted naturalism," as Santayana calls it, was present- and
future entered: it had little place for memory, for reflection on the past. Indeed,
as Santayana proclaims: "Past experience is accordingly real only by virtue of
its vital inclusion in some present undertaking, and yesterday is really but a

term perhaps useful in the preparation of tomorrow. The past, too, must work if it would live, and we may speak without irony of 'the futurity of yesterday' insofar as yesterday has any pragmatic reality" (Santayana in Dewey [1927–1928] 1984, 381). An experience, immediately had, shorn of its past and having little or no connection to past experiences as Santayana thinks Dewey claims, is but a tool for presentism and conventialism: in Santayana's estimation, a philosophy predicated upon the liberal, corporatist, and capitalist forces of the United States.

Allow me to summarize the criticisms:

1. Dewey has no place for quales, primitives, or objects that lie outside of an experience. Everything that is must be said to already be a part of an experience. Therefore, Dewey cannot account for the "real" outside of an experience. Further, Dewey's reduction of all knowledge and interest to the practical concerns of the inquirer leads to hedonism and political intrigue (Russell).
2. Dewey must admit that because of his dualistic conception of experience and knowledge, all inquiry must end not in the discovery of truth, rather a satisfying experience. Inquiry, on this reading, is beholden to an experience (White).
3. Dewey has hypostatized experience by granting only immediate experience reality. This betrays Dewey's attempt to discover, using naturalistic methods of inquiry, what an experience consists of, and ties experience firmly to the present (Santayana).

In turning to past apologists of Dewey's reading of experience, it is important, I think, to note that many are attempts to defend the view that Dewey claims experience as primordial. Though Ernest Nagel speaks not at all about Dewey's "experiential" texts, he is, in this regard, an anomaly. Most scholars, past and present, who take up Dewey make it a point to discuss how inquiry in particular is treated in *Experience and Nature* and *Art as Experience*. And when they do, they invariably have to contend with what at first glance seems a radical shift in emphasis: a shift toward experience as being the central common feature of humankind. The turn to experience and to art is itself a turn to the qualities of an experience and, specifically, to its immediacy and its wholeness. There is an increased emphasis on the traits of an experience. These traits ("qualitative individuality and constant relations, contingency and need, movement and arrest" (Dewey [1925] 1981, 308–09)) are said to be primordial: they are found in any and every experience. Hence, they are termed "generic." When one experience is spoken of as qualitatively superior to another, it is the fullness and expressiveness of these traits that is in question. S. Morris Eames, a longtime teacher at SIU Carbondale, did much in the way of supporting this reading of experience. His scholarly articles show evidence of this. Eames contends that

the precognitive experience out of which emerges reflection, inquiry, or cognitive experience and the postcognitive experience to which reflection or inquiry returns constitute problems for Dewey's philosophy that have not been adequately analyzed and solved. There is a certain vagueness in Dewey's description of primary experience and the relation of primary experience to the cognitive process is a crucial issue. (Eames 1964, 407)

Eames's solution is, in his estimation, patent.

The only answer I can see to the foregoing problem is to claim that the primitives of primary experience [what I am calling immediate experience]—qualitative immediacy *and* existential involvements and connections—are the ultimate grounds upon which any verification of judgments can rest. Because it is difficult to correctly formulate relations so that they might mirror the connections given in an experience, there is always room for error. This is why, I think, Dewey claims that formulated judgments are always open to revision in the light of future experience. And since it is not easy to extract from experience and nature the connections that lie hidden below its surface meanings, our formulated judgments must continually be tested in our ongoing experience. (Eames 1964, 416)

There is a history of this reception in the discipline of education as well as in philosophy. Much of it can be traced to Elliot Eisner and his colleagues' work at Stanford University in the 1960s on the mapping out of a curriculum of the arts. In searching for a model to express the need for a view of art that is manifestly centered on qualitative rather than quantitative reasoning, Eisner and his colleagues chose Dewey's notion of qualitative immediacy and wholeness as worked out in *Art as Experience*. The problem was the inability of (scientific) inquiry to capture all that was going on in the creation of, and reflection upon, works of art. Dewey. As two of Eisner's colleagues, Francis Villemain and Nathaniel Chapman put it:

Learning is properly conceived as occurring only in a problematic situation, where some end-in-view is being sought. But the fact must be recognized that ends-in-view are to be found in a spectrum ranging from problems dominantly qualitative to, at the other extreme, problems which are predominantly theoretical. (Villemain and Chapman in Eisner et al. 1967, 451)

The claim is put forth that experience and art are primordial.

> An examination of his theory of experience and his vision of the *summum bonum* shows him to be a philosopher of art above all else. . . . In the Dewey view of the nature of experience, the aesthetic is so central that we cannot have an experience without it. Indeed, it is the defining characteristic of "an experience." (Villemain and Chapman in Eisner et al. 1967, 451)

The problem with scientizing inquiry, as these philosophers and educators see it, is not merely that Dewey becomes positivistic or scientistic. As it stands, this claim is uninteresting. The problem is rather that ends become separated from means, and growth, that quintessential end for education and democracy, becomes an impossible feat. Growth must begin and end in a state of affairs. This state of affairs, for these educators, is the immediate, qualitative whole. The goal becomes to increase the quality of this whole through the means of inquiry. By scientizing inquiry, the detachment of inquiry from growth—the improvement of an experience—is occasioned. The solution is to contextualize and what I shall call "aestheticize" the role and scope of inquiry. And what this means is that inquiry must be seen as subservient to, and not over and above, the immediate qualitative whole that an experience consists of.

Part Two:
The Present-Day Debate on Experience

The present-day debates on what Dewey meant by experience and whether his talk of experience is ultimately bankable, are by no means settled. In fact, many of the earlier criticisms and supports of Dewey are found in the present ones. Not surprisingly, the participants rely heavily on textual examples to stake their claims, and little beyond polemics is occasioned. Here again, I shall demonstrate the affinities of older thinking with the newer, through an examination of select present-day criticisms and apologies of Dewey's talk of experience. I turn to (once again) H. O. Mounce, as well as Richard Rorty. The others comes from two educators; E. D. Hirsch, the famed writer of *The Schools We Need and Why We Don't Have Them* and *Cultural Literacy*, and Diane Ravitch, author of *Left Back*. Hirsch claims that Dewey's progressivist notions of inquiry in education have limited the importance of abstract learning, book learning, and the role and scope of higher thinking in general. Ravitch similarly claims that progressivist methods, anticipated by Dewey's theory of inquiry applied to education, occasioned a failure of the schools to cultivate children's intellects.

Mounce locates in Dewey's talk of experience a problem. As Mounce puts it, if inquiry into an experience can deal only with conditions and relations, as suggested by Dewey in *Experience and Nature*, and an experience is primarily a qualitative affair in which inquiry constructs relations, then "the world as experienced, in its qualitative reality, always goes beyond anything that can be put into words" (Mounce 1997, 167). Of this, Mounce claims: "The world transcends explicit statement but it is not transcendent; it transcends knowledge but not experience. Quite the contrary; in immediate qualitative experience it is given to us in its full reality" (Mounce 1997, 167). What this leads to, for Mounce, is a failure of inquiry and a fortiori, a failure of inference and of knowledge. For if immediate qualitative experience is the true reality, the 'brute fact,' then inquiry becomes imperiled precisely because it no longer has access to substances and to matter. It can deal only in relations and conditions. As such, it can only remodel an experience in hindsight. It cannot and does not provide the fullest expression of reality. "Reality, being revealed only in experience, will find its fullest expression in the re-creation of experience, which is art" (Mounce 1997, 173). Science can no longer help us to show that there is a reality beyond experience because there is nothing beyond experience. Science thus has little to reveal and as such, is "hardly more significant than any number of other human activities" (Mounce 1997, 173). Science is thus usurped by art. The aestheticization of experience, the desire to grant qualia, qualitative immediate wholes, and traits preeminent, indeed ontological, significance at the expense of inquiry, inference, relation, and thought, is occasioned. And because of this, Mounce claims, Dewey's talk of reality becomes none other than a mystery. Reality transcends statement but is not itself transcendent.

Richard Rorty develops a variant of this charge. He is critical of Dewey's metaphysics: the metaphysics Rorty sees as looming large in Dewey's most ambitious work, *Experience and Nature*. Rorty charges that Dewey's generic traits, those traits common to all experiences—"qualitative individuality and constant relations, contingency and need, movement and arrest" (Dewey [1925] 1981, 308–09)—were as close as anything could be in Dewey's writings to "universal." The turn to generic traits was, according to Rorty, a means for Dewey to get around the philosophical dualisms implicit in any attempt to describe the interaction between "mind" and "phenomenon." Rorty claims that Dewey took two paths to overcoming this dualism. The first was to "point out that the dualism is imposed by a tradition for specific cultural reasons, but has now outlived its usefulness" (Rorty, 1982, 82). The second was to "describe the phenomenon in a nondualistic way which emphasizes 'continuity' between lower and higher processes. This is the Lockean way—the way which led Locke to assimilate all mental acts to raw feels, thus paving the way for Humean skepticism" (Rorty 1982, 82).[6]

Rorty maintains that one cannot both claim generic traits and a thoroughgoing naturalism and historicism. One or another of these positions has to give way.[7] Rorty thinks that Dewey attempted a resolution to this dilemma by blowing up notions like "transaction" and "situation" (Rorty 1982, 84). The net effect of this was to engage in

> constructive metaphysical system-building. The system that was built in *Experience and Nature* sounded idealistic, and its solution to the mind-body problem seemed one more invocation of the transcendental ego, because the level of generality to which Dewey ascends is the same level at which Kant worked, and the model of knowledge is the same—the constitution of the knowable by the cooperation of two unknowables. (Rorty 1982, 85)

Thus, Rorty claims that Dewey reintroduces metaphysics through his turn to generic traits as the experiential building blocks of further refined mental processes.[8]

Several educators are in the business of offering educational solutions for the ills of society, and chide schools and educators for following the failed legacy of Progressivism and Dewey. Though most of the critics' attention is focused on the failure of Dewey's theory of inquiry to solve social problems, or even worsen them (a concern that will be dealt with in chapters 4 and 5), educators occasionally aim their guns at Progressivism and Dewey's theory of inquiry *simpliciter*. A good example of such criticism comes from E. D. Hirsch. Hirsch is professor of English (now retired) at the University of Virginia, Charlottesville. He is well known for his work *Cultural Literacy: What Every American Needs to Know* (1987), as well as *The Dictionary of Cultural Literacy* (1990).

Hirsch expends a great deal of effort discussing an American core curriculum for the schools. The "core" of the core curriculum, if you will, is the transmission of certain knowledge from teacher to student. Hirsch argues that this knowledge is not "content neutral" (Hirsch 1987, 19). It carries with it a certain pedigree that sets it apart from other knowledge. That this core knowledge changes in response to the needs of the citizenry, Hirsch is quite clear. Hirsch's view of knowledge is in distinction to Romantic notions of knowledge, notions that Hirsch does think posit knowledge as being content neutral. Much of the argument in *Cultural Literacy* is an attempt to overcome what Hirsch sees as the Romantic Movement in education. This is a movement that, from Rousseau to our present age, has placed emphasis on method over content, and in so doing has corrupted public education.

Hirsch has an ambivalent attitude toward Dewey. Often, Hirsch praises Dewey. For example, "the reorientation of the schools to practical social goals was intended as a generous and humane goal in the writings of John Dewey."

Often enough though, this praise is tempered by a concern. Thus Hirsch continues, "Despite his opposition to book-centered instruction, Dewey assumed that children would become highly literate under his learning-by-doing principles of education, although that assumption turned out to be incorrect, Dewey was in some respects on the side of the traditionalists, many of whom, for their part, continue to honor his aims of pluralism and social utility" (Hirsch 1987, 122). Hirsch accepts some principles of Dewey's, such as the supposed social utility of pedagogy and the belief that "human values can be taught through many sorts of materials, traditional or untraditional" (Hirsch 1987, 126). But Hirsch dismisses others as being dangerous. He believes Dewey's antibookishness has led to the decline of American literacy.

When one turns to Hirsch's latest book, *The Schools We Need*, one finds Hirsch speaking of the vast difference between Dewey and William Heard Kilpatrick, and citing Robert Westbrook's damning statements on Kilpatrick as evidence.[9] He also states: "The integrationist tradition, represented by Dewey, [William Chandler] Bagley, and others was the finest and soundest tradition of pedagogical thinking in the United States" (Hirsch 1996, 124). But the criticisms that Hirsch heaps upon certain research methods, combined with his aversion to the naturalistic, problem-solving method, betray his allegiance. For example, Hirsch argues of progressivists that

> two doctrines of educational naturalism that have become fallacies by being taken to extremes are 1) the doctrine of developmentalism, or natural tempo, which holds that there is a natural age . . . for introducing bookish content . . . 2) the doctrine of holistic learning, or natural pedagogy, which holds that natural (lifelike, project-like, thematic) methods of instruction are always the most effective teaching methods. (Hirsch 1996, 84)

And further:

> The only truly general principle that seems to emerge from process-outcome research on pedagogy is that focused and guided instruction is far more effective than naturalistic, discovery-learn-at-your-own-pace instruction. But within the context of focused and guided instruction, almost anything goes, and what works best with one group of students may not work best with another group with similar backgrounds in the very same building. Methods must vary a good deal with different age groups. (Hirsch 1996, 174)

Hirsch goes on to suggest that there is certain hubris connected to the claims of developmentalism and naturalism. Specifically, Hirsch claims that it is wrong of the champions of these methods to claim it as superior to others. Hirsch seems eager to allow, within the context of focused and guided instruction, room for various methods and materials. But this supposed "Deweyan" compromise only serves to underscore a fundamental difference in their respective views. For Dewey thought that naturalistic pedagogy and the naturalistic method thereby to be beneficial for American democracy. Hirsch thinks otherwise.

Hirsch charges natural pedagogy with "encourag[ing] a tendency already strong in American culture—to connect academic achievement more with social determinism and natural talent than with focused hard work" (Hirsch 1996, 87). And Hirsch charges critical thinking with ushering in a divorce of thought from content under the guise of problem-solving skills.

> But although giving *specific* metacognitive tips within subject-matter instruction is known to be a useful teaching practice, one may question the current claim that teaching general "higher-order skills" is an *improvement* over subject-matter study. The enthusiasm for metaskills could easily become an updated, "research-based" version of the progressivist antisubject-matter tradition that has already caused our schools to decline. (Hirsch 1996, 137, emphases Hirsch's)

Though Hirsch does not single Dewey out in his chastisement of progressivism and the naturalistic method, it does not require a stretch of the imagination to conclude that Dewey, through his staunch advocacy of the what Hirsch deems a singular and naturalistic method, must also bear the brunt of criticism.

Diane Ravitch is a historian of education at Columbia University and a researcher at the Brookings Institute. As I have mentioned, Ravitch's biggest concern is with the curricular changes that have led to the loss of the "academic" school. Ravitch sets her sights on certain progressivist movements and players, notably the "project method" of William Heard Kilpatrick. In her book *The Troubled Crusade*, she rails against what she sees as Kilpatrick's "utilitarian message . . . the emphasis on experience and projects" (Ravitch 1983, 51). She finds the project method to be little more than an instrument for "a cult whose principles were taught as dogma and whose critics were treated as dangerous heretics" (Ravitch 1983, 79). Legions of schools and teachers, Ravitch argues, had taken up the project method and other fashionable progressivist approaches. The surge of optimism in these methods and approaches was so great as to drown out the critics of progressivism. These critics, such as William Chandler Bagley of Columbia University and Robert Hutchins of the University of Chicago, saw in these methods little more than a rank instrumentalism that resulted in the consumerism of education, the vulgarization of democracy, and the loss of a grand cultural heritage. Ravitch concurs with these critics, arguing that progressivism, though now past, has left its legacy in areas such as school reform, curriculum studies, and policy analysis, where critics of the return to a liberal arts curriculum reside.

One might surmise that Ravitch's critical preoccupation with Kilpatrick also extends to Dewey. Until recently, it did not. Ravitch is often keen to spare Dewey from the very opprobrium that she launches at Kilpatrick. For Ravitch, it is not so much that Dewey is responsible for the predicaments of public education as much as Dewey was naive and slow to respond with his criticisms of progressivist intransigence.[10] Ravitch argues in *The Schools We Deserve*, that

> with hindsight, we can see that the Dewey's [John and his daughter Evelyn, co-authors of *Schools of Tommorrow*] predictions had a mixed fate. While some teachers may have continued to use rote methods, by the mid-1930s the education profession as a whole had accepted the importance of such things as physical health and recreation, vocational education, arts and crafts, and the use of activities and projects in the classroom. However, some of the Dewey's emphases produced unexpected, and sometimes, undesirable outcomes. (Ravitch 1985, 299)

Ravitch goes on to discuss the teachers' and schools' resistance to Dewey's experimentalist approach. She argues here that Dewey's experimentalism was not so much a failure as not attempted. She is quick to point out the distance that separates Dewey from Kilpatrick. While Dewey's methods were never seriously entertained, Kilpatrick's were. All of this suggests that, in Ravitch's mind, there are at least two progressivisms at work.

Arguments become sharper in Ravitch's book *Left Back*. In addition to reiterating Dewey's naiveté, two new arguments are put forth. One of these arguments can best be captured with the term "failure of nerve." Ravitch chides Dewey with not being quick enough to respond to the damaging claims of other progressivists. Dewey, she argues, waited until 1938 to launch his criticisms of progressivism; whereas, she argues, the excesses of the progressivists had been known to him for a long time. Specifically, Dewey is charged with not paying attention to the "anti-intellectualism inherent in courses such as 'social living' and 'basic living' (Ravitch 2000, 308).

The other argument deals specifically with Dewey's experimentalism and is the more compelling for this reason. Of experimentalism, and of Dewey's supposed preoccupation with scientific method, Ravitch claims:

> Dewey's writings encouraged those who thought that education could be made into a science; those who wanted to create child-centered schools based on the interests of children rather than subject-matter; those who believed that learning by doing was more valuable than learning from

books; those who expected vocational and industrial education to train poor and minority children for their future jobs; and those who wanted the schools to serve as an instrument to improve society. These disparate, sometimes discordant ideas had been discussed for years, but Dewey's intellectual eminence certified them as the dominant doctrines in the new professional schools of psychology. (Ravitch 2000, 59)

Ravitch does here suggest that other progressivists undermined Dewey's intentions. One can surmise from the preceding quote that, though science lent itself to the evils of consumerism and vocation-centered pedagogies, nevertheless it was not Dewey's intent to have things so. But she then turns to a more specific indictment of these other progressives—an indictment that requires no stretch of the imagination to be equally applicable to Dewey. She states: "First was the idea that education might become a science and that the methods and ends of education could be measured with precision and determined scientifically. This was the basis of the mental testing movement" (Ravitch 2000, 60). Given Dewey's supposed preoccupation with making the social sciences more akin to the physical sciences, this accusation is stinging. It is tantamount to suggesting that the importation of science and scientific methods to education is of a piece with the further urge to testing, with all of its attendant evils. Dewey and progressivism's scientific method, so seen, is the harbinger of educational darkness.

In turning to apologies of Dewey's talk of experience, what is most striking is that there is no taking back what Dewey has said about experience: experiences, and not thoughts, are primary. This conclusion sets the stage for the turn to the qualitative immediacy of an experience—the precognitive facet of an experience—together with its attendant generic connections, as the *fons et origo* of an experience. This manner of reading Dewey makes its triumphant stand in the work of Thomas Alexander. His book *John Dewey's Theory of Art, Experience, and Nature: The Horizons of Feeling* has done a great deal to stem the tide of criticism among Dewey scholars and has garnered many enthusiasts. Alexander goes so far as to claim of one generic trait—continuity—that this "means growth." It is the trait that links nature and world together (Alexander 1987, 61).[11] This continuity extends to what counts as meaning and, specifically, the capacity of meaning to outrun intelligence and inquiry. Alexander puts it this way:

> Meaning and value initially belong to a continuous domain of interaction that is aesthetically undergone prior to any cognitive mediation, though this material may be mediated and refined instrumentally [later]. That is, human beings experience the world as filled with meaning or value not primarily as the result of consciously deliberate or instrumen-

tal inquiry, but as a qualitative whole of continuous interaction that has the promise of consummatory experience. . . . Both meanings and values are directly embodied in the existential components of their experiences [traits and qualities]. These meanings and values exhibit a wide and differentiated spectrum; language can at best only crudely designate various generic parts of that continuum, which manifest themselves in the upsurge of the present in radical individuality and incommensurable freshness. One reason the arts have such power is their ability to lead us toward these experiences that are above and beyond the uses of strictly cognitive language. (Alexander in Gavin 2003, 134)

This sentiment of Alexander's is shared by many of Dewey's experiential interpreters, as will be shown.

The shifts toward experience lead Dewey to embed inquiry in an experience. This in turn leads many of Dewey's more contemporary interpreters to scorn the attempts by some to claim that science was the approach privileged in carrying out the task of inquiry. Michael Eldridge epitomizes this scorn very nicely. In discussing the way Dewey has been handled by not-so-sympathetic critics, he claims: "One of the ways in which interpreters divide Dewey up is to distinguish between his metaphysics of experience and his instrumentalist theory of knowledge. But for Dewey there was a single phenomenon—experience—that could be understood metaphysically, aesthetically, politically, or epistemically" (Eldridge 1998, 38).

What is at stake in claiming that inquiry is embedded in an experience is that, first of all and rightly, inquiry is context—bound—it takes place within a context of other practical matters—and that the process of inquiring transforms the context as it is carried out. J. E. Tiles sums up this matter well.

He [Dewey] repeatedly affirmed that coming to know results in changes in the situation and in the initial experience which elicited inquiry, but this was not a claim that coming to know should be allowed materially to affect either the answer to specific questions posed in inquiry or the test of (hypothetical) answers by subsequent experience. It was the claim rather that the formation of the question, answer and the subsequent treatment of experiences as confirming or disconfirming that answer, all take place in a wider context of practical concerns. That wider context does not remain unaltered by such a procedure, even as efforts are made to isolate and control phenomena so as to yield a "warranted" answer. (Tiles 1990, 124)

A second claim is that inquiry, far from being reducible to the procedures used in the natural sciences, is much broader than Dewey's critics and sympathetic scientific supporters assume. As well, there is much more to experience than methods. In point of fact, methods are but one aspect of experience and are only invoked when there is something problematic about an experience. In many experiences they are not even present.[12] Larry Hickman nicely sums up this nonscientistic reading of inquiry.

> Dewey did not seek to measure all experience by technoscientific analysis. . . . He did not even think that technoscientific inquiry should serve as the pattern for all forms of inquiry. Rather, it was his view that much of human experience, especially within the domain of simple aesthetic delight, has no need of inquiry because it is not problematic. Further, even where inquiry is called for, the methods of the technoscientific disciplines constitute only one important source of insight among others . . . into ways of understanding and improving upon a pattern of inquiry that is more general than that employed in the technoscientific disciplines. His theory of inquiry . . . is thus considerably broader than his theory about the methods of the technosciences. (Hickman 2001, 73).[13]

Raymond Boisvert is closely allied with these thinkers in his rejection of science as the model of inquiry. As such Boisvert, in his first major publication, *Dewey's Metaphysics*, takes a distinctively Aristotelian approach to Dewey's talk of experience. What counts as metaphysics for Dewey is Dewey's talk of "forms." According to Boisvert, forms have the following characteristics: "Dewey . . . holds that forms do not exist separately [from matter]. They cannot have existence apart from the interaction of organism and environment. Secondly, forms are viewed as results, not as pre-existing givens. Finally, another way of stating this is to say that forms and materials are correlative" (Boisvert 1988, 130). Now these forms are further considered in light of what Dewey has to say about generic traits. These ur-traits arise only from the interaction between form and matter.

The question of inquiry arises at this point. For if all form and matter is inextricably bound, and inquiry investigates the relations between these bound forms and matters, is inquiry then detached from these forms? And can it be studied on its own without recourse to subject matters? Dewey, Boisvert argues, must answer both yes and no. "Dewey is not saying that formal logic cannot be studied as a distinct branch of logic or that the validity of its laws is to be questioned. What he is saying is that this fact of being capable of separate study should not lead to the belief that its *source* is independent of experience" (Boisvert 1988, 182). This I take it is merely a reminder that all logic is developed out of past attempts at problem solving. But Boisvert is at pains to claim that forms, as characteristics, traits, and results of experience, are *ontological* inasmuch as these forms are sources within experience and, as such, one cannot avoid deriving characteristics, traits, and results from an experience. This presents problems for Dewey's claim that logic has little to do with metaphysics.

> If by "logic" Dewey meant formal logic, it would appear that his argument for the separation of logic and ontology might have some merit. The problem with his analysis lies precisely in the fact that when he uses "logic" he means primarily methodology. This peculiar usage entirely alters the possibility that logic can proceed in isolation from ontology [the traits of experience] since the methodology is not formalistic; it involves the special character of the subject matters being dealt with. (Boisvert 1988, 184)

What Boisvert is saying, then, is that inasmuch as traits of experience are involved in the very process of inquiring, ontology cannot therefore be separated from inquiry.

Boisvert later drops the claim that Dewey's talk of generic traits is somehow helpful in discussing the constituents of experience. He thus parts with Alexander's reading of their implications. This is done because

> recognition of generic traits can too readily be understood as a neutral ticking off of attributes . . . Dewey, it is true, goes to great lengths to indicate how this identifying of traits is inseparable from "criticism" or evaluation. Still, there is a kind of static, almost non-Deweyan, quality about identifying generic traits as the extent of metaphysical discourse. (Boisvert in Hickman 1995, 156)[14]

Boisvert prefers that we "map" experience with other characteristic marks that Dewey uses: "event" and "social." "An 'event' has no existence outside of or prior to its varied transactions with other events. . . . The 'social' goes all the way down" (Boisvert, in Hickman 1995, 160). For Boisvert, the purpose of choosing these marks over generic traits is that they not only more fully capture the organic and interactional nature of an experience, but also that they better grasp the "dimensions of the real" (Boisvert, in Hickman 1995, 159). And what are these dimensions? They are interaction, complexity, temporality, and irreducibility. These dimensions are to be found in any and every experience.

What Boisvert drives at is that reality outstrips any particular meaning given to it. Boisvert, in discussing Dewey's contribution to aesthetics from *Art as Experience*, claims:

> But reality . . . is always richer and fuller than any single network of meanings can be. This intersection between sedimented meanings and

underemphasized or undisclosed possibilities is the site where imagination plays its role. . . . "Imagination" is the term used by Dewey to identify the human capacity for discerning such opportunities. (Boisvert
1998, 128)

For Boisvert, inasmuch as the dimensions of experience, as above, can only be
meaningful ex post facto, there will always be the capacity of experience to be
broader, fuller, and more significant than an inquiry into it. Inquiry, though
necessary, is certainly not the sufficient condition of the having, doing, or enjoying of an experience. The dimensions of an experience are producible without it. This leads Boisvert to caution the new reader on her quest to discover
Dewey's works.

If I have been successful, readers will want to turn to Dewey's texts themselves. Those wishing to do so would be well advised to begin with the
works highlighting "experience" in the title: *Experience and Nature, Experience and Education*, and *Art as Experience*. My own view is that the
reader who begins there will find a richer vein of material to carry over
into the twenty-first century than one who begins with Dewey's logical
works such as *How We Think* or *Logic: The Theory of Inquiry*. Beginning
with the latter has two drawbacks. The first is that to use them as a starting point reinforces the attitude that epistemological concerns are the
main issues dealt with by philosophers, a position which Dewey . . . rejected. Second, Dewey's logical works reveal him as still overly influenced by the Cartesian fascination with "method." They provide the
source of formulations, which if read critically, mislead commentators.
(Bosivert 1998, 161)

Boisvert has become even more "Rortyan" of late. In a recent essay, he
castigates Dewey not only for being overly instrumental, but for conflating
method with experience.

For the Dewey we must pass by is the Dewey still captivated by the picture of time characterized by sharp ruptures amenable to single-label
descriptions. It is also the Dewey who thinks that something called "instrumentalism," that is, the understanding of intelligence as paying attention to causes and conditions, is a new arrival on the human scene.
Here is were the sleight of hand mentioned earlier causes an important
confusion. "Intelligence" as paying attention to human experience in
light of revising that experience has been practiced by philosophers for
all time. But "intelligence" as best exemplified by the scientific method
is a relative newcomer, dating from the late Renaissance. Because Dewey

runs the latter together with the former, he distorts unfairly the accomplishments of the past. He can also too easily be read as suggesting, not methods of intelligence properly coordinated with subject-matters, but rather a single method applicable to all. Here, I contend, is that aspect of Dewey which most needs to be jettisoned as we move into the twenty-first century. We who come after him must be categorical. (Boisvert in Gavin 2003, 96)

Upon turning to educators, one notes that the positivist reading of Dewey has occasioned much scorn. Indeed, it is not a stretch to say with Nel Noddings that "possibly the greatest objections to Dewey's work from the perspective of today's educators is that he . . . put such great emphasis on the power of scientific thought to solve our problems" (Noddings 1995, 38). The claims of the critics seem to bear this point out. These objections are various and some of these have been discussed earlier. But it must be said that many have attempted to answer these objections. By far the most developed responses have come from those who (with Raymond Boisvert) ask us to look carefully at Dewey's experiential and aesthetic works. For in these, it is argued, the tempering of scientific inquiry occurs.

Here I turn to two Dewey scholars in education who attempt just this. Phillip Jackson is somewhat of a celebrity in educational circles, chiefly as a result of writing *Life in Classrooms*. Jackson is also a Dewey scholar of sound reputation. His reading of Dewey is avowedly unscientistic: it plays up Dewey's talk of experience and art as being central to philosophy and education and, in so doing, plays down the concerns of (scientific) inquiry. Much of this play can, I believe, be traced to Jackson's own quandaries that have developed out of a careful reading of Dewey on just this topic.

Jackson's first critical encounter with the issue of Dewey's science occurs in his work *The Practice of Teaching*. Here, Jackson claims it is dubious to suggest that a post hoc [after the fact] notion of the characteristics of a good teacher can be proffered. What does this mean? Jackson thinks Dewey's turn to science to tell a good teacher from a mediocre one is circular. This is because science can only pronounce on the merit of a teacher after having decided on just what those qualities are. So to Jackson:

The chief difficulty with all such post hoc theories lies in their circularity. We begin with the observation that some teachers seem to be doing quite well without training, and we proceed to explain that "anomaly" by ascribing to such persons some special powers or gifts. How do we know they are so endowed? Because we observe them doing well despite a lack of training. We can avoid this logical deficiency if we are sufficiently careful, but to do so requires an independent test of the explanatory hypothesis, a move seldom made by those who, like John Dewey, put their views forward not as hypothesis but as established fact. (Jackson 1998, 8–9)

Jackson then segues into a discussion of the merits of scientific inquiry in estimating just what a good teacher consists of. Jackson makes a critical estimation of the place of science in pedagogy.

> Are there truly, as Dewey claimed, "laws known to and laid down by pedagogical science"? If so, what might they be? Indeed, is there any such thing as a "pedagogical science"? Dewey must have believed there was, or he would not have used the term as he did. But was he correct? We certainly don't find the expression in wide use today. Why not? The most sensible explanation I can think of is that the term is pretentious when used to describe what we today can say with confidence about how to teach. (Jackson 1998, 8)

Jackson's skepticism with regard to the accomplishments of scientific inquiry finds expression in his later work *John Dewey and the Lessons of Art*. It is not that Jackson finds scientific inquiry mischievous; rather, scientific inquiry can only properly be considered as important when it is seen in light of its function. And this is to serve in the improvement of the qualities of an experience. Jackson, like S. Morris Eames and Thomas Alexander, sees Dewey's "generic traits" as the primordial elements of an experience. Jackson claims that it is the capacity of all human beings to have these traits (qualitative individuality and constant relations, contingency and need, movement and arrest) that allows for all experience to have about it an aesthetic component. What makes an experience predominantly aesthetic is the degree to which it is responsive to these traits. And this is in turn depends upon what Jackson calls (after Dewey) the "expressive meaning" of an object (Jackson 1998, 27). Expressive meaning is cultivated in two ways: inferentially and imaginatively. In an aesthetic experience, these run together. Jackson quotes Dewey's *Experience and Nature* in his estimation of the inferential aspect of expressive meaning. Dewey here claims that "the business of reflection is to take events which brutely occur and brutely affect us, to convert them into objects *by means of some inference as to their possible consequences*" (Dewey [1925] 1981, 245 in Jackson 1998, 28). Imagination, by contrast, is the arrangement of the meanings gleaned by inference. It is what Dewey calls "ideal experimentation.": "[m]eanings may be infinitely combined and rearranged in imagination, and the outcome of this inner experimentation—which is thought—may issue forth in interaction with crude or raw events" (Dewey [1925] 1981, 132 in Jackson 1998, 28 italics Jackson's). Inference is the tool that, when used imaginatively to rearrange meanings, leads to new meanings, which are then brought to bear on brute facts and events.

This leads Jackson to claim that art-centered experiences differ from intellectual ones. The difference concerns their respective ends. Both make use of inquiry. Both call for reflection. But art-centered experiences are said to be more closely allied to the having of an experience and more representative of what Dewey means by instrumentalism: that is (in Jackson's estimation) the oneness of experience and nature. As Jackson puts it, they are

> more immediate and instrumental. They are chiefly concerned, in other words, with the integral nature of the experience rather than with conditions that lie beyond its temporal boundaries. Intellectual experiences, on the other hand, are focused more on problems whose sources lie elsewhere and whose solution promises to be of maximal value when put to use in future contexts. (Jackson 1998, 51)

Art-centered experiences are said to end in the satisfaction of the having of a qualitative whole: intellectual experiences are said to end in the solution to a particular problem. With this, Jackson makes a strong distinction between the ends (and the qualities) of the two respective experiences.

The distinction is played up further. Jackson once again restates the claim that art experiences are self-enclosed whereas all other experiences (and a fortiori scientific/intellectual experiences) are deficient.

> Art centered experiences are distinguished by their unity and wholeness. They are consummatory. They are accompanied by feelings of fulfillment and satisfaction. They are self-sufficient and meaningful. They do not point beyond themselves. Lesser forms of experiencing, by way of contrast, contain but fragments, mere shards, of what Dewey would call *an* experience. (Jackson 1998, 124)

The implication seems clear: art experiences have something that other experiences do not, and this something is the fuller meaning that arises out of imaginatively resituating prior meanings into a new one with attendant consequences (fulfillment and satisfaction) for the immediate qualities in the having of the experience. The claim is *not* that immediate qualities come with their meanings stamped upon them: rather it is that, through the resituation of meanings (an imaginative undertaking), this new meaning is able to influence the immediate qualities of that *present* experience. What one ultimately achieves is a heightened sense of the presence of the generic traits of nature.

The bringing together of art and inference transforms "the masterful exercise of intelligence." Jackson concludes that, when considered broadly,

Dewey's theory of inquiry comes to look quite different from what scientistic thinkers have made of it.[15] Jackson's "masterful exercise of intelligence" is an amalgam of the following:

> A host of personal dispositions, habits, and attitudes—among them patience, persistence, open-mindedness, careful observation, unflagging attention to detail, reflection, experimentation, imagination, an abiding faith in one's own capacity to pursue the truth, an enduring delight in that pursuit, and even—all cautious properties aside—an undying love of it. (Jackson 2001, 81)

The implication is that all of these ingredients are necessary in the exercise of intelligence. But the equal implication is that the fuller the experience and the more aesthetic it can be made, the more intelligence is exerted. And this capacity in turn falls on the presence of a heightened awareness of the genetic traits (already present) in the having of the experience.

Jim Garrison is another who shares this experiential and aesthetic reading of Dewey, though he develops somewhat different conclusions than do Boisvert or Jackson. His research interests are broad and include constructivist learning and teaching theory, and critical thinking in education. But perhaps the most trenchant interest for Garrison is the question of how to aestheticize the curriculum. Aestheticization of the curriculum, for Garrison, is the attempt to cultivate just those experiences that Dewey calls "consummatory." A richer, fuller, and more complete experience is what Garrison wishes for his students to have. This experience is at once tied to a claim for democratic teaching and learning. This is the claim that only by increasing one's human contacts can one's experiences become consummatory. Characteristically, Garrison is suspicious of cultivating experiences that are designated as nonconsummatory. Garrison finds these sorts of experiences borne out of those attempts to fragment the curriculum or prefer one aspect or element of the curriculum to another. Garrison is particularly sensitive to the hypostatization of logic and science as the one right way to facilitate student experiences. Consequently, he spares no effort to criticize those he sees as complicit in this endeavor.

Garrison's approach to Dewey is phenomenological: he plays up Dewey's talk of immediate experiences, qualities, and wholes as discussed in *Experience and Nature* and *Art as Experience*. In an early paper with Emaneul Shargel, Garrison draws the reader's attention to the variously shared themes of Dewey and Edmund Husserl. In so doing, Garrison and Shargel claim that, for Dewey,

> existential experience for Dewey is a "gift." . . . In this instance Dewey appears, as he so often does, far more radical than Husserl, declaring of prereflective existential experience that "it indicates that being and hav-

ing things in ways other than knowing them exist and are preconditions of reflection and knowledge. (Dewey [1925] 1981, 18–19 in Garrison and Shargel 1987, 258–59).

For Garrison, Dewey does not think knowing exhausts experience (or meaning). Rather, what Garrison calls "prereflective existential experience" suggests it as that which lies outside of reflection and cognition.

Garrison rejects the idealist reading of Dewey that suggests that experiences are exhausted in the thinking of them. He is, in point of fact, a realist in his reading of Dewey, though this label must be qualified. It is not that he thinks Dewey (pace Russell) claims objects/events/elements to be existing outside of our experiences, only waiting to be discovered. It is rather that these objects and events are discovered in and through the transaction of person(s) and nature. To talk of objects and events outside of experience is, for Garrison, only meaningful insomuch as the qualities of an experience suggest them. The transaction is the experience that then allows for discovery to occur.

> For Dewey, human nature was a seamless part of nature. This brings us to what I feel is the font of understanding for Dewey's philosophy of science and research: As Dewey saw it, we are participants in an unfinished universe rather than spectators of a finished universe. That is why our actions, our behaviors, our social constructions, deconstructions, and reconstructions have ontological significance. (Garrison 1994, 8)

Garrison takes pains to remind the reader that, for Dewey, inquiry deals with practical affairs. Inquiry begins with a problem at hand and is finished only when a solution to that problem is tested and deemed acceptable. The object of science is not to offer transcendental solutions to practical problems or to turn toward "atemporal, fixed, inner causal structures antecedent to events with the generative force to cause events" (Garrison 1994, 10). This, Garrison tells us, is scientific realism. And this is just what Garrison thinks Dewey sought to avoid. And it is this realism that Garrison sees in the so-called scientistic readers of Dewey.

Garrison is more rhetorical than Phillip Jackson in claiming that Dewey subordinates science to art. What allows Garrison to make this move is his phenomenological reading of Dewey's notion of experience. In particular, it is Garrison's focus on "the precognitive background" from which inquiry forms, that drives this particular estimation of the scope of inquiry. In his book, *Dewey and Eros*, Garrison states:

> Inquiry emerges from a largely pre-cognitive "background"; evolves into a statable cognitive problem in the foreground of inquiry; and concludes

with the solution to that problem, the answering of the question, and the satisfaction of that need. This process of inquiry is a continuous and un-broken emergence from background to foreground wherein the cognitive foreground remains permanently dependent on earlier precognitive in-tuitions. (Garrison 1997, 101)

Speaking of the precognitive background in more detail, Garrison claims that "the immediately experienced qualitative whole is vague, inexact, and inde-terminate, yet it influences the later discriminations of thought. . . . The qual-itative whole seizes us. . . . Qualitative experience is thus first had, and only later, if ever, known" (Garrison 1997, 102).

The conclusion that emerges from the strong claim of immediate experi-ence as primordial is that science, as inquiry, is subordinate to art, as experience.

> Dewey's naturalistic and emergent theory of inquiry allows us to see that thinking is not a set of context-independent forms, principles of formal logic, or calculations. It also allows us to see that inquiry is inherently a creative, productive, and constructive process of transforming some ac-tual, although undesirable, situation into some desired possibility. The aesthetic artifacts of creative imagination, and all that precede it, are testable by further inquiry. Inquiry on such an account is an artistically creative endeavor. (Garrison 1997, 97)

What is desired in the transformation sought by inquiry is stabilization: the movement of disequilibrium to equilibrium. The object that restores equilib-rium becomes (subliminally?) the object of desire. Imagination, as with Phillip Jackson, is the means to accomplish this task.

> With the loss of integration we have a vague, unconscious feeling of ac-tual or impending disequilibrium. We are in doubt and ignorant of how to continue. When reflective imagination alights upon an idea (or ideal) for restoring equilibrium, that idea then becomes an object of desire. Once we have an object of desire we become interested in identifying means in our environment for obtaining the end-in-view. Selective in-terest then drives selective attention to extract the necessary discrimi-nations from the otherwise infinitely complicated world that we find our-selves in. (Garrison 1997, 98)

The upshot of Garrison's claim is that there is not a single logic, appli-cable to all, at every time and place. Rather, there are many logics, driven by experiences had and imaginations proffered.[16] What determines the logic as used is the context in which the logic is used. And this context is (in part) the precognitive background that each and every student possesses in the having of an experience. Put another way, the precognitive background, by way of its distinctiveness, lends itself to the formation of different logics that are of benefit to those specific situations in which they are used. Garrison uses an example to make this claim.

> Often when students make even grievous errors it turns out that their reasoning was intelligent and logical. There is a logic of intelligent error. The teacher perceptive enough to detect this logic may greatly facilitate learning by detecting systematic errors that are often easily correctable. Sometimes the failure to obtain a predetermined answer occurs because the student uses *creative* rather than *conforming* intelligence. Unfortunately, many educators seem obsessed with the stupidity of this error. (Garrison 1997, 98, italics mine)

The point of this claim is to suggest that there is not only a logic of correctness, if you will, but a logic of error. Presumably, this means that there is a logic of the systematic sort that Garrison mentions further on in the passage, as well as a nonsystematic one, though Garrison is not clear on what this might look like. In any event, Garrison uses the above statement to segue into his abiding concern: the misreading of Dewey's theory of inquiry by scientistic interpreters.

> Oddly enough, educational theorists and researchers usually interpret Dewey's theory of inquiry and instrumentalist logic in a manner that makes him resemble the logical positivists or other idolaters of scientistic methodology. This tendency is ironic, since Dewey opposed positivism from the start. There is no quicker way to dismiss this false impression than by going straight to his aesthetics. (Garrison 1997, 98)

Prima facie, Dewey's sympathizers have a strong case for the removal of the label of scientism and positivism from Dewey. They clearly and forcefully contrast Dewey's talk of the strong role for science in human affairs with his equal talk of the subordination of science to experience and to art. But this turn to experience and art, and this subordination of inquiry, creates problems of its own. The experiential readers of Dewey do poorly with the concern that, in having immediate experience both outstrip and subordinate inquiry, inquiry becomes merely a tool for the promulgation of more and further satisfying immediate experiences. Jackson hints at a solution to the problem through identifying the importance of imagination and reflection as improving in turn the satisfaction of an immediate experience. But he does not address how meaning is to influence an experience that, in its immediacy, is already had. Finally the issue of the denigration of abstract, theoretical thinking is moot for all sympathetic readers heretofore mentioned: for there is no abstract and theoretical thinking in the manner vaunted by Hirsch, Ravitch, or Bertrand Russell. This would be an unsatisfying conclusion for these critics and the question would no doubt be taken as begged. Dewey's statements on the role and scope of abstract, theoretical thinking need to be unpacked.

The central problem of the construal of qualitative wholes and generic traits as the ground of an experience is that inquiry has its function and purpose exhausted in the satisfaction of an immediate experience, to which it is constrained. This is tantamount to proclaiming that the generic traits of an experience are not only the raison d'etre of inquiry, but of individual, social, and democratic living. Construed as such, the conclusion is that Dewey advocates for a behavioristic view of human nature: a view that suggests that the goal of life is to search out and have, satisfaction. On the reading of Dewey's sympathizers, an inquiry that has its purpose exhausted in the facilitation of increasingly satisfying experiences (traits, qualities, and wholes) becomes inquiry's singular endeavor. With respect to its function and its purpose, it emerges as monistic, despite sympathies to the contrary. It is this aestheticized conception of inquiry that I wish to challenge. I claim that Dewey does not maintain this view. But it is unclear how one can get from the goal of satisfying one's experience through the increased having of generic traits, to the aims of growth, community, and democracy. If inquiry is to be absolved of the critics' charges, attention must be paid to this problem. I urge in this next section that inquiry in an experience be read as it was in the previous chapter: as a set of techniques, habits, attitudes, and tempers, and further, that inquiry is necessary (though not sufficient) for both present and future qualitative experiences: While this does not contradict outright either Jackson's or Garrison's claims about inquiry, it does strongly advocate for that which they gloss over. And this is that no increasingly satisfactory experience can do without the rich fund of meanings that inquiry has *previously* developed. Likewise, inquiry cannot do without the satisfaction of an experience had. Inquiry and the experience to which it is ostensibly beholden are both means and ends to each other. And this is what I claim constitutes growth; one of Dewey's avowed aims.

Part Three:
Rereading Inquiry in Experience

It has been said that Dewey advocated a theory of inquiry not scientistic enough. Experience is said to outstrip inquiry; and experience, or elements of it, are said to be primordial, leading to accusations of foundationalism. Experience (and growth) is so vague in an enterprise such as this, that inquiry emerges as easily malleable to experience's satisfactions and needs. As such, science is said to be in the role of improving and satisfying experiences, with subsequently little to ground normative claims beyond the satisfaction of an achieved desire. As well, Dewey's theory of inquiry fails to deal with issues such as the existence of nonobservable particulate matter. Finally, Dewey's talk of inquiry betrays an anti-intellectual bias: to wit, the denigration of abstract, theoretical, and contemplative thinking in favor of a practical and operational one.

The first claim is that experience always outstrips inquiry and as a result, inquiry is beholden to the experience of which it is a part. This claim requires careful exegetical work, together with a choice about which of Dewey's readings on the role of inquiry (reflection, cognition, thought, and meaning) in experience, to privilege. On the one hand, there is the reading of Dewey that suggests that any inquiry into an experience is merely in the service of that experience, with the consequence that inquiry is in the service of an increasingly satisfying experience predicated upon the augmentation of qualitative, generic traits. This is the claim put forth by Dewey in certain of his texts and statements, and is echoed by S. Morris Eames, Tom Alexander, Jim Garrison, and Phillip Jackson. This is also the famous criticism of Dewey's talk of experience by George Santayana and it finds variants in the arguments of Richard Rorty, to the latter thinkers' chagrin.

My reading of Dewey suggests that any augmentation of qualitative, generic traits is itself dependent upon the prior stock of meanings built up through inquiry, such that prior inquiries play a large role in subsequent experiences. These experiences are augmented in much the same way Dewey claims that meanings augment each other: more satisfying experiences portend more investigation of ways to bring about their recurrence, leading to further and more robust meanings, leading to further satisfying experiences. This is in fact a claim that Dewey makes in response to certain critics of *Experience and Nature*. After debating the merits of the two ways of reading experience, I will choose the second over the first. I will then be in a position to claim that inquiry in an experience, far from being a peripheral or subordinate concern to experience, emerge as a requirement for experience. I shall deal with the claim that Dewey's theories of inquiry and experience are unable to account for the existence of nonobservables, such as those studied by particle physics, following. Then I turn to the third claim: that Dewey's theories of inquiry and experience somehow denigrate abstract and theoretical thinking.

The Inconsistency of Dewey on Experience

Before I begin discussing the specific issues raised by Dewey's critics, it will do once again to contrast some of Dewey's statements with one another. I begin with statements of Dewey's supporting a reading of inquiry as predominantly experiential.

The way of approach that sets out from that which is closest at hand, instead of from refined products of science no more signifies beginning with the results of psychological science than it does with those of physical science. Indeed, the former material is further away from direct experience than that of physics. It signifies beginning back of any science, with experience in its gross and macroscopic traits. Science will then be of interest as one of the phases of human experience, but intrinsically no more so than magic, myth, politics, painting, poetry and penitentiaries. (Dewey [1925] 1981, 369)

Scientific method, or the art of constructing true perceptions is ascertained in the course of experience to occupy a privileged position in undertaking other arts. But this unique position only places it the more securely as an art; it does not set its product, knowledge, apart from other works of art. (Dewey [1925] 1981, 284)

When this perception [of art as consummatory experience] dawns, it will be a commonplace that art—the mode of activity that is charged with meanings capable of immediately enjoyed possession—is the complete culmination of nature, and that "science" is properly a handmaiden that conducts natural events to this happy issue. (Dewey [1925] 1981, 269)

The poetic as distinct from the prosaic, esthetic art as distinct from scientific, expression as distinct from statement, does something different from leading to an experience. It constitutes one. (Dewey [1934] 1987, 91)

Scientific method tends to generate a respect for experience, and even though this new reverence is still confined to the few, it contains the promise of a new kind of experiences that will demand expression. (Dewey [1934] 1987, 342)

Here we have Dewey claiming that science, and scientific inquiry, is but one facet of experience, even a "handmaiden" that may lead to further, promising experiences, but not encompassing one. Further, science is said to have a different task than does art: the task of stating, not expressing, meanings. In these passages, Dewey seems to be claiming a weaker place for science than he does in passages urging the strong role and scope of scientific inquiry discussed in chapter 2.

Once again, the facility of choosing passages that either support or condemn a position is demonstrated. Unfortunately, as with much of the proscientific scholarship, the antiscientific and experiential scholarship often resorts to just this practice. But this is not helpful, for (again) it does not resolve the tensions created by the seeming inconsistency. It rather begs them. And Dewey's critics, particularly Richard Rorty, are alert to such question begging. To clear this impasse requires a reading of Dewey that maintains the force of his statements on the importance of inquiry in general and the contexts in which a scientific inquiry is helpful in particular, together with the force of his statements on the proper place of inquiry in experience and in art.

The First Claim: The Exhaustion of Inquiry in Immediate Experience

A chief criticism of Dewey is that Dewey exhausts the claims and function of inquiry in immediate experience. What this means is that inquiry is completely in the service of the satisfaction of an (immediate) experience, as it is just those qualities of an experience (Dewey's "generic" traits) that are to be satisfied, because satisfaction of qualities is just what counts in a more fulfilling experience. This places inquiry in the role of handmaiden: a role supported by several of Dewey's interpreters (Eames, Alexander, Jackson, Garrison) and by Dewey himself, in several key passages and texts. The problem that White and Mounce have is this: if inquiry is indeed beholden to a satisfying experience in the manner in which critics think Dewey claims, then satisfying experiences, rather than shared (normative) interests will be privileged. An individualistic, moral egoism, where people satisfy immediate desires, rather than shared, public concerns, is the logical result. Such egoism, again, cannot successfully adjudicate conflicting normative claims or moral disputes. On this account, it is not much better than the grounding of ethics in the pleasure principle. Further attempts to explain away the worst consequences of this have been largely unsuccessful, as Raymond Boisvert's examples demonstrate.[17]

The solution to this problem is to read Dewey as suggesting that the satisfaction of (immediate) experiences was not the terminus ad quem of inquiry. This is a controversial claim, and no doubt generates a controversial solution to the problem. For Dewey does indeed claim, in several key texts, that it is the satisfaction of (immediate) experiences that is at stake in inquiring into matters at hand. What I am suggesting is that this not be the last word on the subject: rather, I closely examine just what is at stake in the claim that the fulfillment of experience is the goal of all inquiry. I propose that prior inquiries set the stage for what counts as a current, and future, satisfying experience. What count here are the meanings that prior inquiry has constructed. Previously settled meanings, objects, and events, so judged by inquiry, augment the satisfaction of an experience, which leads to further inquiry.[18] The qualities of the further experience are augmented precisely because a network of already built-up meanings has prepared the way for the organism's increasing satisfaction.

I shall begin by outlining two arguments: the first is roughly the line taken by Dewey's apologists: that Dewey meant by the increasing satisfaction of experience, the heightening of qualities (quales, wholes, generic traits) and that this occurs prior to any inquiry, reflection, cognition, into that experience. That is, the qualities had before inquiry into them determine what counts as a satisfying experience. The second is that, even though heightening of the qualities of an experience is the goal of inquiry, this can only be interesting inasmuch as what prepares the way for this heightening is none other than the fund of meanings built up through prior inquiries and that this suggests that (prior) inquiry plays a role in present (and future) experience.[19] This is my claim, and I defend it in what follows.

Dewey's talk of wholes, quales, and traits as primordial has a long history in his work. For example, in an early essay "The Postulate of Immediate Empiricism," Dewey claims:

> Experience is always of *thats*; and the most comprehensive and inclusive experience of the universe that the philosopher himself can obtain is the experience of a characteristic *that*. From the empiricist's point of view, this is as true of the exhaustive and complete insight of a hypothetical all-knower as of the vague, blind experience of the awakened sleeper. As reals, they stand on the same level. As trues [sic], the latter has by definition the better of it; but if this insight is in any way the truth of the blind awakening, it is because the latter has, in its *own* determinate *quale*, elements of real continuity with the former; it is *ex hypothesi*, transformable through a series of experienced reals without break of continuity, into the absolute thought-experience. *There is no need of logical manipulation to effect the transformation, it is just by immediate experiences, each of which is just as real (no more, no less) as either of the two terms between which they lie.* (Dewey [1905–1906] 1977, 164–65, italics mine)

But the telling account of quales, wholes, and traits is found in his experiential texts, notably *Experience and Nature* and *Art as Experience*. In *Experience and Nature*, Dewey tells us that

> esthetic and moral experience reveal traits of real things as truly as does intellectual experience, that poetry may have a metaphysical import as well as science, is rarely affirmed, and when it is asserted, the statement is likely to be meant in some mystical or esoteric sense rather than in a straightforward everyday sense. (Dewey [1925] 1981, 27)

Just what are these traits of real things that aesthetic and moral experiences reveal? Dewey calls these "common traits of existence" and identifies them as qualitative individuality and constant relations, contingency and need, movement and arrest. . . . This fact is source both of values and of their precariousness; both of immediate possession which is causal and of reflection which is a precondition of the secure attainment and appropriation. Any theory that detects and defines these traits is therefore but a ground-map of the province of criticism [philosophy], establishing base lines to be employed in more intricate triangulations. (Dewey [1925] 1981, 308–09)

Note the claims in the above passage. Qualitative traits are the source of values and instability: the source of causality and reflection. Inquiry is of course included in this nominal sense of reflection. A theory of inquiry is (as Raymond Boisvert maintains) a ground-map that directs us, through the tool of criticism, to the qualities themselves. Prima facie, it seems as if reflection and a fortiori, a theory of inquiry, is a second-order function, relying upon and further mapping out first-order qualities.[20] And things bode worse for those inimical to the reading of inquiry as not subservient to generic traits. In his essay "Affective Thought," Dewey tells us that "reasoning is a phase of the generic function of bringing about a new relationship between organisms and the conditions of life, and like other phases of the function is controlled by need, desire, and progressive satisfaction" (Dewey [1926] 1984, 105–06). And Dewey claims in Art as Experience that

the undefined pervasive quality of an experience is that which binds together all the defined elements, the objects of which we are focally aware, making them a whole. The best evidence that such is the case is our constant sense of things as belonging or not belonging, of relevancy, a sense which is immediate. It cannot be a product of reflection, even though it requires reflection to find out whether some particular consideration is pertinent to what we are doing or thinking. For unless the sense were immediate, we should have no guide to our reflection. The sense of an extensive and underlying whole is the context of every experience. (Dewey [1934] 1987, 198)

In this passage, Dewey tells us that the sense of something is akin to an immediate feeling had. Reason is but a phase of experience, a phase controlled by and answering to need, desire, and satisfaction. It is the quality of an experience that binds elements, objects, and feelings within that experience. The very fact of an immediate sense is what guides our reflection, and not the converse.

Nor do things get better with respect to that one area of experience that has hitherto seemed impermeable to immediate qualities: thinking. In the essay "Qualitative Thought," Dewey discusses the primordial nature of a "qualitative situation" and claims that this situation forms "a larger and inclusive sub-ject-matter" (Dewey [1929–1930] 1984, 247). The qualitative situation "forms the universe of discourse of whatever is expressly stated or of what appears as a term in a proposition. The situation cannot present itself as an element in a proposition any more than a universe of discourse can appear as a member of discourse within that universe" (Dewey [1929–1930] 1984, 247). All of this leads Dewey to claim that "the situation controls the terms of thought, for they are its distinctions, and applicability to it is the ultimate test of their validity" (Dewey [1929–1930] 1984, 247). Dewey's interpreters sympathetic to the aes-theticization of experience certainly seem to have the day: inquiry, reflection, and thinking do seem subordinated to immediate experiences, qualitative traits, and situations. If this is right, if Dewey can only be read as placing in-quiry in the service of immediate experience, then Dewey's critics are correct, and Richard Rorty's eschewal of Deweyan metaphysics on the presumption of inflexibility on the part of generic traits stands fast. Must Dewey be forced to admit that inquiry, inasmuch as it is in the service of increasing satisfying ex-perience, cannot be a reliable guide to construct suitable, normative claims? I answer no.

Dewey in fact responded against this reading of inquiry as somehow sub-ordinate to immediate experience. And he did so only two years after writing *Experience and Nature*. Shortly after writing this text, Dewey was taken to task for supposedly having placed experience, rather than inquiry, at the helm of the ship. Santayana, as I have alluded to, accused Dewey of a dominance of the foreground, meaning that for Dewey, only the immediate can be real since all that we can account for in experience is traits and qualities.[21] As well, Everett W. Hall speaks of Dewey's confusion of meanings on "meaning." As discussed previously, the complaint is that in limiting meaning to reflection and lan-guage, what is excluded ex hypothesi, must also be granted a meaning. To as-sert the reality of the nonlinguistic and nonmeaningful is to grant these mean-ing. Dewey responded to both of these critics. In Dewey's essay "Half-Hearted Naturalism," Dewey argues *pace* Santayana:

> I hold that everything which is experienced has immediacy, and I also hold that every natural existence, in its own unique and brutal particu-larity of existence, also has immediacy, so that the immediacy which characterizes things experienced is not specious, being neither an un-natural irruption nor a supernatural imposition. To have traits, however, is not to be them, certainly not in any exclusive sense; and a consider-able part of my discussion of special topics is an attempt to show *that the characteristic traits of the subjects dealt with are to be accounted for as "inter-sections" or "interpenetrations" . . . of the immediate and the nexional or me-diatory.* (Dewey [1927–1928] 1984, 77, italics mine)

Here Dewey maintains that the immediate and the mediate interpenetrate; that is, they are not separate, first the immediate, then the mediate. Rather, they cooccur and coexist. Inquiry is not supervening on immediate qualities. The passage also suggests that perhaps immediate qualities are not temporally prior to an (immediate) inquiry into them.

In Dewey's response to Hall entitled "Meaning and Existence," Dewey chooses to privilege one of his varied positions from *Experience and Nature:* the position that immediate qualities are free from meanings. In so doing, he claims the following:

> I also hold that when it is a question of critical search for valid meaning, namely for that meaning we are entitled to treat as the genuine meaning of the events in question, we are obliged to have recourse to antecedent conditions. *For when a question arises as to what the consequences really are, we must take into account a course of events and sometimes a long one.* (Dewey [1927–1928] 1984, 86, italics mine)

What Dewey claims is that antecedent conditions—and (it seems) a fortiori the products of prior inquiries—play a role in the formation of new meanings.

But the distinction between prior meanings and present, immediate experience cannot hold, if it is to be claimed that only meanings engage meanings, but not (immediate) experiences and meanings. Despite his sometime insistence that meanings do not dwell in the realm of immediate experiences, Dewey does indeed claim that we can have something like an immediate meaning. Dewey tells us: "The sense of a thing, on the other hand, is an immediate and immanent meaning; it is meaning which is itself felt or directly had. When we are baffled by perplexing conditions, and finally hit upon a clew [sic], and everything falls into place, the *whole* thing suddenly, as we say, 'makes sense'" (Dewey [1925] 1981, 200). This suggests that Everett Hall is correct in questioning Dewey's consistency on the topic of meaning. Inconsistency notwithstanding, this passage gives the second reading of Dewey a ray of hope. For it suggests that meanings just may "go all the way down." That is, that there may be multiple "levels" of meaning: some meanings immediately had, while others requiring inquiry to develop. If this is the case then perhaps the connection between qualities, immediate meanings, and meanings developed in and through inquiry is closer and tighter than supposed. I now turn to defend this claim.

I believe that Dewey's argument about the wholeness of an immediately beheld, organic situation proves too much. Take as an example the following: Someone walks into the Palazzio Vecchio and gazes at Michaelangelo's *David.* Let us say that she has a "consummatory experience." Now presumably this means that an experience, in its immediacy, has been had. Further, in this experience, all the elements of our being that are displayed in special emphasis and partial realizations in other experiences are merged. . . . And they are so completely arranged in the immediate wholeness of the experience that each is submerged . . . it does not present itself in consciousness as a distinct element. (Dewey [1934] 1987, 278)

Note what gives this immediate experience its consummatory status. It is the "partial realizations in other experiences" as merged in the new one that is credited with the (ex post facto) judgment of the quality of this experience. Presumably, these partial realizations would include knowing something about art and artworks: having seen, read, or heard about Michaelangelo and his sculpture *David*: knowing its "cultural worth," its status as a coveted and much-loved art object. I am not claiming that this exhausts what must be considered in such a realization, for I do not mean to exclude the location (the Palazzio Vecchio) or the environment (the lighting, the surroundings), or the physical qualities of the sculpture. But I am claiming that prior meanings, formed in earlier inquiries into the subject matter, play a (strong) role in the having of a further (in this case, consummatory) experience.

The qualities of an experience cannot be disconnected from the meanings that those qualities usher. Qualities had beget inquiry into them: the (human) organism desires to reproduce the satisfaction obtained in a consummatory experience, and augment that satisfaction further. In this respect, Dewey's account of experience does not fall far from the Hobbesian tree. But there is more to Dewey's account than simply the increasing satisfaction of experience. Inquiry manipulates objects and events such that new or different qualities emerge. As such, qualities combine in such a way that a consummatory (or any deeply satisfactory) experience is had. The qualities depend upon prior inquiry inasmuch as it is prior inquiry into qualities (their permanence, continuity, individuality, as Dewey suggests) that sets the stage for the increasing satisfaction of present and future qualities. These qualities do not exist in a vacuum, and neither does inquiry. They are bound together in a relationship in which qualities beget inquiry, which leads to increasingly satisfying qualities. The qualities are means for further inquiry, just as inquiry is the end for further, satisfying experience: the inquiry and the satisfying experience (wholes, qualities, traits, and events) had are both means and ends to one another. As such, we must read out of Dewey any strong separation of immediate qualities from inquiry into them and read into Dewey the claim put forth in his rebuttal to Santayana: to wit, an interpenetration of immediate experience and inquiry. This is to be combined with the claim (mine and Dewey's, in his response to Hall) for a strong place and role for prior (settled) accounts of inquiry as aiding in the having of an increasingly satisfying experience.

I wish to return to the criticism of inquiry as beholden to desire and sat-isfaction of an immediate experience. The criticism can be obviated. If prior, settled accounts of inquiry play a role in present and future, immediate expe-riences, then these experiences are already imbued with (the results of) inquiry. How so? As inquiry is the conscious manipulation of generic traits and quali-ties, it orders and controls these traits. The results of this ordering and control do not impact the experience had: this much is admitted. For this experience is already passed. But future experiences, experiences to be had, can and will benefit by the manipulation that inquiry does on the present having of generic traits. The traits of an experience, after an inquiry into these, emerge in a new light in the having of a future experience. They are given meanings that, prior to the inquiry, they did not have. When a new experience occurs, or (more properly) some variation of a prior experience, this experience will be aug-mented because the prior meanings that inquiry has constructed alter the traits of this one. Traits once ignored are given attention. And traits that seemed scattered or disconnected are made whole. The result is the satisfying (imme-diate) experience. The claim regarding the subordination of inquiry to an im-mediate experience, on this account, misses the mark: for a new experience is beholden to prior inquiry for the very quality of satisfaction.[22] Because the premise of the conclusion that inquiry is subordinated to immediate experi-ence cannot be defended without also admitting that immediate experience serves inquiry (meanings), it cannot be claimed that Dewey's account of in-quiry is merely a variant of moral egoism. But to see how the public actually determines inquiry and the satisfaction of experiences thereby, I shall have to ask the reader to wait until chapter 4.

Before I close, there is an objection to reading Dewey in the manner that I suggest. This comes from Ralph Sleeper. As it is a forceful one, I should like to quote it at length.

> By seeming to locate all objects of knowledge where they are real, Dewey appears to be locating them within experience. It is thus possible to read his thesis of continuity [the thesis that Alexander develops] as simply a new version of idealism, as denying that it is possible to have knowledge of independently real objects in an independently real world. According to this reading, Dewey is claiming that our knowledge of existences is re-stricted to those that present themselves in experience—a version of pre-sentative realism, or even an objective idealism. . . . It is a reading that clearly supports the conclusion that, for Dewey, the subject-matter of metaphysics must be experience itself. Moreover, additional support for such a reading can readily be found in Dewey's frequently repeated con-tention that thought is existential and not separate from the activity of

inquiry. Finally, it could be maintained that, since Dewey argues consistently that knowing always begins with apprehension and proceeds by *means* of apprehension, its objects are always tainted, so to speak, by the apprehending mind—which is another way of saying that Dewey has failed to free himself from the idealism with which he began. On this reading, synthesis would be simply experiential for Dewey; it would be merely an updated version of Hegel's synthesis, but set in the context of experimental method rather than the dialectic of world process. Dewey's insistence that the object of knowledge is changed during the process of inquiry and that change is real can only mean that experience is changed, that the object of inquiry is changed by means of inquiry to the end of ever greater fulfillment of its intrinsic reality. (Sleeper 1986, 91)

Sleeper's suggestion to obviate this reading of Dewey is to downplay Dewey's talk of continuity.

It is clear that Dewey views continuity as merely a feature of specific situations and circumstances, a feature that certain other situations and circumstances lack. Neither existence nor experience are terms denoting anything thought to be uniformly continuous. . . . They are terms as often associated with discontinuous events as with those continuous events that stand out, by virtue of their brilliance and focus, as having meaning. . . . The process of inference is indeed characterized as being a continuous event, but the continuity referred to is not categorical at all, but rather, piecemeal, and situational. This is not transcendental realism, but transactional realism, for knowing is here regarded as a transaction that takes place between an organism and its environment, and its occurrence denotes changes in relationships as existential events, actual changes in the real world. (Sleeper 1986, 91–92)

The fear is that, should the "real" of existents be placed within experience, the charge of objective idealism would apply to Dewey. Objects on this account would change through the use of inquiry such that a closer and closer approximation to reality is occasioned. On this account, Dewey comes to look a lot like Hegel, and his notion of experience, similar to Hegel's absolute idealism. The solution is to (once again) claim that continuity is not a "category" of thought, rather a condition of transaction. As such, it is generic. But this turn, as I have demonstrated, evinces its own set of problems. Furthermore, it is unnecessary. The problem with this argument is that it falsely concludes that, since nothing can be said to reside outside of an experience, any real object is real, but only within an experience. As inquiry is said to transform experiences, real objects will transform as well, and thus reality itself becomes conditional on inquiry, and thereby precarious. The problem is that Dewey's pronouncement that nothing is *known* outside of experience is conflated with that of nothing *exists* outside of experience. When Dewey is read carefully, the conclusion is that experiences themselves, made up equally of the known and the unknown, are only partially amenable to transformation. Inquiry may order and control elements within an experience. But it cannot *have* these elements. Nor can it control the unknown elements outside of it. The fear that Dewey's talk of existential reals as falling completely inside of inquiry thus portending the reconstruction of objects such that they fulfill a (preordained?) intrinsic reality, is overwrought.

The Second Claim: Inquiry and Nonobservable Matter

The concern about Dewey's handling of such nonobservables as those postulated in recent particle physics is shared by both Bertrand Russell and Ernest Nagel. Russell's solution is to reject the supposed notion of Dewey's that there is nothing lying outside of experience. This solves the problem of how we can say that there is such a thing as an atom (or more currently, a quark or neutrino). Thus, Russell's stance is a realist one: he believes that existentially real objects are present regardless of our interactions with them. Nagel of course adopts a much weaker version of Russell's realism: though he does not go all the way with Russell in claiming that existentially real objects are present despite no experience of them, he does claim that the philosophy of science must make room for nonobservables, and that Dewey's theory of inquiry does not. Both thinkers agree that Dewey's inquiry and logic cannot handle the problem of nonobservable matter. I shall draw on Dewey's *Logic* once again, in addressing this concern.

In the section of the *Logic* entitled "Immediate Knowledge," Dewey addresses the problem of primitive data under the umbrella term "atomic realism." Dewey here refers to the notion that complex objects can be reduced to primitive data and can further be propositionalized into "this" and "that." Dewey characteristically denies the warrants of atomic propositions.

> The fallacy in the theory of logically original, complete and self-sufficient atomic propositions is thus an instance of the same fallacy that has been repeatedly noted: The conversion of a function in inquiry into an independent structure. It is an admitted fact that ideally, or in theory, propositions about irreducible qualities are necessary in order adequately to ground judgment having existential reference. What is denied is that propositions are complete and self-sufficient logical character in isola-

tion. For they are determinations of evidential material in order to locate the problem in hand and secure evidence to test a solution. (Dewey
[1938] 1986, 151–52)

The problem of positing nonobservable matter is not one that arises as a result
of the presence or absence of existential material. Dewey makes this quite clear
in his allusions to the importance of irreducible qualities. Rather, the problem
is with the aim and scope of the propositions that are constructed to relate the
material. Propositions that take the matter under consideration to be exhausted
by a descriptive characterization as completed of it, are unwarranted. This is to
commit the "psychological fallacy": to wit, taking a part (in this case, a quality
or qualities) from a whole (in this case the environing conditions in which the
qualities were ascertained) and pronouncing it as complete and final.

The further point to note in this passage is that Dewey, when he does
speak of matter, refers not to self-enclosed and complete objects, rather qualities. For Dewey, what can be measured of matter are the qualities produced out
of the transaction of investigator and subject matter. Qualities are not only
measurable; they can be manipulated: differing qualities can be gleaned in and
through experimentation upon subject matters. Objects are logical and cognitive conclusions that follow from the manipulation of qualities in such a manner that predictable results are obtainable. Only then do objects become observable in the sense that scientists use the term. As Dewey puts it:

> It follows, then, that when objects or qualities are cognitively appre-
> hended, they are viewed in reference to the exigencies of the perceived
> field in which they occur. They then become objects of *observation*, ob-
> servation being defined precisely as the restrictive-selective determina-
> tion of a particular object or quality within a total environing field. . . .
> But when the results are carried over into logical theory and taken to pro-
> vide the basis for a theory of data in their logical status and bearing, com-
> plete distortion results. For isolated objects or qualities are then taken in
> their isolation to be the *givens* or *data*. (Dewey [1938] 1986, 152–53)

Dewey does have an answer to this concern. And it is that only on the
faulty premise that matter such as nonobservable elements has as its corollary
logically, self-sufficient wholes, in isolation from the perceptual field and from
the investigator's manipulation of qualities, can nonobservable elements be said
to exist outside of experience. This unsubstantiated claim renders this criticism
of Dewey's logical theory dubious. Dewey can respond by simply saying that this
commits the "psychological fallacy." Note that in responding, Dewey does not
claim that there is no nonobservable matter. Nor does he claim that matter does
not exist outside of our experience of it.[23] What Dewey does claim is that we

cognize such matter only after consciously manipulating the qualities of "something" that then is given the status of observable. It is by contextualizing the qualities, by relating them to other concerns, interests, and conclusions—in short, by placing them in a (temporal) continuum of qualities and objects—that they derive the specific meaning of observable that Dewey suggests. The qualities had beget the inquiry that leads to the logical and cognitive construction of the object (atom, quark, neutrino) which is then used to further manipulate qualities. The pattern, again, is circular. In so doing, we are able to draw the inferences that lead us to conclude that matter external to our senses does indeed exist. Dewey does allow for nonparticulate matter, but he does not allow for nonobservable matter in isolation from the qualities had and operations undergone in coming to conclude that nonobservable matter is existential.

The Third Claim: The Denigration of Abstract Thinking

Russell, Hirsch, and Ravitch advocate one or another form of the argument that Dewey somehow denigrated abstract thinking in his zeal to operationalize inquiry. Each of these criticisms takes a slightly different form. To recall Scheffler, thinking yoked to the search for a solution to a problem curtails free thinking and occasions a failure of the imagination, thereby. For Hirsch, problem solving neglects the rich storehouse of valuable (abstract) methods and thinking built up through the past. For Ravitch, the turn to fashionable Deweyan and progressivist methods of instruction such as activity or project-based learning, took away from the more important tasks of imparting knowledge to children. For Russell, neglect of rationalist logic portends the impossibility to conceive of solutions to problems such as nonobservable matter and the logic of causality. In short, to operationalize thinking is to deny its abstractive properties and this inhibits thinking from rising beyond the mundane.

Dewey's reply to these criticisms seems inadequate: for Dewey denies just what the criticisms want to maintain. And this is that abstract thought is privileged over and above practical thought. And what gives it this privilege is not its capacity to solve the problems of men, rather its self-stated superiority. And this turns on a metaphysical conclusion about the worth of abstract thinking. Abstract thinking has been previously privileged, Dewey claims, because it is saddled with a metaphysical status: a pronouncement that it is somehow better because more rarefied. Rarefied thinking precedes the imagining of rarefied objects, such as experimentally unapproachable predicates. This in turn leads to abstract thought as having a more prestigious social status. As Dewey puts it in a justifiably famous passage from *Experience and Nature*:

> For reflection the eventual is always better or worse than the given. But since it would also be better if the eventual good were now given, the

philosopher, belonging by status to a leisure class relieved from the ur-
gent necessity of dealing with conditions, converts the eventual into
some kind of Being, something which is, even if it does not exist. Permanence, real essence, totality, order, unity, rationality, the *unum, verum
et bonum* of the classic tradition, are eulogistic predicates. When we find
such terms used to describe the foundations and proper conclusions of a
philosophic system, there is ground for suspecting that an artificial sim-
plification of existence has been performed. (Dewey [1925] 1981, 33)

This criticism can be located in many different works of Dewey's. But this argument against abstract thinking is, as it stands, merely a negative one. That
is to say, it is a reductio ad absurdum, in that it demonstrates the trouble that
abstract thinking gets into without due attention to the criticism itself. Clearly,
this will not extinguish the criticisms. More must be offered. I claim that
Dewey does have a place for abstract thinking, though this thinking is manifestly different from what the critics have made of it in their own work. To recall the argument of the first chapter, for Dewey, abstractions are logical forms.
Abstractions are equally universal propositions. Abstraction takes the logical
form of an if-then proposition. Abstract propositions are, as mere possibilities,
nonoperational with respect to a defined, existential problem. They become
operational inasmuch as they further direct generic ones. Dewey states it nicely
in the *Logic*, using the example of freedom as a universal proposition:

> Take the proposition "Only if men are free, are they justly blamed." Nei-
> ther the existence of freedom nor of just blame is affirmed. While it may
> be said that the existence of men is *postulated*, it is not implied nor is it
> expressly affirmed. The relation affirmed between freedom and just
> blame, if it is valid at all, will still be valid if all human beings are wiped
> out of existence. Freedom, justice, and blame designate abstract charac-
> ters. Nevertheless, the proposition formulates possible operations which,
> if actually performed, are *applied* to the actual conduct of men so as to di-
> rect observations into the conditions and consequences of actual cases
> of blame. Apart from such application, the proposition represents merely
> an abstract possibility depending upon a definition of freedom and jus-
> tice which, as far as existence is concerned, might very well be arbitrary.
> (Dewey [1938] 1986, 302)[24]

This rather Aristotelian-sounding description of universal propositions as possibilities and operationalized propositions as actualities serves well to underscore the point of universal propositions: they do not have any direct intended
reference to existence. Rather, they are relevant to inquiry itself.

This can only appease the critics so far, though. For as ideas "they are not intended to be themselves realized but are meant to direct our course to realization of potentialities in existent conditions—potentialities which would escape notice were it not for the guidance which an ideal, or a definition, provides" (Dewey [1938] 1986, 303). Ideas as abstractions are indirectly at the service of existent situations and problems. There seems to be no getting around this. It seems there is no place for abstract thought in Dewey, if abstract thought is to be for the sake of thought itself. Even at the level of Dewey's idea of abstraction, this thought seems to be in the service of inquiry, which is, in turn, in the service of the existent situation at hand.

There is another possible route to be taken. As previously noted, Phillip Jackson has said of imagination that it arranges the meanings gained by inference (Jackson 1998, 28). Prima facie, this seems to meet at least some of the requirements of abstraction that Dewey's critics are looking for: imagination is ideational; it arranges meanings, not objects; it seems to involve no experimentation or operationalism. Does Dewey's notion of imagination satisfy the critics' requirements? In *Art as Experience*, Dewey says of imagination:

> There is a conflict artists themselves undergo that is instructive as to the nature of imaginative experience. The conflict has been stated in many ways. One way of stating it concerns the opposition between inner and outer vision. There is a stage in which the inner vision seems much richer and finer than any outer manifestation. It has a vast and enticing aura of implications that are lacking in the object of external vision. It seems to grasp much more than the latter conveys. Then there comes a reaction; the matter of the inner vision seems wraithlike compared with the solidity and energy of the presented scene. The object is felt to say something succinctly and forcibly that the inner vision reports vaguely, in diffuse feeling rather than organically. The artist is driven to submit himself in humility to the discipline of objective vision. . . . The interaction of the two modes of vision is imagination; as imagination takes form the work of art is born. (Dewey [1934] 1987, 272–73)

Dewey makes a similar pronouncement on the part of the philosopher:

> It is the same with the philosophic thinker. There are moments when he feels that his ideas and ideals are finer than anything in existence. But he finds himself obliged to go back to objects if his speculations are to have body, weight, and perspective. Yet in surrendering himself to objective material he does not surrender his vision; the object just as an object is not his concern. It is placed in the context of ideas and, as it is

thus placed, the latter acquire solidity and partake of the nature of the object. (Dewey [1934] 1987, 273)

Here, Dewey advocates a synthesis of idea and object and pronounces this syn-thesis as imagination. Note that in the synthesis, the idea is not subordinated to the object: rather, it is made more robust as a result of the communion. For now, in addition to a bare idea, a fund of meanings is built up that could only have arisen as the result of the communion of idea with object. Indeed, this fund of meaning (Dewey's "context of ideas") serves to augment both the idea and the object. And this augmentation will serve to augment further ideas. Dewey's stark talk of imagination seems to fly in the face of Dewey's talk of uni-versal propositions as shorn of existential content, as he puts forth in his Logic. Is there inconsistency here, or is Dewey talking of something entirely different when he discusses imagination?

    The answer, I claim, is that there is no inconsistency and that imagina-tion can adequately account for the synthesis of objects and universal proposi-tions. How is this so? First, the notion that abstract thought pays allegiance to none other than itself must be given up. Abstract thought, characteristically, pays attention to other abstract thoughts. And these in turn, far from arising out of nowhere, are built up from the (logical) objects arising as a result of the settled outcomes of prior inquiries. In other words, previously built-up objects and relations (meanings) serve as the material upon which abstract thought works. The relation of abstract thought to logical object/relation and existen-tial object is inextricably bound, though not viciously circular. Existential ob-jects/events beget logical objects/relations (meanings) that supply the material for further universal propositions (abstract thought). Abstract thought denotes possibilities which, when operationalized through manipulation of the quali-ties of material objects by relations, may result in a transformation of a logical object/event and meaning. These meanings then become the material for fur-ther thought. The ontological form-matter distinction can only be held as a functional device: in truth, there is no ontological distinction. And this is the second point to be made. For only if one sees abstract thought as existentially detached from logical objects and relations, does one note a problem with the operationalization of abstraction. The criticism of abstraction in the service of human problems turns on a begged premise: and this is that abstraction is, by its very nature, isolated from existents. To say that abstract thought can never (even indirectly) be in the service of existential situations is to fall prey to a reductio ad absurdum. For abstract thought detached from existential situa-tions can provide no account of the material upon which abstraction works. This is because abstraction is but mere form, shorn of content and function: it is mere form and as such, an idle fancy. Though Dewey's critics would no doubt agree to disagree with Dewey on the abstract nature of some modes of think-ing, they can do so only at the risk of being unable to account for the warrant of the abstract nature of thinking beyond a claim that it is justified only in and for itself. And this is plainly unworkable: it cannot help us to make clear the relation between abstract thinking and the material that it thinks, whereas Dewey's account can.

Part Four:
Inquiry, Growth, and Education

On the above reading of inquiry, there cannot be an existential distinction be-tween qualities had in an experience and the (subsequent) reflection into them. This is so because inquiry is already at work in the having of an experi-ence, inasmuch as prior meanings, built up from prior inquiries, play a role in the satisfaction of a present experience. Further, inquiry cannot be said to denigrate abstract thinking. This is so because abstract thinking has for its ma-terial, itself: that is to say, other abstract thoughts. Far from being exiled, ab-stract thoughts are necessary (though intermediate) conceptions that ulti-mately improve the chances for a successful outcome of inquiry. Finally, Dewey is able to account for the existence of nonobservable matter, with the caveat that any such matter cannot be presumed to correspond in its existence to a fixed logical form. Nonobservable matter runs together with the conceptions that think it.

What we have here is a very robust and context-bound notion of inquiry that, though not scientistic, is nevertheless every bit as involved in the order-ing of the data of experience as a scientistic theory would promise to be. In what remains, I wish to consider this robust notion of inquiry in relation to some recent developments concerning theories of knowledge, and then to Dewey's statements on growth and growth's chief means—(formal) education. Doing so will put me in a position to argue that a (naturalized) *telos* of inquiry is growth and further, that this growth is dependent on education; a formal means to facilitate the building up of a fund of meanings such that increasingly satisfying experiences can be had. Growth is thus coeval with the notion of ever-expanding linkages of inquiry, meanings, and satisfying experiences.

I wish to return once again to Michael Williams and his characterization of epistemology in his *Problems of Knowledge*. For the foundationalist argument of knowledge—the argument that there must be something prior to something else, something that grounds, buttresses, or holds up, ideas, concepts, and re-lations—is endemic not only to older varieties of empiricism and positivism: It creeps into talk of coherence theory and of holist thinking in general.

Williams's chief concern in dealing with foundationalism is to challenge the skeptical conclusion that the external world is imperiled if there cannot be found a certainty upon which one's perception and knowledge can count. So-lutions to this dilemma have historically been phenomenalist: that there are primitives, sense data, or sensibilia that are present in every act of knowing. Williams is dubious: "The skeptic claims that we know nothing about the world: our knowledge extends no farther than experience. The phenomenal-ist tells us not to worry. Of course we know all sorts of things about the exter-nal world, because the external world is only a construction out of experience" (Williams 2001, 139).

The problem with phenomenalism in particular and foundationalism in general, is that it splits knowledge into a two-level affair: reflection, thinking, conceptualization, on the one hand; having, perceiving, and/or sensing prim-itives on the other. Williams claims:

> To be able to recognize the relevance of and respond appropriately to challenges to observation reports, I must know a good deal about my per-ceptual capabilities. It follows that I cannot come, by observation, to know anything, unless I already know lots of things. This consequence is fatal even to modest or 'two-level' versions of foundationalism. Ac-cording to 'two-level' views, basic beliefs have an intrinsic initial credi-bility that can be reinforced (and perhaps occasionally degraded) by our subsequent development of a systematic, reflective view of our epistemic abilities. But if Sellars is right, there is no autonomous first level, how-ever modestly conceived. We need reliability—knowledge to have any observational knowledge of particular facts. (Williams 2001, 176)

What Williams suggests in place of granting primacy to phenomena and the priority of the first-level view of knowledge, is that phenomena and talk of phe-nomena serve the very same purpose as talk of second-level concepts: that is, explanation. Williams puts it this way:

> It is important to see that the prime function of sensation-talk is ex-planatory. Sensations are causal intermediaries between events in the world and our seeing and reporting that things are thus and so. They are not evidence for how things are. It is true that we can have noninferen-tial knowledge of our sensations, just as we can have such knowledge of our thoughts; and it is true that we know that our impressions are nor-mally reliable indicators of how things are in our surroundings. But our knowledge of how things are in our surroundings is not hostage to any "reliability inference." Observational knowledge is causally mediated but

epistemically direct: that is, non-inferential in the sense explained earlier. (Williams 2001, 184).

Dewey is in full agreement with all of this. Dewey's talk of experience is talk not of known primitives, but of events, traits, quales, and wholes that are had. Such talk is inimical to the claim that known primitives are the building blocks of knowledge. Further, all knowledge, as Williams claims, is not inferential or relational: there is also direct, observational knowledge. We might label this "the immediacy of meaning."

It is wise to dig deeper and see what Williams has in mind when he discusses the traditional sources of knowledge.

In the first place, they are generic: the sources of knowledge are "the senses" or "Reason." Secondly, they are ultimate. Such authoritative faculties are sources of what Richard Rorty calls "privileged representations," beliefs that are the basis of all further inference because they themselves possess a special credibility, derived from their pedigree. In identifying such beliefs, we reach rock bottom: questions of justification cannot be pressed any farther. The picture of knowledge as belief that derives from authoritative sources thus creates a strong prejudice in favour of substantive foundationalism. It also builds in a kind of metaepistemological foundationalism. Once questions about justification are raised to the level of epistemological theory, citing a generic source, the pedigree that gives basic beliefs their special status, is the last word. (Williams 2001, 168–69)

This is what Williams calls epistemological realism, and he sets this in opposition to pragmatism, the view that the context helps to determine both the methods and the knowledge that arises therein. Much traditional talk of the sources of knowledge, Williams says, invites us to epistemological realism. This gets us into trouble, because it places the entire weight of the capacity to know onto either a phenomenal or conceptual foundation. And if the foundation turns out to be questionable, the project of knowing collapses. "If there are certain ultimate, generic sources of knowledge, which fix our 'epistemic situation,' epistemically responsible believing must pay these sources due respect. If it turns out that our ultimate sources are not really up to the job, our epistemic situation is intrinsically defective and we cannot know anything. Or if we cannot show that they are up to the job, then for all we know, we know nothing" (Williams 2001, 171).[25] This, Williams claims, invites skepticism about our capacity to know, and is itself reminiscent of Sellars's metaphor of knowledge as an elephant resting upon a tortoise, immediately introducing the question What supports the tortoise?

Dewey's talk of generic traits and the immediacy and qualitative whole of an experience can be seen as part of a response to this quandary. Generic traits just are present in any and every experience, and what counts as an experience is the quality of that immediate having, which is in turn a function of the presence or absence of these generic traits. This is very close to William's notion of epistemic directness. One must be very careful, though, to not construe these traits or qualities as anything like foundations, sources, or known primitives if one does not have in place a further means for their support. And since these traits and qualities are considered primary, what support they have must be, I claim, from the meanings accrued from past satisfying experiences. Otherwise, one is trapped between the Scylla of what supports the primitives, and the Charibdis of where to locate the beginning of knowledge. And, as Sellars famously said, neither of these will do.

What remains is to discuss the connection between inquiry, experience, and Dewey's talk of growth. Dewey has (at least) three senses of growth. The first may broadly be called "organismic," and is the sense of growth that humans share with other creatures. The second is "judgmental," and has to do with our ability to expand our capacities to form the habits of inquiry. The third is experiential, and is the sense of growth that I wish to discuss most fully here. A few words are, however, in order about the first two senses of growth, as these are intertwined with the sense important to having an experience. The first sense of growth connotes biological maturation, both in terms of physical traits and species-related tasks. To say, for example, that a tiger cub has successfully grown is to say that it is physically mature (an adult) and that it is capable of performing the tasks that are considered the proper ends of tigers (hunting, killing prey, mothering cubs and protecting young, etc.). The primary condition of growth in this sense is "immaturity," which is to say, "a being can develop only in some point in which he is undeveloped" (Dewey [1916] 1980, 46). Immaturity "designates a positive force or ability—the *power* to grow" (Dewey [1916] 1980, 47).

Now human beings differ from other animals in that they are not born with an abundance of physical gifts already developed; rather, what humans have going for them is an abundance of social linkages. Consequently, a human infant is much more dependent on his or her parents or group than an animal. But, as Dewey says, "From a social standpoint, dependence denotes a power rather than a weakness; it involves interdependence" (Dewey [1916] 1980, 49). Human young learn to overcome obstacles through putting instinctive reactions together with environmentally created wants and needs. This conjunction is what Dewey famously, here and elsewhere, calls a habit. As human beings are said to have great plasticity, a "specific adaptability of an immature creature for growth," human beings can form a potentially infinite number of habits. These habits are the result of learning from experiences and, specifically, the "power to modify actions on the basis of the results of prior experiences, the power to *develop dispositions*" (Dewey [1916] 1980, 49). For, as Dewey says, "without it, the acquisition of habits is impossible" (Dewey [1916] 1980, 49).

And this takes us to the second sense of growth: the growth of judgments. While it may seem as if there is a great distinction between the sort of growth that the individual has in terms of physical maturation (coordination of muscles, bladder and bowel control, fine and gross motor control, etc.) and that of ideas, concepts, analysis, synthesis, and other so-considered intellectual habits, this is in fact not at all the case. Not only do these skills achieve their maturity on the basis of learning from experience, they too, require dispositions to develop. Judgments, as with other skills learned, begin as a set of responses to contingencies and problems and mature as a result of adaptation to the needs of the organism. Thomas Dalton makes a convincing argument for the parallel in judgment and human development largely on the basis of Dewey's observance and participation in research conducted by the psychologist Myrtle McGraw on infant balance, proprioception, and reflex learning. McGraw identified alternate phases in infant balance control, in which "older traits and emergent capabilities are actually recombined and reintegrated in slight different ways . . . to alter the form or configuration of a total pattern" (Dalton 2002, 222). Now Dalton claims that this had an impressive influence on Dewey's writing of the *Logic*. For Dewey is said to have "believed that the alternating phases McGraw identified, through which development progresses, demonstrated that judgment emerges through overlapping stages of comparison through contrast, reorientation, and redirection that increasingly delineate the scope of effective thought and action" (Dalton 2002, 222). Specifically, Dalton notes that, for Dewey, "uncertainty instigates a process of 'requalification' through 'groping,' as Dewey calls it in the *Logic*, involving the identification of the limits or boundaries of an indeterminate situation . . . that is comparable to the diffuse writhing and wriggling movements that McGraw found infants making in their initial attempt to explore the limits of their immediate environments" (Dalton 2002, 222).

Dalton continues: "Similarly, Dewey characterized this initial stage of the dialectic of inquiry as involving an attitude of 'bare acquiescence' or assent to the limits of a situation. . . . Significantly, Dewey considered each step in the process of judgment to be mediated by an attitude as evidenced by the shift of mood in verb tenses from the indicative 'is' to opative 'may be' to imperative 'must be' (Dalton 2002, 222–23).

The next stage of judgment involves the effort to differentiate specific characteristics and kinds against the background of more general phenomena. Generic propositions are invoked at this point, according to

Dewey, to distinguish traits according to whether they belong to one kind or another. . . . McGraw's infants illustrated this stage in their deliberate efforts to attain balance by controlling the frequency and direction of their movements, contributing to one form of locomotion rather than another. . . . Finally a point is reached, after experimental operations have been performed as specified by "universal propositions," when extraneous elements (i.e., hypotheses proven incorrect or movements deemed inessential) are eliminated. When remaining traits are sufficiently integrated (as exemplified by a stable pattern of walking, involving the seamless integration of stance, stride, and gait), then final warranted judgments can be embodied in propositional form. Dewey characterized this stage of inquiry as a "reaction from some into all," when phenomena sharing the same qualitative attributes as one kind are integrated to form generalizations applying to all such kinds. (Dalton 2002, 223)

The final sense of growth that I wish to discuss is the growth of the ability to have an experience. In many ways, this sense of growth is cumulative; it relies on the other two senses and indeed, subsumes them. In *Experience and Nature*, Dewey discusses growth and its relation to the generic trait, continuity. Dewey says, "The reality is the growth-process itself; childhood and adulthood are phases of a continuity, in which just because it is a history, the later cannot exist until the earlier exists . . . and in which the later makes use of the registered and cumulative outcome of the earlier—or, more strictly, is its utilization" (Dewey [1925] 1981, 210). And in *Experience and Education*, Dewey claims that "growth, or growing and developing, not only physically but intellectually and morally, is one exemplification of the principle of continuity" (Dewey [1938–1939] 1988, 19). Growth is the biological and cultural manifestation of the generic trait of continuity. One might say it is continuity writ large. As such, it occupies a privileged position in Dewey's experiential, social, and educational writings. Growth implies transformation of the organism. One can speak of growth as occurring when the biological organism, in response to its environment, undergoes desired change. This transformation of response is what Dewey, in various places, calls habit (Dewey [1938] 1986, 38), (Dewey [1922] 1983, 31). Habits involve a change in the total organism, and not simply the organism's cognitive or motor apparatus. Dewey, in discussing the response of a child to a flaming candle, likens the transformation of behavior to a whole, rather than a reflex arc (Dewey [1896] 1972, 108–09). Growth occurs similarly when the whole organism, inclusive of the transaction of person and environment, reconstructs habits previously formed such that a new habit is developed for that situation (and possibly others).

It is in this way growth-as-continuity emerges as a self-sustaining and self-perpetuating *telos* of inquiry. Growth as the adjustment of the organism to its environment through the transaction of organism and environment requires for this adjustment a means by which reliability and predictability of present and future adjustments can occur. This means is inquiry. Inquiry, through analytic discrimination and synthetic construction, through ordering and control, through experimentation, hypothesis testing, and evaluation, aids the organism in this adjustment and proffer growth. Inquiry emerges as the conscious manipulation of the environment such that order, control, and continuity thereby can occur. Problematic situations drive inquiry inasmuch as these situations require the inquirer to attend to the details of the situation in a much more precise and careful manner. Experimentation occurs and new techniques are attempted. If all goes well, the problematic situation is solved (or dissolved) and a new "habit" of inquiry, an inquiry that is better suited to solving just this sort of problem, is constructed. Growth occurs in the transaction of organism and its environment (the solution to a problem that inhibited the satisfaction of the immediate experience) as well as within inquiry (an improvement upon an older method of inquiry that did not function well in the new context). Increasingly satisfying experiences (experiences that betoken continuity) are dependent on the adjustment of the organism to and with its environment. Ceteris paribus, the adjustment of the organism is dependent upon the awareness of increasingly satisfying experience as had. In point of fact, it is reasonable to suggest that growth and adjustment are similar terms for different functions: at the point of intersection of organism and environment, growth connotes adjustment; at the point of intersection of inquiry and an experience had, growth connotes a build-up of increasingly satisfying meanings which can be brought to bear on further experiences.

If growth is viewed in this way, it becomes clear that, in the language of experience, the fund of meanings that prior inquiries have built up, and in the language of habit, the fund of habits that prior inquiries have built up, are embodied in satisfying and new experiences and habits, respectively. In the case of experience, which is our concern here, what this suggests is that the fund of meanings that is built up out of prior inquiries leads, when related to a new experience, to growth-as-continuity. This is so because any new experience had is situated (related) to the complex of objects, concepts, and judgments arising from, and constructed out of, older experiences; this new experience is given immediate, additional satisfaction. This additional satisfaction propels its qualities above those of prior experiences. One can say that an experience, though had as a (self-subsisting?) whole, has been rendered continuous with other experiences (grown) inasmuch as the augmentation of its qualities is due (in part) to the meaningfulness adjudged of prior experiences.

Growth-as-continuity is to be read as a self-generating, self-perpetuating process that implies the increasing satisfaction of the qualities of an experience through the manipulation, order, and control of one's environment and—inasmuch as these, too, arise of the transaction of organism and environment—one's judgments. This obviates the criticism of growth that it is beholden, in some Hobbesian sense, to desire. For when one asks the question Desire for what? one sees that desire cannot encompass some base motivation, instinct, or drive, such as pleasure or happiness (though happiness and pleasure do arise out of the satisfaction of an experience had). This is because the satisfaction aroused owing to the presence of the generic traits, which arises as a result of having a transactional "whole," is itself predicated on inquiry and the ability to order and control qualities such that continuity can emerge. This satisfaction is an end that in turn becomes a means to the further development of meanings, which prefigured, in turn, augment the qualities of an experience yet to be had. There is no base desire beyond the traits one seeks that counts as satisfying in the having of *that* experience, and since this having is thoroughly context laden, there can be no prior judgment as to what counts as the traits had for *that* person in *that* experience. These traits arise with, and not before, the experience had. In fine, there can be no existential separation of elements: satisfying experiences are had as a whole, and continuity is a quality, not a precondition, of this whole. This includes the trait of continuity, the trait that Alexander lauds. For continuity connotes the having of an immediate and unified whole. But this is predicated on the prior work that inquiries have done to relate and build meanings that in turn make the having of this whole possible. Continuity emerges (in part) as the product of prior meanings built up through inquiry.

Thus far, inquiry has been discussed in relation to growth. But little has been said about the conditions in and under which inquiry can be facilitated, developed, fostered, to lead to the happy occasion of growth. The task of facilitating inquiry, and growth thereby, falls to education. Education is the formal means for the development of the habits and attitudes of inquiry such that growth can occur. Now Dewey defines growth in *Democracy and Education* as "the cumulative movement of action toward a later result" (Dewey [1916] 1980, 41). This very broad definition implies the capacity of the biological and social organism to respond to its environment, to adapt or adjust to the environment, and to use the settled results of these adjustments for present and future reorganization and reconstruction. Dewey is of course writing in the context of childhood and schooling. Growth is here wedded closely to the biological development of the human organism, the psychological (habitual) development of the human organism, as well as the social development: a point and purpose of education is to foster the growth of all these sides of the human being. But Dewey allows for "modes" of growth, modes that are "appropriate to different conditions" (Dewey [1916] 1980, 50). Growth itself differs as a result of the physical and social maturity of the individual growing, as well as the problems and situations that the individual faces.

Growth has its telos in further growth. "Since in reality there is nothing to which education is relative save more growth, there is nothing to which education is subordinate save more education" (Dewey [1916] 1980, 51).[26] This famous tag is equally a caveat to inquiry. For inquiry is in the service of growth. Inquiry exists as the means with which to order and control experiences such that valuable habits are produced that will enable further, satisfying experiences to emerge. Inquiry, to promote future growth, cannot allow itself to become rigid and dogmatic. The means for flexibility arises out of the context-bound and self-correcting nature of inquiry, as was demonstrated in chapter 2. Dewey of course, often calls this experimentalist inquiry, "scientific." And scientific inquiry is not only to have a profound role in the ordering and control of the educational environment, but is the chief habit that education seeks to develop. As Dewey puts it:

> It is its [education's] business to cultivate deep-seated and effective habits of discriminating tested beliefs from mere assertions, guesses, and opinions; to develop a lively, sincere, and open-minded preference for conclusions that are properly grounded, and to ingrain into the individual's working habits methods of inquiry and reasoning appropriate to the various problems that present themselves. (Dewey [1910–1911] 1978, 28)

Inquiry organizes traits of experience through attentive observation, control, and ordering. The settled results of these orderings are facts. Facts become the basis for (further) evidence. Facts are now isolated, now resituated, now reconstructed through inquiry. Inquiry is equally reconstructed through the enlargement of the heightened status of generic traits, more satisfying interrelations of facts, and more refined habits of doing and undergoing. It is inquiry that is educated, and to educate inquiry is to construct new meanings. To construct meaningful facts about the world is to expand the fund of meanings that one has. To expand the fund of meanings one has is to enrich present and future experiences. Inquiry is the primary means by which growth is occasioned, and inquiry is a habit that is (and must be) developed, brought to bear on environmental and social, situations. To develop this habit is precisely what is meant by education.

A further criticism has been that growth is too vague a notion to adequately describe change for the better. Thus far, this criticism stands fast. This is obviated only when it is made clear just what can increase the satisfaction of an experience had. Here I shall argue that what leads to the having of increasingly satisfying experiences is the very capacity to have, as best as possible, another's experience as my own, and, ceteris paribus, my own as another's. Thus, we can only augment our experiential qualities in "conjoint association," as Dewey puts it, and this means we must live, work and interact together in communities to realize this potential. Formal education—that is, schooling—not only should facilitate the development of the habits of inquiry but also provide the conditions of this facilitation through the bringing together of children having varied experiences, with the goal of having these experiences shared. It is this sharing of experiences that augments the satisfaction of experiences had and occasions growth. This claim informs the focus of chapter 4.

IV
INQUIRY, GROWTH, AND COMMUNITY

Thus far, I have attempted a reading of Dewey's inquiry as self-correcting and his notion of experience and the inquiry therein as tied intimately to growth. Here, I look at Dewey's notion of community. I look at issues surrounding Dewey's notion of community in detail, and suggest (again) that inquiry needs to be reread, and further, that through linking community closely to Dewey's aim of growth, a more workable defense of the criticisms extant emerges. As education is for Dewey predominantly a social affair, and as education occurs in (social) institutions, it is apropos to discuss the linkage of inquiry to education in this chapter. I shall therefore look at the one practical, pedagogical experiment that Dewey was engaged in during his lifetime: that of the Laboratory School at the University of Chicago. I shall examine the relationship between inquiry, growth, and community, as told by Dewey and his biographers. The prevailing concern in doing this is to see whether the theory and practices arising out of the Laboratory School are of a piece with the rereading of Dewey's theory of inquiry that I am suggesting. I shall discuss the relationship between inquiry and democracy, as well as the democratic practices of the school, more fully in chapter 5.

Part One:
A Short History of the Debate on Community

Notwithstanding the criticisms of Dewey's logic and metaphysics, there is no single facet of Dewey's broad scholarship that has come under such indictment as his notions of community and democracy. This is particularly true in the case of educators; as education (for Dewey) is primarily a social endeavor, it is reasonable to expect the bulk of the criticism to be directed here. The perennial concerns of the critics—that Dewey somehow argued for an expert society; that his notion of community was not robust enough to dismantle existing institutions; that Dewey was wedded to corporatist, capitalist, and bureaucratic interests—for many, continue to dog the thinker. Central to these concerns is the role that science and inquiry play in solving human problems. Often, when criticisms of Dewey's notion of community and democracy are proffered, they manifest as criticisms of the role and scope of science in constructing the sort of society that Dewey envisions. Here I shall look at two older critics of Dewey: Bertrand Russell and Klarence Carier, formerly a historian of education at the University of Illinois.

In claiming that Dewey's conception of moral judgment hinges on one's achieving one's desired ends, Bertrand Russell, in a statement previously cited, claims:

> The pragmatist may say, in reply, that the success which is a test of truth is social, not individual: a belief is "true" when the success of the human race is helped by the existence of the belief. This, however, is hopelessly vague. What is "the success of the human race"? It is a concept for the politician, not for the logician. (Russell [1939] 1989, 153)

Russell, after stating his reservations regarding Dewey's inquiry, comes to the conclusion that "the pragmatist's position, if I am not mistaken, is a product of a limited skepticism supplemented by a surprising dogmatism. . . . In spite of his skepticism, he is confident that he can know whether the consequences of entertaining a belief are as such to satisfy desire (Russell [1939] 1989, 154). What leads Russell to condemn the method of pragmatism so vigorously is not simply its lack of a role for contemplative thought, or not taking precepts seriously enough. Russell is fearful that the method of pragmatists will, under the influence of practical needs and desires, become little more than an instrument for personal and social satisfaction. This becomes most obvious in his accounting of Dewey in the famous *History of Western Philosophy*. After invoking many of the arguments earlier published in essays and reviews on Dewey's theory of inquiry, Russell sums up his major concern with pragmatism.

> It has seemed to me that the belief in human power, and the unwillingness to admit "stubborn facts," were connected with the hopefulness engendered by machine production and the scientific manipulation of our physical environment. . . . It seemed to me that I was saying the same thing when I wrote "Dr Dewey has an outlook which, where it is distinctive, is in harmony with the age of industrialism and collective enterprise." (Russell [1944] 1979, 780)

After claiming that Dewey's outlook is amenable to, if not of a piece with, the industrial temper, Russell concludes (ironically enough, given his stature as the preeminent public intellectual of his day) that philosophers ought not to be in the business of society making. No doubt Russell, who witnessed with terrible sadness the birth of the Soviet Republic under Lenin, is frightened of the philosopher's utopia coming true in the Western world. Russell, ever mindful of Dewey's supposed making the satisfaction of desires the aim of inquiry, makes his strongest condemnation of pragmatism yet.

In all this I feel a grave danger, the danger of what might be called cosmic impiety. The concept of "truth" as something dependent upon facts largely outside human control has been one of the ways in which philosophy hitherto has inculcated the necessary element of humility. When this check upon pride is removed, a further step is taken on the road towards a certain kind of madness—the intoxication of power which invaded philosophy with Fichte, and to which modern men, whether philosophers or not, are prone. I am persuaded that this intoxication is the greatest danger of our time, and that any philosophy which, however unintentionally, contributes to it is increasing the danger of vast social disorder. (Russell [1944] 1979, 782)

By far the scholar most critical of pragmatist and progressivist impulses in education has been Clarence Karier. Clarence Karier was until recently a historian of education at the University of Illinois. Despite the label of historian, Karier sees himself as no meer chronicler of historical facts. Central to Karier's concerns is the importance of history being a public enterprise to ward off the infection of ideology. "In the final analysis, historical knowledge must be public knowledge, open to critical review and subject to acceptance or rejection on the basis of various criteria" (Karier 1968, XI). Karier's aim is a practical one: to challenge the assumptions of late American liberalism and corporatism (which he sees as synonymous) and the role of education therein. Thus, he spends a great deal of energy expounding the role and scope of liberal educational policies and their tragic consequences for democracy. Karier locates many of the failures to that time period when American society turned toward science and the belief in social efficiency for liberation of its ills. This was the progressive era.

In the progressive era, Karier argues, enlightenment optimism reigned supreme. "America had always been an optimistic nation. That optimism was expressed in terms of the Enlightenment and was sustained in the nineteenth century by the wealth of the frontier and the opportunities it afforded" (Karier 1986, 290). This optimism was heavily wedded to the belief in science as the solution to social problems. This led to the construction of the great edifice of monopoly capitalism, with all of its attendant regulative and bureaucratic minutiae. And this was fed, in part, by education. "The educational frontier, itself, was realized as a consequence of a growing monopoly capitalism, which provided the surplus wealth necessary to sustain and develop the system" (Karier 1986, 290). Dewey, as the supposed mainspring of progressivist ideas, is handled in a balanced and thoughtful manner in Karier's first work *Man, Society, and Education*. Karier, at once realizing the challenges of Deweyan pedagogy in an era of monopoly capitalism, nevertheless heaps praise upon him.

Although Dewey's name is often associated with the Progressive Education Association founded by Dewey and other Teachers College graduates and faculty to spread the influence of progressivist methods and especially the child-centered wing of the movement—a wing which advocated an extremely permissive approach to education—throughout his lifetime Dewey remained a severe critic of its excesses. Repeatedly he warned against a hit-or-miss impressionistic curriculum and suggested that unless progressive educators evolved an intellectually coherent curriculum, they would fail. In general, and failing to heed his warning, progressive educators like William Heard Kilpatrick and others used Dewey's criticism of the traditional school as a basis for advocating their own child-centered views. At least this was Karier's view in 1968. (Karier 1968, 147).[1]

By the time of his next important work *The Roots of Crisis*, Karier had taken a new tack.[2] No longer is Dewey the lone member of the progressive era who fought in earnest for the reigning-in of the excesses of child-centered pedagogy. Dewey is now considered the leader of the very movement that brings American thought into the fold of monopoly capitalism and the regulated state. Karier condemns Dewey for his public role in supporting World War I and supporting government intervention in the affairs of the Polish community, detailed in a report to the Military Intelligence Branch of the federal government, 1917–1918, entitled "Confidential Report on the Condition of the Poles in the United States." This report was sponsored by Albert Barnes and was ostensibly to look at impediments to democratic living on the part of immigrant groups. The Polish community in Philadelphia was chosen. Dewey and a number of graduate students from Columbia descended on the Polish community and began to interview sources and collect data. Dewey had been assured by Barnes that the study was to be scholarly: Barnes misled Dewey. He had not told him that the study was being done for military intelligence to discover the extent of Polish unrest and pro-German sympathy on the issue of the war. It was too late for Dewey to back out when the news arrived, and he completed two preliminary and one final report. Speaking of the war, Karier argues: "In the closing days of the war, Dewey pointed with pride to the intelligent mobilization and management of the nation in crisis. He then looked to the future with hope that the same intelligence might be applied in developing a new social science that would help shape the new order in the future along similar lines" (Karier 1973, 91). And of the Polish affair, Karier comments: "Dewey was committed to the economic growth and progress of that [corporate] society, even though such progress might require manipulating Polish workers . . . Dewey viewed ethnic and religious differences as a threat to the survival of society, to be overcome through assimilation" (Karier 1973, 93). Further, Karier, together with David Hogan, charges Dewey with abandoning procedural democracy in his handling, as president of the New York City branch of the American Federation of Teachers, of a teacher's union grievance in 1930. Of this, they claim, "The emphasis on prior commitment to organic unity, along with a de-emphasis on the political procedures of democracy, reflected Dewey's own fear of conflict and quest for unity" (Hogan and Karier [1972] 1992, in Tiles, 399).[3]

Dewey's scientific method comes under especial condemnation. Karier sees Dewey's talk of scientific inquiry as beholden to the larger capitalistic forces at play in the regulated state. "To Dewey, as to many who followed him, science and technology was the new theology. All humanity was tied to a quest for 'The Great Community,' where men would ultimately learn, as Dewey put it, to 'use their scientific knowledge to control their social relations'" (Karier 1973, 89). This urge to control social relations, Karier argues, betrays a non-democratic task. "Rejecting confrontation politics, Dewey turned to science and what he termed a method of intelligence. His ideal was the new scientific socialism, not democratic socialism. . . . The new theology, for Dewey, had become science and technology, which in a way, had become a creator of new values and ends" (Karier 1973, 101). But these ends, according to Karier, were not human ones. Rather, they were corporate and bureaucratic ones. This led Karier to conclude that inquiry becomes little more than a tool for indoctrination of the masses into a corporate mindset. Inquiry was said by Karier to be set up as something beyond the society of which it was a part and to which it was beholden. This charge is synonymous with the charge of transcendentalism. In one of Karier's more fanciful moments, he said, "Plato had his logic, Dewey his scientific method" (Karier 1973, 99).

The establishment of scientific inquiry was tantamount to the establishment of a technique that was ready-made for subsequent use by the regulated state.

Means had become ends and the perfection of technique, not the perfection of man, had become the standard. As their lives increasingly became objectified, depersonalized, and systematized, and as the technological system was used more and more not only to create means, but also ends, independent of human will, Americans reached a critical state in the idea of enlightened progress. (Karier 1973, 29)

All of Dewey's talk of inquiry is said to be of a piece with a means-consequence instrumentalism that takes for its ends not social problems but the survival value of the American nation. Such an end, Karier concludes, is parasitic on large segments of society. In the final estimation, Karier concludes of pragmatism that "when stripped of its restraining humanitarian ethic and reduced to cold, hard operationalism, [it] came dangerously close to a Facist perspective on thought and action" (Karier 1973, 83).

In summary, these two past critics of Dewey's notion of community argue two points:

1) Dewey's notion of inquiry in conjunction with the community implies a scientization of the aims and means of social institutions and can and does lead to social control, industrialism, and bureaucracy (Russell, Karier).

2) Dewey's talk of inquiry in community is a cloak for powerful, entrenched interests beholden to capitalism (Karier).

Part Two:
The Present-Day Debate on Community

Sadly, there is little early interpretive support for Dewey's notion of community extant, beyond the characteristic defense of his claims regarding the public as found, for example in the Schillp volume on Dewey. Many if not most supporters of Dewey seemed more interested in defending his logical and experiential works than his works on the public, although several books on Dewey and education are extant. Book-length apologies for Dewey's talk of the public and community are a recent phenomenon, though they are now beginning to proliferate. So I shall have to turn to some of these later claims for Dewey's theory of inquiry as it plays out in the broader community. But before I do this, I shall have some words to say about Dewey's present-day critics.

It is in the spirit of Russell's "cosmic impiety" that John Patrick Diggins writes perhaps the most vociferous polemics on pragmatism in general, and Dewey (and James) in particular, of this past two decades.[4] The work in question is *The Promise of Pragmatism*. Diggins is most suspicious in Dewey's supposed denigration of authority.[5] This, for Diggins, is manifest in Dewey's seeming disdain for "historical knowledge." As Diggins, mustering his full rhetorical force puts it:

Dewey derived from James and Peirce flashes of insight into epistemology, ontology, and metaphysics, and from these brilliant fragments he constructed a whole philosophical universe, a systematic, unified theory of man and society in which there would be no essential need for historical knowledge and belief. In the writings of Dewey authority found its

most profound and consistent antagonist and modernism its most vigor-
ous and thoughtful champion. (Diggins 1994, 206)

Diggins condemns what he sees as Dewey's failure to integrate "historical
knowledge" into his anthropology. The problem for Diggins is that of Santayana's: without due attention to both the successes and failures of past politics, one is left unable to militate against dilemmas in the present. And for Diggins, there are glaring contradictions in modern-day politics that he thinks can
only be addressed in a nonnaturalistic fashion. One might say that for Diggins,
one has to get outside of Dewey's unified theory to see these contradictions.

   Diggins looks to the historical past for assistance with present-day social
problems. To the extent that Dewey bases his social hope in practical activity
rather than historical suppositions, Dewey is said to repudiate the role of certain authority in the lives of the people.

> Dewey had his work cut out for him. Where classical writers looked to
> transcendent ideas or the historical past for true knowledge, Dewey
> looked to probable hypotheses and present problems as the place where
> useful knowledge asserts itself. . . . Dewey's pragmatic naturalism, locat-
> ing the origins and validity of ideas in human experience, arrived at a
> conclusion that turned upside down the assumptions of classical thought:
> authority, like truth, is neither given by nor revealed to the theoretical
> intellect, but instead is produced by human activity. (Diggins 1994, 221)

Diggins does not dispute that Dewey does have a means of legitimating authority. His concern is not that Dewey is lacking a theory of authority. It is
rather that his means of legitimacy is not found in a turn to the historical past
but the "reflective enterprise that enables man to take his bearings in a chaotic
world" (Diggins 1994, 226).

   The turn to the "reflective enterprise" is what concerns Diggins the most.
And this concern is most telling at the confluence of authority and inquiry.
Diggins sets up his argument against Dewey's theory of inquiry by first telling
the reader what traditional authority has hitherto provided. "Traditionally authority implied, among other things, the capacity to give credence to a judgment, make pronouncements on moral and political issues, and declare the
lawfulness, rightfulness, or truthfulness of propositions and assertions" (Diggins
1994, 234). Yet Dewey's theory of inquiry supposedly cannot rely on any of
these. For Dewey's inquiry "must suspend judgment until the process of verification takes place. . . . While Dewey's theory of knowledge offers 'plans of action' relating to the future, knowledge is really acquired in the past, after the
event, when experience renders its judgment" (Diggins 1994, 234). And so,
where an earlier authority could pronounce upon moral, social, and political

matters, Dewey's notion of authority cannot. And it cannot precisely because its very methodology is faulty. "If pragmatic knowledge must always be from hindsight, of what value is it in guiding our thoughts prior to acting?" (Diggins 1994, 234). Diggins responds to his own rhetoric by answering, characteristically, "very little."

All of this leads Diggins to conclude that Dewey was too fond of the notion that science can somehow ameliorate long entrenched political problems. As he puts it in the essay "Pragmatism and Its Limits":

> The idea that democracy can be likened to a science in that both enterprises allegedly involve inquiry is a belief so accepted that the time has come to question it. . . . Dewey assumes that democracy and science are so compatible that they can only reinforce one another. . . . To equate democracy with science meant that politics could only issue in specialization, routinization, and bureaucratization. Science cannot address issues of justice, meaning, and value, and politics cannot escape the world of power. (Diggins 1998, 208)[6]

The problem is one of blindness to the institutional aspect of democracy: science cannot help us to see that the furtherance of democracy through face-to-face interaction, as Dewey thinks of it, necessitates an increasingly bureaucratic counterpart. Diggins claims that "nowhere in his writings did he seem to understand that more democracy means more politics, and with more political participation the American people end up with more institutions and agencies, more structures and systems, even, and especially those that have become alienated from the very people who consented to their creation" (Diggins 1998, 209).

Aaron Schutz has an interesting variant of this argument. Schutz agrees that scientizing politics leads to increasingly bureaucratic structures. But he goes further than Diggins in his criticism of Dewey's supposed naiveté regarding the issue of power. For Schutz not only locates Dewey's failure to deal with institutional power in regards to the supposed scientization of democracy, he also criticizes Dewey's notion of face-to-face communities as failing to address the "how" of dismantling systems, discourses, and institutions entrenched through power. Schutz thinks Dewey fails at multiple levels: at the level of inquiry certainly, but also at the level of his conception of the public. Schutz states: "To the extent to which Dewey's practice of democratic dialogue . . . is one that middle-class students are more equipped to engage in—partly because of its emphasis on enhancing the distinctiveness of participants in collective action—this hierarchy may end up leaving these students in ultimate control of communal actions. . . . While people can learn myriad 'secondary discourses,' students whose primary discourses are most similar to that taught in schools will have less trouble achieving fluency, and will experience fewer conflicts between the new discourse and their primary discourse. . . . And even if schools could, somehow, teach students to overcome their primary discourses, such an effort seems more that problematic. To the extent to which the kinds of practices Dewey recommended are inseparably intertwined with the cultures of particular dominant groups in our society, such an approach threatens to return us to the ideas of cultural 'deficiency' that many have struggled so long in education to overcome" (Schutz 2001, 292).

It will do to once again summarize these criticisms. First, because inquiry is either too scientistic or not scientistic enough, it can result in bureaucracy, rationalization, industrialism, and/or totalitarianism (Russell, Diggins, Karier). Second, inquiry either supports the further marginalization of the public, or is impotent to suppress it (Diggins, Karier). Finally, a community of inquirers cannot form in a robust enough manner to obviate these tendencies (Diggins, Karier, Schutz). I shall take each of these claims up one at a time. But for now, I wish to turn to those sympathetic to Dewey and to Dewey's notion of community in particular. As I shall show, even Dewey's sympathizers have concerns about the capacity of Dewey's notion of community to do what he intends.

Unfortunately, neither the early nor present-day scientific readers of Dewey (Nagel, Phillips, McCarthy) address the issue of increasingly bureaucratic and rational control under the aegis of scientific inquiry, though Leonard Waks does claim that only through scientizing democracy, can the problems of men be solved. But the potential (and actual?) abuses of scientific inquiry are simply not mentioned. The non "inquiry as scientific" readers of Dewey, surprisingly, fare little better. It will do to take a closer look at these readers and see what they are able to make of Dewey's talk of community.

Jim Garrison does conclude that a strongly scientistic reading of Dewey could occasion these fears, but placates the reader with the declaration that this is not how Dewey thought of inquiry. The problem with this claim is that if inquiry is beholden to immediate experience, as Garrison suggests, then how is inquiry to account for the needs of the public in the face of its reduction to a satisfying experience? Presumably, Garrison would say (rightly) that the goal becomes an attempt at a sharing of as many experiences as possible so that what counts as a satisfying experience for one counts as well for many. And this is correct, as far as it goes, but this theme is underdeveloped. What is developed is rather the distinction between authoritative models of the state, of community, and democracy, and Dewey's differing claims from these. Speaking of Dewey's nondualistic, nontranscendental aim of philosophy, Garrison claims: "A substantial difference is that Dewey thought Plato's separation of the theoretical and the practical is a dangerous dualism. . . . He also explicitly denounced the Platonic distinction between abstract theory and concrete, everyday practice" (Garrison 1997, 13). And further:

In Dewey's view the philosophy-versus-practice distinction serves the purposes of king of various kinds (including some bureaucratic and technocratic experts and theoretical authorities) who assume some higher realm of reality and knowledge beyond reflection on ordinary practice. Dewey thought that Plato's metaphysics and epistemology emerged of out oppressive social practices. (Garrison 1997, 20)

Garrison spends a great deal of time discussing Dewey's transactional realism and how this improves upon the older, Platonic dualisms of mind and nature, and cites Dewey's talk of experience and of traits, qualities, and wholes as primordial. To cultivate just these traits in their immediacy is the point of education. And Garrison chooses the teacher as the prophet who would facilitate this enterprise. Garrison, however, does not provide a bridge to get from the claim that education ultimately deals in the augmentation of satisfying experiences, to the need for, and role of, the greater public. If the abundance of generic traits is the task of education, then it becomes unclear, beyond the provision of a teacher, as to why one needs a public at all. Education (as with experience) seems to be, on this reading, a solipsistic endeavor.

The difficulty in defending Dewey's notion of community and the place of inquiry therein has vexed otherwise sympathetic commentators. Little more than soothing rhetoric, that Dewey did not mean for inquiry to be the means for increasingly rationalized, corporatist, and bureaucratic control, is often offered up in response. Dewey's biographer Robert Westbrook says of the role of science in society that

Dewey's call for scientific intelligence was not a call for the rule of intelligent scientists but for the egalitarian distribution of the capacity for scientific thinking and its incorporation into democratic decision making in the polity, workplace, and elsewhere. He continued to be wary of centralized state power and though he firmly believed that experts performed indispensable functions in complex societies, he explicitly consigned them to an advisory role and advocated the subordination of expert administration to fully participatory, deliberative, democratic publics. (Westbrook 1991, 187–88)

Another of Dewey's biographers, Alan Ryan, concurs with the sentiment that Dewey's theory of public inquiry was not beholden to private or state interests. Ryan claims that "What Dewey wanted was more nearly what was offered in the next century by . . . guild socialism" (Ryan 1997, 116). And further, "A democratic state was simply one in which absolutely everyone's interests in this enterprise is taken into account on a free and equal basis (Ryan 1997, 218).

John Stuhr finds in Dewey's talk of inquiry little that can address entrenched power. "Dewey's on-target recognition of the general impact of prejudice on inquiry is not followed by a needed first step toward a hermeneutic re-
habilitation of prejudice and the circularity of inquiry. Rather, it is a misstep
in the general direction of the illusion of the possibility of inquiry free from all
prejudice. And it is a missed opportunity for reflection on the power of practices of inquiry, prejudice, and warrant to constitute ourselves" (Stuhr in Burke
et al. 2002, 281).[7]

Michael Eldridge has argued directly against Hogan and Karier's reading
of Dewey's allegiance to bureaucracy in the Teachers Union debacle of 1930.
Of Hogan and Karier's criticism of Dewey, he writes: "Admittedly, Dewey was
as irenic person who promoted commonality. But his behavior in this and other
episodes was not fearful. . . . Dewey and the grievance committee dealt with
the conflict in an open, thorough manner, exposing conflicts rather than sup-
pressing them. . . . He was insistent that unity must come about through conflict rather than avoiding it" (Eldridge 1998, 96). But in a recent paper, Eldridge
has taken back his favorable assessment of Dewey. He claims that Dewey did
not communicate the results of the committee's report to the president in a
timely manner, and in so doing, ensured (unwittingly) that the conflict would
continue. He charges Dewey with a failure of follow through (Eldridge in Burke
et al. 2002, 262–74). For Matthew Festenstein, "Dewey belongs to that strand
of liberalism, or liberal socialism, for whom the 'anarchy of the market' is an
insult to human intelligence" (Festenstein 1995, 76). Further, "He [Dewey]
sees in classical liberalism's conception of authority the 'false and misleading'
opposition of two abstractly conceived, conflicting principles, that of authority and that of individual freedom" (Festenstein 1995, 77). But this is clearly
not enough if these commentators want to defend Dewey from his critics. True
enough, there are many passages in Dewey that do just what Westbrook and
Ryan want them to. But they and other of Dewey's sympathizers gloss over the
question of how Dewey's theory works.

Festenstein does take Dewey to task for ignoring the problem of connecting the ground-up inquiry that Dewey says is required for public control of
social institutions, to these.

Th[e] image of community reconciles the forces which have eclipsed the
public to the democratic ideal, but only by fiat. The tension between
"original democracy" and the complexities of the Great Society provided
the starting point for Lippmann's and Dewey's reflections: Dewey seems
to be arbitrarily writing the problem with which he began [the problem
of the inchoate public] out of the picture.[8] The bathos of these propos-
als [in *The Public and Its Problems*] flows from the difficulty in establishing how the ethical concept of communication is supposed to "harmo-

nize the development of the individual with the maintenance of a social
state in which the activities of each one will contribute to the good of
all" in complex societies. (Festenstein 1995, 95)

Festenstein thus thinks Dewey does not adequately address the "how" of social
change. This concern devolves into a matter of the procedures and practices required for the dismantling of powerful social institutions that inhibit public
need. This is a variant of Russell's "stubborn facts" argument: that people will
simply resist (democratic) change without the presence of self-evident moral authority. And I agree: Festenstein is correct. Dewey does not provide us with an
authoritative blueprint or a set of procedures or plans; though why this is, and
why this criticism should give us pause, I leave until further on in the chapter.

Part Three:
Rereading Inquiry and Community

Recall the criticisms of Dewey. First, because inquiry is either too scientistic or
not scientistic enough, it can result in bureaucracy, rationalization, industrialism, and/or totalitarianism. Second, inquiry either supports the further marginalization of the public, or is impotent to suppress it. Finally, a community of
inquirers cannot (therefore) form in a robust enough manner to obviate these
tendencies. These criticisms are based (in part) on a mistaken notion of Dewey's
theory of inquiry, what it consists of, what its aim is, and what it can achieve,
to help solve the problems of men. Because Dewey's sympathizers give little in
the way of refutations to these criticisms, other than rhetorical gestures and ap-
peasements that Dewey did not think as they claim, they are generally of little
help in obviating the concerns. Once again, I believe that Dewey needs to
reread in such a way that the linkage between inquiry, growth, and community
is tight. I will take these criticisms up in turn. But before I do, I will begin by
turning to several passages of Dewey's that seem, prima facie, inconsistent.

While it would be absurd to believe it desirable or possible for everyone
to become a scientist when science is defined from the side of subject
matter, the future of democracy is allied with the spread of scientific attitude. It is the sole guarantee against wholesale misleading by propaganda. More important still, it is the only assurance of the possibility of
a public opinion intelligent enough to meet present social problems.
(Dewey [1939] 1987, 168)

Until what shall be taught and how it is taught is settled upon the basis
of formation of the scientific attitude, the so-called educational work of

schools is a dangerously hit-or-miss affair as far as democracy is concerned. (Dewey [1939] 1987, 169)

The combined effect of science and technology has released more productive energies in a bare hundred years than stands to the credit of prior
human history in its entirely. Productively it has multiplied nine million
times in the last generation alone. The prophetic vision of Francis Bacon
of subjugation of the energies of nature through change in methods of
inquiry has well-nigh been realized. (Dewey [1935] 1987, 42)

These statements share a similar sentiment: that science, scientific inquiry, and
the resultant technology, is the best means that society has to solve the problems of men. One could conclude that a sunny optimism is here proffered: indeed, Dewey ties the question of democracy and the question of whether society and the schools therein can exist democratically, directly to the possibility
of fostering a scientific attitude in the public. But consider these cautionary
passages:

It is no longer possible to hold the simple faith of the Enlightenment that
assured advance of science will produce free institutions by dispelling
ignorance and superstition—the sources of human servitude and the pil-
lars of oppressive government. (Dewey, [1938–1939] 1987, 156)

For it is commonly said and commonly believed that science is completely neutral and indifferent as to the ends and values which move men
to act: that at most it only provides efficient means for realization of ends
that are and must be due to wants and desires completely independent
of science. It is at this point that the present climate of opinion differs so
widely from that which marked the optimistic faith of the Enlightenment; the faith that human science and freedom would advance hand
in hand to usher in an era of indefinite human perfectibility. (Dewey
[1938–1939] 1987, 160)

A culture which permits science to destroy traditional values but which
distrusts its power to create new ones is a culture which is destroying itself. War is a symptom as well as a cause of the inner division. (Dewey
[1938–1939] 1987, 172)

In these passages, a more cautious voice is evident. Here, there is no guarantee that science will help society achieve its aim of solving social concerns.
These passages were written on the brink of World War II, and Dewey's concern regarding the directing of scientific analysis and discovery for the purpose

of violent conflict are everywhere evident. Indeed, with the exception of one passage, all of these were written within a year of each other, and several from the same work. The futility of simply citing passages out of context, those that support this or that reading of Dewey, seems to me (once again) self-evident. This is particularly cogent considering that the vast majority of Dewey scholars that do remain generally sympathetic to him, question the feasibility of (scientific) inquiry to do the work set out for itself, and turn to this very tension in Dewey as a symptom of this lack. The questions of Dewey's stance on the strong role and scope of science in allaying social concerns and the resultant implications that this has for Dewey's notion of community needs further attention to deal adequately with these concerns.

The First Claim: Scientism and Social Problems

Perhaps the most common criticism of Dewey (and of pragmatists in general) is that he advocates scientistic investigations and solutions to social problems. Prima facie, this does not seem so egregious: experiment, ordering, and classification of problems such that they might better be solved is an eminently reasonable course of action. The skepticism concerns not science and scientific method per se, rather the wholesale application of scientific method to (presumably) nonscientific problems and, further, the supposed detachment of the scientists (the class of "experts") from the needs, wishes, and desires of the public such that science becomes irresponsive to public concerns and public oversight.

I shall not rehearse my objections and responses to the reading of Dewey's theory of inquiry as scientistic. I ask the reader to turn to chapter 2 for more on the objections and the response. Here, I simply note that the vast majority of these objections have their basis in one or another charge. The first is that Dewey is committing a performative self-contradiction in his espousal of democracy by (furtively) advancing antidemocratic methods. The second is that Dewey flatly called for solutions to social problems through the institutionalization and rationalization of inquiry, and the bureaucratization of the expert class. As these charges seem to me to be intertwined, I shall deal fully only with the second charge. The charge that Dewey's theory of inquiry and supposed fetish for problem solving either has led to, or might lead to, the bureaucratic, rational, capitalistic state ruled by the expert class, is a familiar one, judging by the amount of attention given to it by Dewey's critics. I shall discuss Dewey's stance on the public and on expertise in relation to his statements on authority and freedom. I will proceed first to argue that authority for Dewey equates with *organized* intelligence, and I will discuss what this means. Secondly, I will show that organized intelligence is coeval with *public* intelligence.

This completed, I will argue that authority is the composite of organized public intelligence that all are able to participate in.

Dewey puts the challenge of authority to modern society nicely in his essay "Authority and Social Change."

> We need an authority that, unlike the older forms in which it operated, is capable of directing and utilizing change and we need a kind of individual freedom unlike that which the unrestrained economic liberty of individualism has produced and justified; we need, that is, a kind of individual freedom that is general and shared and that has the backing and guidance of socially organized intelligent control. (Dewey [1935–1937] 1987, 131)

When Dewey talks of individualism, he is describing a phenomenon he sees as a holdover from a previous, laissez-faire-style liberalism; one that, as he says in *Liberalism and Social Action*, places negative freedoms ahead of positive ones (Dewey [1935–1937] 1987, 30). Although this liberalism at one time served well the democratic interests, it now fails to provide an adequate answer to the pressing social problems that are encountered as a result of present and new technological possibilities. Such technological changes bring with them consequences that, if democracy is going to survive and peoples prosper, requires a fundamental shift from an individualist conception of authority as a brute imposition on one's freedom.

"Organized intelligence" is Dewey's chosen response to laissez-faire-style liberalism. Science provides the most reliable evidence we have that organized intelligence can solve complex public problems. In the main, what dictates for Dewey the necessity of placing authority in the method of organized intelligence is its record of accomplishment with respect to scientific and technological innovations.

> Within a limited area, the collective intelligence which is exemplified in the growth and application of scientific method has already become authoritative. . . . When we turn to the practical side, we see that the same method is supreme in controlling and guiding our active dealings with material things and physical energies. (Dewey [1935–1937] 1987, 141)

By making organized intelligence, and in particular, its inquiring feature, the locus of authority, Dewey is suggesting first of all, that anything which is to be given value over other determinations is subject to inquiry. Secondly, should inquiry determine that a change in the initial determination is necessary, owing to new consequences, or new factual data being presented, the value placed on that initial determination must also change. With inquiry, the value of any-thing is contingent and cannot be relied upon as a fixed principle from which to operate. Although, as Dewey argues in *Human Nature and Conduct*, one in-herits her morality to a large extent from her social group via speech patterns (Dewey [1922] 1980, 43), yet the authority of this morality is always contin-gent on further inquiry. If inquiry determines that a particular value or ethical good is untenable, then that value or ethical good must be questioned.

Furthermore, organized intelligence is *public* intelligence. The great masses of peoples do not live in isolation from one another. They form groups and share interests. They belong to communities, societies, and cultures: this recognition contrasts with the autonomy constructed by earlier, laissez-faire, individualist model of intelligence. The driving force behind these earlier models was that of an organized intelligence residing solely in the individual experiencer. However, this, as Dewey argues, presents problems. Chief among these lies the faulty epistemology upon which the model relies. The empiricist view that intelligence arose from the reconstruction of atomistic, isolated events was predicated upon an individualist theory of cognition with little to say about how communities, groups, societies, and cultures come to inquire into a particular problem. "The doctrine of laissez faire was applied to intelli-gence as well as to economic action, although the conception of experimental method in science demands control by comprehensive ideas, projected in pos-sibilities to be realized by action" (Dewey [1935–1937] 1987, 33). A concep-tion of intelligence not fastened to an empirical, atomistic psychology was needed if a new liberalism was to emerge. This new intelligence, as with this new liberalism, is to take its bearings not from an individualistic, spectator theory of the world, but rather from a conception of intelligence and cognition that involved the organism fused into an organic whole with its environment. The focus was not exclusively on environment, nor on perceiver, but rather the transformation of the two through mutual interaction.

Environment is recognized as playing a much larger role in cognition. Environments that were once considered of little consequence can now be shown to have a demonstrative effect upon the interacting individual. Certain environments, for Dewey, lead to further and more satisfying experiences. Im-portant for Dewey is face-to-face contact and communication: the basic tasks of the public. The manner in which this environment comes to affect partic-ular individuals is, of course, via the medium of communication. Through the give and take of communicative exchange, of language, peoples can transform themselves.

> Language grew out of unintelligent babblings, instinctive motions called gestures, and the pressure of circumstance. But nevertheless language once called into existence is language and operates as language. It oper-

ates not to perpetuate the forces which produced it but to modify and redirect them. It has such transcendent importance that pains are taken with its use. . . . In short, language when it is produced meets old needs and opens new possibilities. It creates demands which take effect, and the effect is not confined to speech and literature, but extends to the common life in communication. (Dewey [1922] 1980, 57)

Organized intelligence involves the selective habituation of one's responses in and through this transformation. It involves active reflection and inquiry in determining what the best response to a given social environment might be, and what response is, thereby, to be valued. The procedures of organized intelligence, of inquiry, adopted on a social scale, allow diverse peoples to come together in conjoint communication around a particular social consequence of a seemingly private act. These consequences can then be deliberated upon. It is in this way intelligence is transformed into a public activity.

Inquiry of a public sort, as with inquiry of a scientific sort, is to be free of preconceived notions or goals. As Dewey puts it: "An experimental social method would probably manifest itself first of all in surrender of this notion. Every care would be taken to surround the young with the physical and social conditions which best conduce, as far as freed knowledge extends, to release of personal potentialities" (Dewey [1925–1927] 1984, 360). Further, and most important for my argument, public inquiry is to eschew the tendency to model itself after the physical sciences. "The assimilation of human science [public inquiry] to physical science represents, in other words, only another form of absolutistic logic, a kind of physical absolutism" (Dewey [1925–1927] 1984, 359–60). Rather than modeling itself on the physical sciences, public inquiry's logic is said to

> involve the following factors: First, that those concepts, general principles, theories and dialectical developments which are indispensable to any systematic knowledge be shaped and tested as tools of inquiry. Secondly, that policies and proposals for social action be treated as working hypotheses, not as programs to be rightly adhered to and executed. They will be experimental in the sense that they will be entertained subject to constant and well-equipped observation of the consequences they entail when acted upon, and subject to ready and flexible revision in the light of observed consequences. (Dewey [1925–1927] 1984, 361–62)[9]

Inasmuch as there are public problems, problems that affect a number of (conjointly associated) individuals, the public is to be the locus of inquiry. But this begs immediately the question of who, precisely, constitutes the public? It is well known that, by the time of writing *The Public and Its Problems*, Dewey felt the public at the time he wrote was "lost . . . bewildered" (Dewey [1925–1927] 1984, 308) and "eclipsed" (Dewey [1925–1927] 1984, 304). This was due primarily to the abundance of multiple publics, combined with the lack of an effective means of shared inquiry. What was necessary in Dewey's estimation was a reconstruction of the public via the instruments of inquiry. Indeed, the formation of public interest was itself the communication of the results of public inquiry. In Dewey's estimation, all those who have a stake in the (problematic) consequences of an activity of the one or the many have license to participate in this shared inquiry and thereby reap the results. The entire public, inasmuch as certain broad social policies affect the mass of peoples, have the means to share in the process of deliberative inquiry and the consequences thereby.

The public, however, does not have all of the tools necessary to probe in experimental fashion the consequences of particular activities. Inasmuch as certain factual data demands precision in compilation and evaluation, a certain expertise is demanded of some. Now not every individual who constitutes the body public is capable of performing these tasks. Thus, it falls to specialists to carry out these needed activities. Experts are for Dewey necessary constituents in inquiry of a public nature. Their role, however, is a rather limited one. Specifically, experts in a particular discipline or subject matter are not to prescribe, from the results of inquiry, what is to be done. Rather, the expert demonstrates to the inquiring public the factual data upon which further analysis and pronouncements depend. As Dewey puts it in *The Public and Its Problems*, "It is not necessary that the many should have the knowledge and skill to carry on the needed investigations; what is required is that they have the ability to judge of the bearing of the knowledge supplied by others upon common concerns" (Dewey [1925–1927] 1984, 367). The locus for decision making with respect to the factual data presented by experts is the concerned public. Inasmuch as the public must judge the implications of adopting a certain response to shared social problems, the public must as well be able to carry out the task of inquiry. The authority invested in inquiry and its result demands vigilance on the part of the concerned public with respect to the communication of findings and the judgment passed on various possible alternative solutions to problematic situations. This in turns demands that the public be properly educated with respect to the tools and capacities of and for inquiry. Education, that is, formal schooling, is the chief vehicle of supply for this demand. This I will address more fully in the final section of this chapter.

The question of the development of rational-bureaucratic structures that somehow impedes individuals and communities in carrying out their freedoms is addressed by Dewey's insistence that inquiry is not to be seen as a tool solely in the service of the bureaucratic elite (though Dewey does stress the need for experts to have this tool), rather as a shared function of the need to solve the problems of men. On this reading and use of inquiry, inquiry emerges as a ground-up tool, and not a top-down one. Inquiry is the product and the tool of conjointly associated peoples who recognize, in their shared experiences, shared problems that are amenable to shared solutions. Indeed, inasmuch as inquiry is performed in a top-down manner, it becomes insensitive to the needs of the public. Such is to block the road of inquiry, as it blocks the investigation into the real problems of the public. Inquiry beholden to a few experts and applied in a decidedly presumptuous fashion, is not inquiry at all. Rather, it is dogma. The concerns about the undue scientization of inquiry, represented in the guise of top-down prescriptive pronouncements by an expert, bureaucratic class, is, on this reading of Dewey's statements on public inquiry, misguided.

The Second Claim: Inquiry in Community Supports Entrenched Power

The second criticism is that Dewey's talk of inquiry in community supports the notion of entrenched power. Most sympathetic readers of Dewey take pains to dismiss the criticisms that Dewey's theory of (public) inquiry was somehow beholden to state, industrial, or capitalist interests. One can cite passages ad infinitum to dispute this reading of inquiry. A related, but more difficult problem emerges out of the rhetoric of public inquiry. The concern is this: given that Dewey eschewed both positivistic and transcendental, supernatural assumptions in his theory of (public) inquiry, there is little, if nothing, on which to hitch a strong conception of authority.[10] The concern is that Dewey's notion of public inquiry has little control over entrenched power in social institutions. Here the scientistic reading of Dewey is played down. But what emerges in its place is an inquiry toothless in the face of seemingly insurmountable, entrenched power, and the critics' concerns are begged.

This argument is premised on the claim that, because Dewey's notion of public inquiry is a bottom-up one, requiring the public to band together in conjoint association over shared concerns, it is the public that is ultimately responsible for setting and following the norms, principles, and laws that arise out of the settlement of these problems. But the public is often at odds with itself. Further, there exist already many examples of strongly entrenched power structures that must be dismantled before the public can act in a manner sufficient to solve its very problems. For frequently, the problems that the public must solve concern precisely the problems of the entrenched power of social institutions, through the effect that this power has upon the individuals (and groups) that form the public. A bottom-up response cannot possibly succeed, as it will never (assuming the public can band together to recognize and plan for such a response) have the power equal to that of the institutions, to overcome them. What is required is the realization that no account of participatory democracy will obviate entrenched power: in point of fact, it will strengthen it. Underlying the above argument are assumptions common to both readings of Dewey. The first is that nondemocratic, authoritarian means to democratic ends are necessary to absolve us of the problems of entrenched power. The second is that the experimental enterprise that is (public) inquiry is impotent in the fashioning of the ultimate values that are necessary in the creation of democracy, because the principles arrived at are mutable. These two assumptions are interrelated. The response to the first assumption involves a reductio ad absurdum: that the notion of nondemocratic means leading to democratic ends is untenable as a solution to the problem of entrenched power, and thus the only choice is one in which democratic means and democratic ends function together in the solution to this problem. The response to the second assumption is that the fungibility of principles arising out of shared inquiry does not limit the power of those principles to have an effect upon those institutions of power.

The view that democracy can only occur if fixed and universal principles inhere is tantamount to proclaiming that inquiry into shared values is limited to only those that are (already decided upon as) unassailable. Such a stance not only blocks the path of inquiry and, in so doing, renders the likelihood of the success of inquiry unlikely, but occasions something far more sinister. As Dewey puts it in *Freedom and Culture*:

> If there is one conclusion to which human experience unmistakably points it is that democratic ends demand democratic methods for their realization. Authoritarian methods [and I might add, principles] now offer themselves to us in new guises. They come to us claiming to serve the ultimate ends of freedom and equity in a classless society [The Soviet Republic]. Or they recommend adoption of a totalitarian regime in order to fight totalitarianism [Spain, Italy, and Germany]. In whatever form they offer themselves, they owe their seductive power to their claim to serve ideal ends. Our first defense is to realize that democracy can be served only by the slow day by day adoption and contagious diffusion in every phase of our common life of methods that are identical with the ends to be reached and that recourse to monistic, wholesale, absolutist procedures is a betrayal of human freedom no matter in what guise it presents itself. (Dewey [1938–1939] 1988, 187)

Three sorts of arguments are presented in this passage. The first is a variant of a "slippery slope" argument. Dewey claims that democratic ends are prefigured in democratic methods (means). This claim seems to be that the adoption of undemocratic methods will result in a "critical mass" of undemocratic practices that necessitates the converse of democracy. The second is a (more forceful) reductio ad absurdum of the first: that undemocratic methods can only result in undemocratic ends, as they are (one might say at the level of generic propositions) two distinct kinds that cannot be transposed. The third and most telling is that undemocratic methods to democratic ends betrays human freedom. For Dewey, "The problem of freedom and of democratic institutions is tied up with the question of what kind of culture exists; with the necessity of free culture for free political institutions" (Dewey [1938–1939] 1988, 72). Further:

> The problem of freedom of cooperative individualities [communities of individuals] is then a problem to be viewed in the context of culture. . . . We are concerned with the problems of freedom rather than with solutions . . . the fundamental postulate of the discussion is that isolation of any one factor, no matter how strong its working at a given time, is fatal to understanding and to intelligent action. (Dewey [1938–1939] 1988, 79)

Dewey's notion of freedom is fungible. Freedom, like democracy, is a work in progress. Dewey's account of freedom consists in the freedom of intelligence to inquire into the problems of cooperative individualities by antecedent and fixed methods and principles. Inasmuch as authoritarian methods and principles are said to be in the service of democracy, democracy and freedom is imperiled. And this in turn suggests that only democratic means, as opposed to authoritarian ones, can lead to democratic ends and to freedom thereby.

The question of the fungibility of the principles arising out of public inquiry seems, prima facie, to cripple Dewey's argument that a ground-up inquiry can have an effect on prevailing institutional power and control. It seems natural enough to assume that only robust (because universally held and intuitive) principles can challenge such imposing structures. Indeed, without the strength of these principles, supplied by their very universality and obviousness, the concept of institutions as having an unequal share or control of power would not present itself. This is Diggins's claim in a nutshell. A two-pronged response can be given in reply to this.

The first is that it is the perceived impermeability and universality of principles and methods that results in the entrenchment of power. In the case of the power of social institutions in (then) present-day United States, Dewey claims that it is precisely the lack of inquiry into the present and future of institutions that has heralded the loss of the public's power. As Dewey puts it: "The extreme danger of giving any body of persons power for those whose exercise they are not accountable is a commonplace in democracy. Arbitrary irresponsibility varies in direct relation to the claim for absoluteness on the part of the principle in behalf of which power is exercised" (Dewey [1938–1939] 1988, 128). The solution to this is, characteristically, vigilant public inquiry into the ends of social institutions and the means whereby these ends can be actualized.

What does the construction of shared values in and through public inquiry look like? Dewey supplies us with a model of this in his *Theory of Valuation*. What is specifically targeted for attack in this work is the dualism between ends and means. Dewey is loath to admit a conception of "ends-in-themselves." In fact, he considers ends separated from means "foolish to the point of irrationality." (Dewey [1938–1939] 1988, 214). Likewise, Dewey attacks any separation of "the world of facts" and the "realm of values." (Dewey [1938–1939] 1988, 249). To Dewey these realms are only supposed; they do not exist in the dualistic manner that absolutist moral theories suggest. Indeed, Dewey argues that to force an artificial separation of facts and values is to invite arbitrariness and capriciousness into public inquiry. It sets up a specific valuation as fixed and ahistorical: an absolute to be obeyed. Such, Dewey argues, is the very condition that results in the entrenchment of power, ab initio. It perpetuates the power and authority of one group or class who, through domination via moral imperatives, seek to inhibit certain values of others. (Dewey [1938–1939] 1988, 244). Valuations that are not tested in and through public practice serve as fixed and canonical instruments of domination.

Similarly, Dewey's notion of the public rejects Hobbesian and utilitarian theories that hypostatize desire and make this the end to which one must accede (Dewey [1938–1939] 1988, 206). Consequences, including desires and satisfactions had, while important, are for Dewey instrumental to further action. They exist as means for future conduct. Dewey would say that the public does not commit to the consequentialization of its actions in armchair fashion and then reflect upon the effect that this consequentialization has for the particular act to be performed. Rather, the public views the consequences that have already happened in a particular situation and it forms a plan of action to ameliorate the difficulties that the consequences portend. In this way, consequences become what Dewey calls "ends-in-view;" they exist for the purpose of fashioning from them more and better methods of problem solving and not as "ends-in-themselves" to direct all subsequent behavior. There is a circularity evident here: ends-in-view become means to further ends-in-view: the satisfaction derived from the attainment of an end-in-view is but a prelude, a means, to a further end-in-view and further satisfaction.

As vehement about rejecting the absolutism of ends-in-themselves as Dewey is, he is also equally insistent on bringing together the seemingly disparate terminology that characterizes much discussion of moral theory. Desire, interest, enjoyment are to be unified into an organic whole with these terms representing not isolated and disconnected feeling-states but rather a circular movement in a process of coming to value an idea as an instrument. Dewey recognizes the behavioral base of the human organism. All individuals exist within a nexus of organic activities that produce "affective motor" responses (Dewey [1938–1939] 1988, 200). "Value expressions, then, have to do with the behavioral relations of persons to one another" (Dewey [1938–1939] 1988f, 200). These expressions can be tracked. One way to track them is to observe the particular wants that arise out of an experience. These Dewey aptly labels "desires." Dewey further connects these up with interests. Interests refer to the *transaction* between the desiring individual and her environment. Desires and interests, acted upon, have effects or consequences, which can be measured. The valuation of objects is intimately connected with desire and interest. Valuation of objects through the consequences they produce is a valuation, in turn, of desire and interests. One values as means, ones desire and interests to value, in turn, the object under consideration. Any consequence, while serving as an end for that particular valuation, is but a means to another, further consequence. Desired consequences do not exist as ends-in-themselves. Rather, they are ends-in-view. They alternately serve as both ends and means. Again, the particular end reached is not a final end, but an end that is a means to some other investigation that results in a modified, or novel, valuation.

The process by which valuations result in further modification or change is inquiry. Valuation cannot be said to exist apart from it. How does this work? On the one side, habits and impulses are challenged by examination. Instrumental habits are kept while needless ones are discarded. Impulses are streamed into appropriate desires and interests. The resultant desires and interests are then brought into concert with reflection. Reflection connects desires and interests to the consequence of utilizing an object or instrument for a purpose. In this way, an organic, circular, unity of instrument, consequence, desire, interest, and reflection is created. The value produced via reflection is final. As Dewey puts it:

> A value is final in the sense that it represents the conclusion of a process of analytic appraisals of conditions operating in a concrete case, the conditions including impulses and desires on one side and external conditions on the other. Any conclusion reached by inquiry that is taken to warrant the conclusion is "final" for that case. (Dewey [1938–1939] 1988, 231)

The conclusion of an inquiry is a terminal event, but only in and for the particular situation of which it is a part. It is a product of the bringing together of all of the above ingredients into a unity. The fungible consequences of acting on the value serve in turn as the means for future valuation. Far from being weak in comparison to fixed, antecedently held, universal principles, these values demonstrate their effectiveness in operations to a degree that absolute values cannot: they work precisely because they have been constructed out of the very situations that they are, in turn, to be responsive to. The concern with absolute values is that the demands placed upon the problematic situation by these inhibits an operational solution: there is the (strong) possibility that, inasmuch as the bringing to bear of antecedent principles to human problems will necessitate only one solution—a solution realized only in behavior that is dictated by, and must approximate, the prescription of the principle—any other solution is ruled out. What remains is for publics to realize that they alone have the power to change and to shape, (largely, though not exclusively, through the education of future generations) social institutions. But this is precisely because it is these publics' and not Dewey's task to do this. What the plans and procedures are to be requires inquiry into specific issues and problems. Until this occurs, any estimation of blueprints, plans, or procedures would be presumptuous at best and authoritarian at worst. Dewey does not allow for nondemocratic (noninquired) means to democratic ends.

Part Four:
Inquiry as Growth through Community

At the end of the previous section, I outlined how growth and inquiry are to connect up. Now I must make good on this claim. The claim is that it is only through shared experiences had in communities of individuals that growth, as the increase in one's fund of meaningful experiences, can occur. Individuals, bonded together through shared experiences, use inquiry to solve pressing social problems, to reflect imaginatively on heightened qualities of an experience, to improve traits and qualities of future experiences. This bonding both requires and results in what Dewey calls a community. As such, it is community that furthers the having and undergoing of experiences.

Contrary to prevailing criticisms, Dewey's image of a public inquiry can be very robust. Indeed, in Dewey's estimation there is no social problem that can be solved without public use of inquiry. But what has to be in place for the public use of inquiry to occur is the realization that experimental methods can be and are the best means to accomplish a (the) solution to these, together with a faith in the capacity of a civic-mindedness of the sort laid out in *The Public and Its Problems* and *A Common Faith*. This, no doubt, is taken by critics as begging the question of exactly why we should trust experimental methods, where the civic-minded faith is to come from, and how existing social institutions are to be dismantled. To these questions, Dewey has, I claim, a response. And that response is "education." But then the question becomes one of disentangling corporate interest from the schools such that a nonconstrained inquiry can be fostered. The task is to offer a response to this concern.

Not only is an individualist notion of inquiry into problems of the public absurd, it is devastating.[11] The scorn that Dewey heaps on the then-prominent monopoly capitalism and laissez-faire economic theories, particularly to the extent that these overlook the plight of the less fortunate of society, should give the reader pause.[12] To recover the individual from the ideology of laissez-faire individualism requires a manifestly social use of inquiry. As Dewey puts it, "Recovery of individuals capable of stable and effective self-control can be had only as there is first a humbler exercise of will to observe existing social realities and to direct them according to their own potentialities" (Dewey [1929–1930] 1984, 74).

When Dewey discusses "the great community" in *The Public and Its Problems*, he has in mind one that trades on the blurring of terms such as individual, community, and society. For Dewey these terms are famously ambiguous: they emerge as guideposts to direct attention to a function rather than fixed and absolute states of affairs. Speaking of society in *Individualism, Old and New*, Dewey states:

> Society is of course but the relations of individuals to one another in this form and that. And all relations are interactions, not fixed molds. The particular interactions that compose a human society include the give and take of participation, of a sharing that increases, that expands and deepens, the capacity and significance of the interacting factors. (Dewey [1929–1930] 1984, 82)

And speaking of community in *The Public and Its Problems*, Dewey (similarly) notes:

> Thus we are told that the public is the community as a whole, and a-community-as-a-whole is supposed to be a self-evident and self-explanatory phenomenon. But a community as a whole involves not merely a variety of associative ties which hold persons together in diverse ways, but an organization of all elements by an integrated principle. And this is precisely what we are in search of. (Dewey [1925–1927] 1984, 259)

The search for the unifying principle does not end with a metaphysical absolute, as Dewey thought Hegel (by way of example) attempted to provide. Rather, it ends with the shared consciousness of a need for experimental inquiry into the problems that beset the public *and* the individual such that shared and heightened experiences can emerge from the satisfying conditions that follow the application of the results of inquiry. Note that in the second quote above, what is stressed by Dewey are the traits of interaction and rela-

tion. It is the conscious manipulation of these traits through ordering and control that augments the quality of these traits.

The notion of community for Dewey is more than associative ties. It is a
conscious realization that one's problems, concerns, experiences, attitudes, values, and customs are also another's and, further, that problems, concerns, experiences, and the like can be managed more efficiently and fruitfully when a
shared *method* is brought to bear on these. When a community forms, it does
so (in part) as a result of shared problems, interests, and experiences. But a community grows only in proportion to the expansion of the interaction of individuals. And what counts as expansion is participation in the lives of others
such that one's experiences and interests are broadened and deepened as a result.[13] Community can be seen as both the backdrop against which experiences
are made richer and more fulfilling and the result of the fulfilling of (shared)
experiences.

Growth is akin to a natural end for the (human) organism, much as are
movement, reproduction, and satiation. An individual is said to grow when she
undergoes further and further satisfying experiences. What counts as a satisfying experience is none other than the having and augmentation of generic
traits. Prior meanings, built up through prior inquiries, lend themselves to the
richness and quality of these traits. Not only do many, if not most, of our experiences occur in the presence of others, but our experiences are often shared
or informed by others. All of us to some extent have similar doings, sufferings,
and undergoings. The realization that this is the case is the beginning of the
possibility for control and ordering of experiences through the (public) use of
inquiry. As experiences are shared and are amenable to transformation and
heightening through inquiry, experiences can be enriched.

The enrichment of experiences, through the public use of inquiry, leads
to a more robust fund of meanings, which in turn leads to the having of more
heightened qualities of experience. Individuals realize that their experiences
and interests share similar traits with those of others. Individuals, existing in
and experiencing with, a community of others, realize that, through control
and ordering of traits, they can improve the quality of their experiences. Shared
public inquiry into the social conditions resulting in the underdevelopment of
one's qualities of an experience, as well as the circumstances that impel these,
result in more satisfying experiences. Experiences take on heightened qualities
and additional meanings. These meanings are added to the fund of previous
meanings and are brought to bear on present and future experiences such that
these experiences will also have heightened qualities and meanings. Inquiry as
(leading to) growth takes place in the context of a community and, functioning to assist the members of that community to solve problems and heighten
experiences (which amount to the same thing), emerges as the most powerful

tool for sharing, doing, and undergoing that an individual and a community wields.

To grow is equally to participate in a community where one shares one's experiences with others and has experiences of others shared, in turn. The means for this sharing is education. To educate is a social activity: it does not and cannot take place outside of the context of other inquirers and communicators. As Dewey claims, "Not only is social life identical with communication, but all communication (and hence all genuine social life) is educative" (Dewey [1916] 1980, 5). The problem for education to tackle is "to extract the desirable traits of forms of community life which actually exist, and employ them to criticize undesirable features and suggest improvement" (Dewey [1916] 1980, 83). To do so is to use inquiry of a public sort—a sort that Dewey tells us can only be developed in a public setting. The institution that supplies the bulk of formal education is that of the school. Schools are, of course, social institutions. Education, inasmuch as it is the carrying-out of the task of the schools, is a social institution as much as it is an activity. As such, it is vitally important that education receive the tools to complete the task of assisting the pupil to habitualize inquiry. As Dewey states: "There is only one way out of the existing educational confusion and drift. That way is the definite substitution of a social purpose, controlling methods of teaching and discipline and materials of study, for the traditional individualistic aim" (Dewey [1933–1934] 1986, 180).

The Laboratory School: Background

Up to this point, I have discussed Dewey's theory of inquiry in relation to his aims of growth and community *in abstractio*. And though this is an important task and is no doubt necessary, by itself it is not enough. That is to say, in discussing the relationship between Dewey's aims and education, concrete educational practices must be turned to. And no amount of rereading Dewey dispels the notion that his optimism in the capacity of a public to form, or existing institutions to be dismantled for this purpose is overwrought. The best that one can do, I believe, is to suggest that it is education that Dewey has in mind as the chief vehicle for the transformation of the public, and, with the chief task of education being growth, the development of inquiry in this endeavor is central. This can occur only one child, one school, and one community at a time.

It is well known that Dewey's greatest and lasting contribution to educational practice is his leadership of, and study undertaken in, the Laboratory School at the University of Chicago, 1896–1903. Dewey's involvement, both to a greater and lesser extent in the affairs of curriculum and organization, is also well known and well documented. The Laboratory School, then, is an excellent place to turn for representative examples of these relationships.

Though the history of the Laboratory School is well known and does not need repeating at length, it seems appropriate to provide a short summary of its development. When Dewey arrived in Chicago in 1894, he was granted control of both the departments of philosophy and pedagogy.[14] After having been a high-school teacher, and having been involved in student groups and with student issues at the University of Michigan, Dewey seemed prepared for a role in educational theory and practice. Equally, his strong sense of social justice, particularly in response to the Pullman strike, ongoing the summer that Dewey arrived in Chicago, strengthened his resolve that education was not simply an individual, but a social, affair. As Dewey puts it:

> I believe that much of present education fails because it neglects this fundamental principle of the school as a form of community life. It conceives the school as a place where certain information is to be given, where certain lessons are to be learned, or where certain habits are to be formed. . . . As a result they [the schools] do not become a part of the life of the child and so not truly educative. (Dewey [1895–1898] 1972, 88)

Dewey was to maintain this sentiment throughout his writings on education.

Shortly after his arrival at the University of Chicago, Dewey proposed to President William Rainey Harper his plan for a University-based elementary school. Encouraged by the success of Col. Francis Parker's schools in Massachusetts and Chicago, he thought the time ripe for a school that embodied many of the practices of Parker's school, while having a unique and distinct purpose of its own. As Dewey puts it:

> The conception underlying the school is that of a laboratory. It bears the same relation to the work in pedagogy that a laboratory bears to biology, physics, or chemistry. Like any such laboratory, it has two main purposes: (1) to exhibit, test, verify, and criticize theoretical statements and principles; (2) to add to the sum of facts and principles in its special line. . . . As it is not the primary function of a laboratory to devise ways and means that can at once be put to practical use, so it is not the primary purpose of this school to devise methods with reference to their direct application in the graded school system. (Dewey [1895–1898] 1972, 437)

Dewey is quite clear about the intentions of the Laboratory School in this passage: it exists for the purpose of inquiring into the phenomena of educational theory and practice with a view to providing "means" that can be put into further educational practice. It has as its aim that of inquiring into the existing conditions of education as well as developing methods that can be used to improve upon these conditions. It is, in short, the purpose of the Laboratory

School to use and develop inquiry to help solve the problems of learning and teaching.

The school's first class consisted of 12 students. Over the seven years of operation, the classes grew in size, until the school, at its peak, held approximately 125 students. Most of these were from the Hyde Park neighborhood; many of the early students were children of professors at the university. There was a fairly even mix of boys and girls, though no African American students. Toward the end of the school's run, a number of Eastern European students were enrolled. As to the subject matter studied, the school emphasized what has come to be called "learning by doing." Dewey links this with the (combined) aims of self-expression, communication, and social "constitution."

> The problem . . . is the co-ordination of the social and psychological factors. More specifically, this means utilizing the child's impulses towards, and powers of, expression in such a way that he shall realize the social ends to which they may be made serviceable, and thus get the wish and capacity to utilize them in this way. The starting point is always the impulse of self-expression; the educational process is to supply the material and provide . . . the conditions so that the expression shall occur in its normal, social direction, both as to content and form or mode. . . . Consequently the beginning is made with the child's expressive activities in dealing with the fundamental social materials—housing (carpentry), clothing (sewing), food (cooking). These direct modes of expression at once require the derived modes of expression, which bring out more distinctly the factors of social communication—speech, writing, reading, drawing, molding, modeling, etc. (Dewey [1895–1898] 1972, 230)

The older children also participated in activities, though these were more complex and the inquiry into them more formalized than that for the younger children. While cooking and sewing were provided for the younger children (of both sexes), the older children also tried their hands at plant growing, history, and the construction of a clubhouse (Mayhew and Edwards [1937] 1965, 285, 206, 228–34). In all activities, inquiry was stressed; but it was inquiry built up through shared problems in attending to the material of cooking, sewing, constructing, and modeling. It was not inquiry, predetermined and preformulated, brought top-down to bear on material. When formal concepts and principles were required, they were often discussed as concepts and as principles, ex post facto the undergoing of a shared project. Only in a few specific instances, was it necessary to discuss concepts and principles isolated from a particular context.[15]

In 1900, Dewey was able to convince President Harper to hire the former superintendent of Chicago schools, Ella Flagg Young. With Young at the helm, the school flourished, and was able to accommodate students as old as fifteen years of age. Further, on Dewey's request, Harper hired Dewey's wife Alice for the position of principal.[16] For the next year, events at the Laboratory School ran smoothly. Then, in 1902, Harper announced that the Laboratory School and Col. Francis Parker's school would merge. As Parker was dying and his school was in financial trouble, it was thought that combining the school with Dewey's would obviate the problem of having separate, private, experimental elementary schools. Unfortunately, many problems were occasioned with this merger. The staff of the Parker school was justifiably nervous. Wilbur Jackman, who took upon himself the position of spokesman for the Parker faculty, announced in a pamphlet distributed to the Chicago community that the Laboratory School would become part of the Parker school. This angered Dewey, as he had been promised by Harper that the Laboratory School would remain intact. Further, the staff of the Parker school, after spending a year under Alice Dewey's principalship, complained that she mistreated them. Harper arranged a deal with Jackman that would satisfy the staff from the Parker school: Alice Dewey was to be removed from the position of principal at the end of the school year. Neither Alice Dewey nor John Dewey was consulted, however, and the eventual announcement came as a shock and an embarrassment to both. As a result of Harper's dissembling, Dewey resigned from the leadership of the school and from the University of Chicago proper. With Dewey's departure, Dewey's Laboratory School was brought under the auspices of a university committee and the role of the school as a laboratory for pedagogy gave way to a more traditional, teaching-centered one.

The Laboratory School: Inquiry

By the time Dewey left the Laboratory School, he had developed much of the material that he later used in writing *Democracy and Education*. His writings on education were prodigious: between 1894 and 1903, he wrote no less than fifty papers and books on the topic. The development of his ideas paralleled his participation in the Laboratory School: much of the material from which his thinking arose came out of his interaction with the students and teachers therein. It will do to look more closely at some of Dewey's ideas on inquiry as they arose during this period, with a view to whether inquiry can be shown, in the context of education, to be of a self-correcting nature.

In *Interest in Relation to Training of the Will*, a publication in 1899 for the Herbart Society, Dewey discusses inquiry in relation to the stimulation of a child's interest in the material at hand, and the subsequent effort put forth in response to that interest. Of interest, desire, and effort involved in student learning, Dewey notes this in his text:

> Desire and effort in their legitimate meaning are both of them phases of mediated interest. They are correlatives, not opposites. Both effort and

desire exist only when the end is somewhat remote. When energy is put forth purely for its own sake, there is no question of effort and equally no question of desire. Effort and desire both imply a state of tension. . . . We call it effort when we are thinking of the necessity of a decided transformation of the actual state of things in order to make it conform to the ideal—when we are thinking of the process from the side of the idea and interested in the question how to get it realized. We call it desire when we think of the tendency of the existing energies to push themselves forward so as to secure this transformation, or change the idea into a fact—when we think the process from the side of the means at hand. (Dewey [1895–1898] 1972, 128–29)

Note what is being claimed here. Desire and effort are correlative: they are not opposed to each other. They exist as what Dewey calls "phases of mediated interest"; they exist in a "state of tension" when an end is remote. But when an end is in view, when a problem is discovered, and when a plan is made to reach the end-in-view, the tension is dissolved. Effort becomes imaginative; that is, it involves the thinking through of the situation such that a solution can be practically realized. This allows for the "change [of] the idea into a fact." Two of Dewey's later characteristics of inquiry are presaged in this statement. First of all, inquiry involves interest and desire. This roughly accords with the problem-solving temper or attitude characteristic of Dewey's later talk. Secondly, it involves universal conceptions (imagination and thinking) and generic conceptions (the side of the means at hand).

Other factors involved in Dewey's later notion of inquiry are on display at the time of these writings. Dewey, in his 1899 *Lectures on the Philosophy of Education*, notes that

the child responds especially to the way in which he sees other people looking at things, he responds unconsciously to the estimates which other people put on things, and also to the degree of skill, or workmanship, of power, command, control over the subject with which the teacher approaches it. That factor of real skill, ability to control, seems to me one of the most indispensable factors in the moral as well as the intellectual development of the child. (Dewey [1899] 1966, 183)

Dewey also notes that

it is simply because we have worked out of the positive, direct unity of our experience, and have got hold of the method of breaking up our experience and for picking certain parts of it and classifying them together on the basis of their relation to common principles, that . . . the older student, say in the latter part of the secondary, can get the full force of the meaning of distinct studies at all. . . . By reflective intellect they are made distinct for purposes logical and scientific, but until the mind has reached the point where it is logical and scientific, it cannot grasp the force of these distinctions, and to force them on the mind before that period, is to destroy the natural unity of experience without putting anything in the place of it; anything which the child can appreciate. (Dewey [1899] 1966, 192–93)

Here, a number of other characteristics of inquiry are notable. First of all, inquiry is said to be involved in the command or control over the subject to which it is brought to bear. Secondly, it is involved in the breaking up of experience, or analysis. Classifications according to kinds (generic propositions, though not so labeled) are also invoked. Most importantly, inquiry (the reflective intellect) is said to be developed, not fixed: children can be introduced to the methods of logical and scientific analysis, but only when the "mind" has developed to such a state that it can grasp these methods. To do otherwise, to introduce these methods before the child is ready, is to destroy the unity of experience.

Dewey has, by 1899, most of the characteristics of inquiry present in his thinking on the subject. Inquiry has the characteristics of interest and effort (attitude or temper and thinking and reflection), classification (ordering and generic propositions), imagination (universal conceptions), the unity of experience and control over the subject matter at hand. Most of the ingredients required for what would later become a formalized theory of inquiry were already present at this period. And it has been noted in the previous chapter that Dewey at this time describes inquiry as involving the construction of children's habits, and most notably, the habit of intelligence, a sentiment he carries through to the *Logic*. The characteristics necessary for inquiry to be self-correcting are present as well. Dewey does not, as he does in the *Logic*, describe his inquiry as self-correcting, but considering the developing nature of inquiry set out in these early lectures and writings, he would no doubt at least insist that inquiry has the capacity for change, for refinement, and for growth.

But to see the self-correcting nature of inquiry first-hand, it is necessary to turn to an incident in the history of the Laboratory School. For here is found a wonderful example of a self-correcting inquiry in practice. The first two years of operation at the Dewey school occasioned many changes in the curriculum. Most of the substantial changes concerned the addition of older children, and courses and activities for these. But at least one change stands out: the Laboratory School made a conscious shift in its policy of adhering closely to one (preset) principle of operation to the neglect of others.

In 1898, Dewey and the teachers met for an end-of-year revision of the curriculum of the Laboratory School. The problem was evident to all: in attempting to give the children a flavor of the development of social life, they

chose examples too abstract and far away, and student interest was not stimu-
lated. The teachers attempted to introduce students to social living through
historical examples, and they began with ancient Greece. However, the children could not develop interest in Greek life. As Mahew and Edwards put it in
The Dewey School,

> Full interest was lacking. The difficulty seemed to be that all these things
> persisted in remaining objective and far away from the children in spite
> of the fact that they had once had to do with the reality of living. The
> work was too abstract and detailed for this age of development, too for-
> mal and too remote from present personal interest. The dynamic quality
> was lacking, that which made life moving and vital. It did not furnish
> images enough. (Edwards and Mayhew [1936] 1965, 48)[17]

What was occasioned in the end-of-year meeting was an overhaul of the curriculum. Dewey and the teachers poured over the lesson plans of the previous
year and scrutinized them for gaps between the child's interest and the subject
matter provided. It was decided that an overadherence to a specific principle
as outlined in Dewey's Plan of Organization of the University Primary School
was at fault. This principle concerned the need for the child to analyze and dis-
criminate in her experiences. In the case of introducing the children to ancient
Greek social life, the subject matter and the methods of instruction were set
up to do this. But the subject matter was too difficult and "too far away" for the
students, and they had an extremely difficult time maintaining interest. The
principle of the whole, of the unity of the child's interest with the subject matter, was overlooked in the zeal to incorporate analysis into the teaching of the
social life of past cultures. Further, the activity as carried out involved no coordination of movement, nor any building, constructing, or play. While the importance of analysis was certainly maintained in the plan, the need for unity
was even more pressing. As Dewey puts it:

> In connection with this, it is important that real wholes should be con-
> structed if there is to be educative interest. . . . In other words, normal
> interest requires that technique, both intellectual and practical, be mas-
> tered within the process of active expression, or construction of wholes,
> and relative to the recognized necessities of such construction. . . . (No
> such standard of judgment exists when genuine and necessary wholes are
> not produced as the child's own self-expression). (Dewey [1895–1898]
> 1972, 238)

Upon recognizing the problem and in working together toward a (tentative)
solution, a decision was made by all. The curriculum was to be changed. The

outcome was that the winter 1898–1899 curriculum no longer reflected subjects taught *in abstractio,* shorn of activity or of the child's natural inquisitiveness. Rather, subject matters were always to be hooked to some activity involving all of the senses. Touching, making, and doing were stressed in place of sitting and seatwork.

Dewey took the lessons of the first two years to heart. Five years after the meeting, in "The Child and the Curriculum," Dewey notes with some satisfaction the results of the solution:

> What, then, is the problem? It is just to get rid of the prejudicial notion that there is some gap in kind . . . between the child's experience and the various forms of subject matter that make up the course of study. From the side of the child, it is a question of seeing how his experience already contains within itself elements—facts and truths—of just the same sort as those entering into the formulated study; and what is of more importance, of how interests which have operated in developing and organizing the subject-matter to the plane which it now occupies. For the side of the studies, it is a question of interpreting them as outgrowths of forces operating in the child's life, and of discovering the steps that intervene between the child's present experience and their richer maturity. (Dewey [1902–1903] 1976, 278–79)

I claim that this event evidences the self-correcting nature of inquiry in vivo. A set of operating principles (later, generic propositions) about how to carry out the curriculum comes under scrutiny because the intended results are not forthcoming: a problem emerges out of the results of a prior inquiry. This is manifest in that result's inability to carry out the end-in-view (the learning of social life on the part of the children). This leads to investigation of the problem (the meeting) which no doubt invokes imagination, reflection, and abstraction—in short—reflection, on a group-wide scale. New generic propositions are formed and these require closer attention to the unity of student interest and subject matter than hitherto thought. The results of operationalizing these principles demonstrate that they are much more effective than the prior ones.

In this case, the failure of inquiry was not at the level of abstraction, for Dewey had already set out, in his thinking about the aims of the Laboratory School, the necessity of the unity of interest and subject matter. Rather, the failure was at the level of operation. Rigid adherence to the principle of analysis and discrimination occasioned failure on the part of the children to learn. The principle that real wholes are to be constructed in an educational experience was played down. Thus, the unity put forth in reflection was not reproduced in the classroom. The failure was analyzed and the offender—the failure to take into consideration the organic need for unity on the part of the child—was identified. The outcome was a change in the subject matters and heightened attention to the need for the connection of student interest and the subject matter at hand. Upon inquiring into this problem, it was found that inquiry itself, and specifically the task of operationalizing the generic principles in a situation, fell short. Inquiry recognized this and corrected for it. And the interest of the children improved.

The Laboratory School: Inquiry and Growth

The reading of growth as continuity, as a self-generating and self-perpetuating telos that implies the increasing satisfaction of the qualities of an experience through the manipulation, order, and control, of one's environment and one's judgments, is premised on reading Dewey's experiential texts in this manner. But this reading results from attention to Dewey's experiential texts: little has been said about what growth in Dewey's early educational works looks like. I shall spend time looking at some of the statements Dewey makes in these texts and turn to the self-generating, circular relationship of growth to the qualities of an experience and the role of inquiry therein, in detailing an example that Dewey himself draws from to illuminate his own ideas on the subject.

Dewey's early thinking on growth leads him to associate growth with stages or phases in the development of the child's physiologic and educational capacities. In an early article on the subject, he outlines the importance of the notion of growth for the Laboratory School:

> In its practical aspect, this laboratory problem takes the form of the construction of a course of study which harmonizes with the natural history of the growth of the child in capacity and experience. The question is the selection of the kind, variety, and due proportion of subjects, answering most definitely to the dominant needs and powers of a given period of growth, and of those modes of presentation that will cause the selected material to enter vitally into growth. . . . We cannot admit too freely the limits of our knowledge and the depth of our ignorance on these matters. (Dewey [1899–1901] 1973, 277)

Dewey envisions growth as having three stages. The first is the motor stage. Ideas and actions (movement) are inseparable at this stage. The goal of the curriculum at this stage (ages 5–7) is to "provide an outlet for expression . . . [to foster] the connection between knowing and doing, so characteristic of this period of the child's life" (Dewey [1899–1901] 1973, 277). The goal of the second stage (ages 8–12) is to develop and increase the skill of producing objective results. So to Dewey:

When the child recognizes distinct and enduring ends which stand out and demand attention on their own account, the previous vague and fluid unity of life is broken up. The mere play of activity no longer directly satisfies. It must be felt to accomplish something—to lead up to a definite and abiding outcome. Hence the recognition of rules of action—that is, of regular means appropriate to reaching permanent results—and the value of mastering special processes so as to give skill in their use. (Dewey [1899–1901] 1973, 227)

Finally, in the third stage of growth (ages 12–13) the child is able to undertake specialized study in the context of the traditional disciplines of subject matter.

It comes when the child has a sufficient acquaintance of a fairly direct sort with various forms of reality and modes of activity; and when he has sufficiently mastered the tools of thought, inquiry and activity, appropriate to various phases of experience, to be able profitably to specialize upon distinctive studies and arts for technical and intellectual aims. (Dewey [1899–1901] 1973, 232)

Dewey does not discuss growth in relation to the high school student in this paper; but he does in his lectures on *Philosophy of Education*.[18]

In . . . secondary education, there should be differentiation of subject matter in what we may call the various studies of the school, and those should be presented to the child systematically so that he may see each by himself and each in its relation to the others, so that he gets an encyclopaedic survey of the field of human learning and attainments, and on the other side finds out to what he himself is drawn most easily and successfully. (Dewey [1899] 1966, 173)

For Dewey, growth is a developmental process. The education of the child should parallel the physiologic and social growth that the child is undergoing. In the first stage, the curriculum should be such that learning (knowing) is closely tied to action (doing). In the second stage, more room is given to formalizing the side of knowing. This involves a curriculum that provides for the formation of ends of action (ends in view) and a regular means to accomplish this. In the third stage, subject matter can be differentiated, as the child is said to have mastered the tools of inquiry for different phases of experience. Finally, the high school student is to be immersed in the traditional division of subjects such that she can see the relationships between these. At this level, a broad and connected whole is to be constructed from the various "parts" that are the traditional disciplines. What are stressed throughout these passages are the continuous and developmental nature of growth and the importance of the development of inquiry. Growth is occasioned when inquiry is developed to the extent that various means and ends can be mastered. This leads to what Dewey calls "an abiding outcome"—the satisfaction of an inquiry successfully completed. And this connotes further growth. Even in these early writings on growth, the relationship between growth and inquiry is a bounded one.

But experience as discussed in Dewey's later works has not been mentioned, other than in passing. What is the relationship between growth, inquiry and experience in Dewey's writings on the Laboratory School? Dewey does not downplay experience in these early writings: far from it. Experience is accorded preeminent status in respect of the goals of education. In discussing the relationship of growth to experience, Dewey states:

> There are earlier and later stages, but no lower and higher ones. The experience of the child at the age of four and five is just as intrinsically valuable, is just as much life as that which can be got when the person is in the high school or college; it must be looked at from its own intrinsic standpoint. . . . Of course we should not really ignore the later periods, because life is continuous, and we get light by considering what comes after, but when you come down to the treatment of the child, the subject matter and methods that he needs, the criterion should be the best experience and the best control of power which the child can get at that particular period. (Dewey [1899] 1966, 116)

Concerning the teacher's role in fostering these "best" experiences, Dewey says:

> What concerns him, as teacher, is the ways in which that subject may become a part of experience; what there is in the child's present that is usable with reference to it; how such elements are to be used; how his own knowledge of the subject-matter may assist in interpreting the child's needs and doings, in order that his growth may be properly directed. He is concerned, not with the subject-matter as such, but with the subject-matter as a related factor in a total and growing experience. (Dewey [1899] 1966, 201)

In these passages, Dewey makes clear that the subject matter is not merely a means to a vital experiencing through its being incorporated into the child's present. Beyond this, it further assists with the child's havings and doings. Though Dewey does not talk of meanings here, it nevertheless seems that a rudimentary thesis that what is built up in incorporating subject matters into the child's experiences is meanings, and that these meanings will assist with the child's further experiences, is maintained. A pattern is built up, in which experience is had, inquired into (reflected upon, analyzed, synthesized, controlled) with meanings built up, and these pressed into service for further enrichment of a future experience.

Growth as the augmentation of one's experiences was equally in evidence at the Laboratory School. The curriculum was consciously structured in such a way that the child had opportunities to interact with the subject matter so that growth could be occasioned. There are many examples of this and these can be multiplied endlessly: I choose but one. Lillian Cushman, the art director at the Laboratory School, here discusses how she stages her curriculum such that the expression of esthetic experience can be garnered. I quote her at length:

> The drawing and painting activities of the school were based on the assumption that a creative attitude of mind is essential to a complete art experience. . . . Knowledge and technical skill are significant to the individual only when they are intermediate between a felt need and its satisfaction. . . . Our six year olds, whose studies centered about the farm, registered in their art expression the extent to which farm life has become real to them. Under their small hands clay turned into figures of farmers engaged in their most dramatic occupation, into farm animals, and even such otherwise prosaic things as fruits and vegetables. An older group, which had been studying the settlement of the Northwest, chose as subjects for a bas-relief, scenes from the life of Marquette. . . . These subjects and projects would have held very little interest for a school in which subject-matter is factual rather than living reality. No cut and dried list of projects can mean the same thing to all children. . . . A very young child lives so completely in a world of his own creation that he invests his rude scribblings with a meaning, regardless of their outward form. . . . By the time he reaches his sixth year he observes the external world more accurately and realizes a discrepancy between his crude symbols and the reality. If self-expression is to be sustained, instruction, or rather supervision, should begin as early as this. . . . That esthetic appreciation grows as the child grows may be illustrated by the common tendency of young children to pass through a stage of primitive satisfaction in crude color before they are able to enjoy the subtleties of harmoniously related hue. *Appreciation cannot be taught directly, but rather results from a continuous process of reevaluating experience. This is another way of saying that the growing child is constantly modifying his standards and developing esthetic discrimination.* (Cushman, in Edwards and Mayhew [1935] 1965, 360–61, emphasis added)

In this example, growth is intimately tied to the child's experience. The development of esthetic appreciation is premised on the continuous reevaluation of experience, which is in turn premised on felt needs and satisfaction, mediated by knowledge. Here again, though not expressly stated as such, the relationship between growth, experience, and inquiry is indissolubly bound: felt needs lead to investigation of materials (inquiry) which, if a satisfying experience is occasioned, results in new meanings, new skills and techniques, which leads to further satisfying experiences. And this occasioning, this continuous expansion of esthetic appreciation, connotes growth. The experiential side of growth is connected with the physiologic development of the organism in a circular fashion, as well. Further physiologic development leaves the individual with the capacity to better coordinate psychomotor activities, leading to an expansion of the child's capability to investigate her world. This leads to further inquiry into areas of interest, resulting in the build-up of further meanings, leading to increasingly satisfying experiences; the occasioning experiential growth.

The Laboratory School: Inquiry, Growth, and Community

To say a community has formed is to say that there exists a social network wherein one shares one's experiences with others and others share theirs in turn. To say education participates in a community is to say that it, too, is a social activity, one that fosters the development of experiences (growth) and their subsequent spread to others. To say that growth begets community, and community, growth is to say that shared control and ordering of experiences through inquiry leads to a community bound together by needs and the means to satisfy these, and this satisfaction leads in turn to heightened individual growth. I claim that there is a rudimentary relationship between what Dewey calls "growth-as-experience" on the one hand, and community on the other and, further, that inquiry is bound up in this relationship.

Dewey is famous for his pronouncement that the school is the social center of the child's life. Indeed, this is the overarching theme of his most popular book *School and Society*. Dewey puts the importance of society to the school and school to the society this way:

A society is a number of people held together because they are working along common lines, in a common spirit, and with reference to common aims. The common needs and aims demand a growing interchange of thought and growing unity of sympathetic feeling. The radical reason that the present school cannot organize itself as a natural social unit is because just this element of common and productive activity is absent. . . . Upon the ethical side, the tragic weakness of the present school is that it endeavors to prepare future members of the social order in a medium in which the conditions of the social spirit are eminently waiting. (Dewey [1899–1901] 1973, 59)

Three claims are put forth in this short passage. First, a society is a number of people who work together for "common aims" and "in a common spirit." Dewey's notion of society here is a germinal notion of what is later to become his notion of community. Second, a "growing interchange of thought" and "growing unity of sympathetic feeling" are necessary to carry society on. Not only is growth implied at the level of society, but the means to growth—inquiry—is requisite. Finally, Dewey charges the school with failure because it cannot promulgate the sort of relationships among students (staff?) that are necessary for a community to form. Thus, it cannot adequately "prepare future members of the social order." Here is an implicit claim that the school exists as the means for the establishment and growth of the community.[19]

Dewey makes the relationship between community and inquiry, undertaken in response to and on behalf of social problems, even stronger in passages from his essay "The School as Social Centre." As he puts it:

Now our community life has suddenly awakened; and in awakening it has found that governmental institutions and affairs represent only a small part of the important purposes and difficult problems of life, and that even that fraction cannot be dealt with adequately except in the light of a wide range of domestic, economic, and scientific considerations quite excluded from the conception of the state of citizenship. (Dewey [1902–1903] 1976, 82–83)

Dewey goes on in the passage to claim that only if the schools are transformed such that they are able to take into account the new and diverse meaning of citizenship can they in turn be responsive to society's political problems.

We find that our political problems involve race questions, questions of the assimilation of diverse types of language and custom; we find that most serious political questions grow out of underlying industrial and commercial changes and adjustments; we find that most of our present political problems cannot be solved by special measures of legislation or executive activity, but only by the promotion of common sympathies and a common understanding. . . . The content of the term "citizenship" is broadening; it is coming to mean all the relationships of all sorts that are involved in membership in the community. . . . This of itself would tend to develop a sense of something absent in the existing type of education, something defective in the services rendered by the school. Change the image of what constitutes citizenship and you change the image of what is the purpose of the school. (Dewey [1902–1903] 1976, 82–83)

What can be described as an indissoluble bond between growth, community, and inquiry does seem to be present in Dewey's early talk of community. Though in an inchoate form, there is nevertheless an assumption that the sharing of experiences will lead to more and further growth—of others, certainly, but also of the individual. As well, this sharing of experiences is the stuff of which a community is made. And this community, utilizing inquiry in the quest for solutions to shared problems, further augments the individual's experiences as a result of the solution to these problems, and in this way occasions growth.

But was a public involved in the purported community building under way at the Laboratory School? The answer to this question is a qualified yes.[20] The best example of this is the construction of the school Club House by two extant student organizations: the Dewey Club for discussion and debate; and the Camera Club (Mayhew and Edwards [1935] 1965, 228–33). The Club House was an idea arising from the lack of a home for these two clubs. The construction process was wholly managed by the children and these formed committees to handle the related tasks of architecture, sanitation, costs, and interior decoration. Tied into the construction project was a study of architecture, Chicago city sites, drainage systems, the history of the Great Lakes and trading systems, and local physical geography. Most of the construction of the house was completed by the children with minimal outside help.

One of the groups involved became overwhelmed by the magnanimity of the task and asked for help from the entire school. Thus, the other students were invited to be part of a cooperative effort to finish the construction. A community of students with the task of concluding the work of construction was born. Mayhew and Edwards put it this way:

> . . . many groups and ages and performed a distinctly ethical and social service. It ironed out many evidences of unsocial and cliquish spirit which had begun to appear in the club movement. As the children came to realize the possibilities afforded by the cooperation of numbers, this spirit changed from an exclusive to an inclusive one. (Mayhew and Edwards [1935] 1965, 232–33)

The club was finally finished in the latter part of the last year of Dewey's tenure at the school. Sadly, the children in question had little opportunity to use it, as they matriculated to the University High School the following year. Luckily, the students were unaware of this sad fact until shortly before the building was completed.

This example of community building is the strongest of those mentioned by Mayhew and Edwards in *The Dewey School*. A community of inquirers (the two clubs) came together with a problem: the lack of dedicated space to have meetings. A hypothesis was formed to ameliorate the problem and plans were made to build a clubhouse. The work was carried out, with a division of labor helping to ensure efficient use of time and resources. A problem occurred: one of the clubs could not finish their task. More investigation into the problem got underway. A solution to the problem was reached: to widen the community of builders such that the workload could be shared and the task accomplished. The construction proceeded and completion occurred. Unfortunately, in this instance the satisfaction from planning and building was tempered by the matriculation of the students. Thus, the example must be qualified. Though inquiry and community were involved in the process of constructing the clubhouse, growth, the satisfaction of an experience undergone, was tempered by the realization that the fruits of inquiry and labor would not be available. Some growth no doubt can be surmised to have taken place upon the completion of a finished task and the completion of the clubhouse proper. But to the extent that the students matriculated and were unable to enjoy the fruits of their inquiry and labor, the growth occasioned was probably less robust than if the children had had the opportunity to have their meetings in the building.

The Laboratory School: Inquiry, Growth,
Community, and Democracy

Though Dewey discusses the relationship of the schools to democracy in his later educational writings, there is comparatively little discussion of this in reference to the Laboratory School. Much of what is discussed is of course the relationship between the child and society. But democracy, as a formal arrangement of the community premised on the having of shared problems, is not developed at any length in Dewey's writings about the Laboratory School. Nevertheless, Dewey does discuss democracy and education in at least one article written at the time of the school's operation. In "Democracy and Education," Dewey ties the notion of democracy, in good enlightenment fashion, to the removal of the imposition of external authority. As Dewey puts it:

> Modern life means democracy, democracy means freeing intelligence for independent effectiveness—the emancipation of mind as an individual organ to do its own work. We naturally associate democracy, to be sure, with freedom of action, but freedom of action without freed capacity of thought behind it is only chaos. If external authority in action is given up, it must be because internal authority of truth, discovered and known to reason, is substituted. (Dewey [1903–1906] 1977, 229)

What is accomplished in the freeing of mind is the ability of peoples to make intelligent choices which can in turn inform action such that it, too, becomes intelligent. What is developed here is an inchoate notion of democracy, underdeveloped in comparison to the model in *Democracy and Education*. Nevertheless, both notions share this one attribute: Democracy cannot occur until the capacity to inquiry is freed from the yoke of authoritarianism and dogma.

Dewey's notion of democracy extends to the school as well. For the school is the locus of the development of intelligence. As such, the child, if hindered in her development by rigid and dogmatic instruction, will be unable to develop the necessary means for intelligent action to occur. As Dewey puts it:

> We shall find equally great difficulty in encouraging freedom, independence, and initiative in every sphere of social life, while perpetuating in the school dependence upon external authority. The forces of social life are already encroaching upon the school institutions which we have inherited from the past, so that many of its main stays are crumbling. Unless the outcome is to be chaotic, we must take hold of the organic, positive principle involved in democracy [the freeing of mind], and put that in entire possession of the spirit and work of the school. (Dewey [1903–1906] 1977, 239)

The task, then, is to minimize, as much as possible, the imposition of dogma, authority, and fixed and rigid rules of conduct upon the children such that they can develop, through investigation and activity, intelligent thought and action. In short, the task is to develop inquiry. Democracy as considered by Dewey in his writings regarding the Laboratory School is about the development of a nondogmatic, nonauthoritarian, capacity to inquire.

It is easy to judge all the activities undertaken at the Laboratory School as means to the development of the child's capacity to inquire. But this becomes tautological: for if every activity is a means for this development, the distinction between activities that foster the development of inquiry and those that do not becomes very hard to make. And no doubt, as I have shown in chapter 4, certain activities were not conducive to the development of inquiry. On the whole, though, Dewey's rudimentary notion of democracy was successfully developed and applied in the Laboratory School. Most of the activities were social and involved at least small communities of children working to solve a problem or follow through with an activity. Even those activities and problems that required little more than individual effort ultimately aimed at a social purpose.[21]

But one must not get the idea that, because the development of inquiry was a central aim of the School's, therefore the social element was downplayed. This is far from the case. Dewey, commenting upon the Laboratory School experiment with thirty year's hindsight, says:

It will be noted that the social phase of education was put first. This fact is contrary to an impression about the school which has prevailed since it was founded and which many visitors carried away with them at the time. It is the idea which has played a large part in progressive schools: namely, that they exist in order to give complete liberty to individuals, and that they are and must be "child-centered" in a way which ignores, or at least makes little of, social relationships and responsibilities . . . [rather] . . . It was held that the process of mental development is essentially a social process, a process of participation. (Dewey [1935–1937] 1987, 205–06)

But even this phase, this aim of education as social, required experimentation to determine. It was not a predetermined premise upon which further conclusions would follow. As Dewey puts it:

We had to discover by actual experimentation what were the individual tendencies, powers, and needs that needed to be exercised, and would by exercise lead to desirable social results, to social values in which there was a personal and voluntary interest. Doubtless, the school was overweighted, especially in the earlier years, on the "individualistic" side in consequence of the fact that in order to get data upon which we could act, it was necessary to give too much liberty of action rather than to impose too much restriction. (Dewey [1935–1937] 1977, 206)

Dewey's notion of democracy, as developed in and through the Laboratory School, is inchoate. The relationship between democracy and growth and community, so strongly tied together by the time Dewey writes *Democracy and Education*, is only in a germinal stage here. At the time of these writings, Dewey is primarily concerned with linking democracy to inquiry. Little therefore is said about the linkage of democracy with community and growth. A richer and fuller account of democracy, one that takes into consideration the formalized agreement among a community of peoples to act for the good of all such that each can grow, is still years away. What would remain is for Dewey to inquire into the accomplishments and failures of the Laboratory School and work through these to develop a robust connection between democracy and education, and growth and community.

V
INQUIRY, GROWTH, COMMUNITY, AND DEMOCRACY

Up to this point, I have dwelt on the alleged failure of Dewey's notion of inquiry to be of service to prevailing community concerns. What I have not yet done is to talk more specifically about democracy; that is, inquiry in the context of, and of service to, the concerns of a (presumably) democratic populace. Nor have I discussed fully the place of education in a democracy and the complex relationship that each has to the other. What is meant by democratic and why it is important to have such a model for community and a foritiori, inquiry, as well as how and why democracy and education are and must be bound up together, is the focus of this chapter.

Critics of Dewey, notably Clarence Karier and John Patrick Diggins, have accused Dewey's theory of inquiry and community of being pressed into the service of corporate, capitalist interest. Statements of Dewey's that seem to proclaim humanity and human beings as a resource for the production and dissemination of material goods seem, prima facie, to support these criticisms. Likewise, earlier critics find Dewey's tendency to argue away the effects of, for example, such legislation as the Sedition Act of 1917, an act of capitulation at best and betrayal at worst. For Dewey's critics, all of this augurs badly for his allegiance to democracy: if the reigning interests are able to affect control of the populace through socialization, (formal) education, and legislative fiat, then democracy—a state in which the populace can freely inquire as to the best solutions to pressing social concerns—cannot take place. Dewey's theory of inquiry becomes, in this regard, a tool that can be used for ill: a readily available means to construct an antidemocratic society because void of any specifically moral self-constraining means.

In chapters 2, 3, and 4, I demonstrated why inquiry cannot and ought not to be read as such. I claimed that inquiry is and must be seen to be self-correcting, and responsive to the contexts in which it is used and from which it is developed. Dewey's theories of inquiry, growth, and community are robust enough to see the way clear to dismantling existing roadblocks to associated living. Here, I discuss Dewey's notion of democracy in terms of what counts as a democracy and why after all, a democracy is needed if persons are to grow and communities can come together to solve the problems of men.

Part One:
A Short History of the Debate on Democracy

I begin by expanding upon the criticisms of the previous chapter. Doing so allows me to draw out the implications of these for Dewey's strong talk of democracy as the surest means to expand, and have expanded, one's experience, and to occasion growth, thereby. This will involve attention to Dewey's notion of democracy and the inquiry therein, with regards to what many supporters and critics of Dewey agree represents his least successful campaign: the support of the war effort of the period 1915 to 1918. I claim that, though Dewey may have been mistaken in his support of the war effort, nevertheless this is not sufficient to claim that either his theory of democracy or his pragmatism is faulty. And to the extent that Dewey's talk of democracy is defended by sympathizers, it leaves much of the criticism untouched.

Later arguments, as with most criticisms of Dewey, share a pedigree. In this particular instance, it is the criticism of Dewey's alleged failure to buttress his pragmatism sufficiently that it is unable to be pressed into service for the war effort. The tendency for pragmatism to bend to the rhetoric and ideology of war is, for Dewey's critics, tantamount to proclaiming pragmatism a value-neutral theory of inquiry that can be used to support antidemocratic political agendas as well as prodemocratic ones. To be able to be used in such a way is to draw no other conclusion than that of Dewey's pragmatist theory of inquiry being a failure. And this state of affairs has historical precedent.

One of the earliest of the criticisms of Dewey's talk of democracy and the method therein comes from Randolph Bourne. Bourne, a one-time student of Dewey who became a leading social critic and close friend of Dewey's daughter Evelyn, was a proponent of Dewey's pragmatism, in both political and educational respects. He was an early and enthusiastic supporter of the pragmatic revolution in education, and specifically of the so-called Gary Plan, made famous by William Wirt's experimental school in Gary, Indiana.[1] A young magazine writer with a keen sense of justice and a prolific output, he was Dewey's closest ally in the years immediately following 1910. Sadly, he died during the influenza epidemic of 1918. But the year before his death, he turned against Dewey and against the pragmatism that Dewey proffered. This rupture was a result of Bourne's increasing estimation that the war in Europe, World War I, was unjust, and that the United States ought not to intervene. Dewey, initially antagonistic toward the burgeoning call for American support of the war, began to think otherwise, and this led to a rancorous public debate. Though the focus of the debate primarily centered on the war, Dewey's pragmatism itself came under fire. A sad consequence of the debate was Bourne's removal from the *Dial*, a magazine that was to be the last refuge for Bourne's essays. Dewey had a hand in his dismissal: he had just been offered to write for the *Dial*, and insisted to the publisher that Bourne be removed before he commenced. Martyn Johnson, the publisher of the *Dial*, complied, and Bourne was let go.[2]

Bourne's scathing criticism of pragmatism's response to the war is best exemplified in his essay "Twilight of the Idols." By the time he wrote this essay, Bourne had taken a Nietzschean turn, and in so doing, decided that pragmatism and particularly Dewey's version of it lacked vision—the imaginative wherewithal to see through the wrong that joining the war effort occasioned. As Bourne puts it:

> The defect of any philosophy of "adaptation" or "adjustment," even when it means adjustment to changing, living experience, is that there is no provision for thought or experience getting beyond itself. If your ideal is to be adjustment to your situation, in radiant co-operation with reality, then your success is likely to be just that and no more. You never transcend anything. You grow, but your spirit never jumps out of your skin to go on wild adventures. . . . Vision must constantly outshoot technique, opportunist efforts usually achieve less even than what seemed obviously possible. (Bourne [1917] 1964, 61)

This lack of a vision makes the methods and techniques the pragmatists apply easily conformable to existing interests. I shall quote Bourne at length here.

> What is the matter with the [pragmatic] philosophy? One has a sense of having come to a sudden, short stop at the end of an intellectual era. . . . Is there something in these realistic attitudes that works actually against poetic vision, against concern for the quality of life as above machinery of life? Apparently there is. The war has revealed a younger intelligentsia, trained up in the pragmatic dispensation, immensely ready for the executive ordering of events, pitifully unprepared for the intellectual interpretation or the idealistic focusing of ends. The young men in Belgium, the officers' training corps, the young men being sucked into the councils at Washington and into war-organization everywhere, have among them a definite element, upon whom Dewey, as veteran philosopher, might well bestow a papal blessing. They have absorbed the secret of scientific method as applied to political administration. They are liberal, enlightened, aware. They are touched with creative intelligence toward the solution of political and industrial problems. . . . What is significant is that it is the technical side of the war that appeals to them,

not the interpretative or political side. . . . It is true, Dewey calls for a more attentive formulation of war-purposes and ideas, but he calls largely to deaf ears. His disciples have learned all too literally the instrumental attitude toward life, and, being immensely intelligent and energetic, they are making themselves efficient instruments of the war-technique, accepting with little question the ends as announced from above. . . . Their education has not given them a coherent system of large ideas, or a feeling for democratic goals. They have, in short, no clear philosophy of life except that of intelligent service, the admirable adaptation of means to ends. (Bourne [1917] 1964, 59–60)

This paragraph of Bourne's represents well what would become, in successive generations of critics, determining points of contention with Dewey's theory of inquiry. Above all, it is the instrumental character of pragmatism, and specifically, the turn to technique, to method, and away from vision, from imagination and creativity, that portends the failure of will. Pragmatist education is in no wise excluded from this denouncement: inasmuch as education is the means to facilitate the development of these methods and techniques, it too, is complicit in the failure.

Bourne targets pragmatist education elsewhere in the essay:

Dewey's philosophy is inspiring enough for a society at peace, prosperous and with a fund of progressive good-will. It is a philosophy of hope, of clear-sighted comprehension of materials and means. . . . It is scientific method applied to "uplift." But this careful adaptation of means to desired ends, this experimental working out of control over brute forces and dead matter in the interests of communal life, depends on a store of rationality, and is effective only where there is strong desire for progress. It is precisely the school, the institution to which Dewey's philosophy was first applied, that is of all our institutions the most malleable. And it is the will to educate that has seemed, in these days, among all our social attitudes the most rationally motivated. Bourne [1917] 1964, 55–56)

Bourne continues,

For both our revolutionary conceptions of what education means, and for the intellectual strategy of its approach, this country is immeasurably indebted to the influence of Professor Dewey's philosophy. . . . But nations, of course, are not rational entities, and they act within their most irrational rights when they accept war as the most important thing the nation can do in the face of metaphysical menaces of imperial prestige. (Bourne [1917] 1964, 56)

Bourne here charges Dewey with a failure to recognize that, even with education's ability to facilitate the means of democracy—that is, methods and techniques—this by itself is not enough. Without due attention to what cannot
be decided by rational means—to wit, the rights of nations—the triumphs of
method are premature, and the attempt to provide rational means to irrational
entities results in failure.

Bourne presses further. For Bourne, it is not simply that education is unable to provide the sort of means that can counter a nation's irrational urges,
though it surely includes this. It is the inculcation of method, of technique, in
students, which serves to inhibit the facilitation of the irrational. Bourne had
by this time come to read and accept much of Nietzsche's rhetoric on the base
nature of peoples, and the need for the irrational as the fundamental motiva-
tor of humankind, and had further accepted the limits to which techno-
rational thinking could alleviate national and social concerns. For Bourne, the
overbearing presence of method in education and in society renders the likelihood of democracy unlikely. How so?

> But when the emphasis [of pragmatism] is on technical organization,
> rather than organization of ideas, on strategy rather than desires, one be-
> gins to suspect that no program is presented because they have none to
> present. This burrowing into war-technique hides the void where a dem-
> ocratic philosophy should be. . . . Is the answer that clear formulation of
> democratic ends must be postponed until victory in the war is attained?
> But to make this answer is to surrender the entire case. For the support
> of the war by radicals, realists, pragmatists, is due—or so they say—to the
> fact that the war is not only the saving cause of democracy, but is im-
> mensely accelerating its progress. Well, what are those gains? How are
> they to be conserved? What do they lead to? How can we further them?
> Into what large idea of society do they group? To ignore these questions,
> and think only of the war-technique and its accompanying devotions, is
> to undermine the foundations of these people's own faith. (Bourne
> [1917] 1964, 58)

The wholesale turn to technique and method, as Bourne believes Dewey
insists, is for Bourne tantamount to undermining the very faith in democracy
that is necessary for democracy to survive. It is to surrender the faith and the
vision of democracy as "end" for mere "means." It equally suggests that what
schools should be working toward is not simply the acquisition of the tools of
inquiry, but the facilitation of imagination, of vision, of faith, together with a
caveat to students regarding the potential for overindulgence in method and
technique. Education, if it is to be properly democratic, must be wary of,
and indeed resist, the all-consuming tendency to embrace inquiry as the point

and purpose of the school. For Bourne, to not do so is to place the school in the position of fostering a set of methods and techniques that can and would be used for undemocratic ends. In such a scenario, education paradoxically becomes a means to social planning, engineering, and control.

Clarence Karier evidences a variant of Bourne's charges. For Karier, in addition to the criticisms that he levels against Dewey's representation of liberal, bourgeois class interests, is the criticism of Dewey attempting to "make the world safe for democracy" by fiat (Karier 1977, 20). Here, Karier ties Dewey's prowar sentiment to his express wish for a corporate, bureaucratic, expert-controlled society through social engineering. As Karier sees it:

> With America's entry into the war, Dewey hesitated no longer. He argued for aggressive American involvement in shaping both the world and American democracy. He saw the war as a pragmatic opportunity not only to make the world safe for democracy, but also to reconstruct the American community toward his unique vision of an industrial democracy . . . he believed that the increase in state power to regulate and control production and consumption resulting from the war would result in the decline of capitalist power and the rise of state power. Dewey's confident faith in the coming development of industrial democracy rested, however, not so much on the great increase in the power of the state, but rather on the growing influence of the scientifically oriented knowledgeable professional to use that power in the service of the larger community. The new professional expert thus would serve as a midwife at the birth of a new American industrial democracy. (Karier 1977, 20)

Thus far, the criticisms leveled against Dewey are:

1) Pragmatism supports the reigning interests of society (capitalism, industrialism, entrenched power interests), whatever they are. It is a method to maintain and enforce social control (Bourne, Karier).
2) Schools indoctrinate children into this system of life (Karier).

Dewey has had support on the war issue from sympathizers. Sydney Hook, Dewey's one-time student and life-long friend and champion of pragmatism, is perhaps the most vocal of these earlier apologists, and the only one that confronts the accusations head-on. He deals specifically with the criticism of Dewey's war-related articles in his volume *John Dewey: An Intellectual Portrait*. Speaking of Dewey's critics, Hook says, "One facile literary critic [Hook does not say who] has seen in Dewey's philosophy little but a continuation of 'the pragmatic acquiescence' to the dreary compromises, the externalism, and cruelties of American life which had received an earlier expression in the philosophy of William James" (Hook 1939, 227). Hook goes on to claim:

The chief reason, apparently, for this blanket judgment on Dewey, aside from a misreading of a text, is his failure to oppose America's entry into the World War to save democracy. By a strange irony, this very critic, at the present writing, is frantically beating the tom-toms for another world war for peace and democracy. Stranger still, in a retrospective evaluation, he justifies America's entry into the last war, so that, in to his latest pronouncements, Dewey should be applauded for having acquiesced in the acquiescence of the American people. (Hook 1939, 227)

Beyond attempting to turn the tables on the unnamed critic, Hook offers this support:

It is true that he [Dewey] did not actively oppose the War. His knowledge of the economics and politics of imperialism was inadequate, and he placed too much confidence in Woodrow Wilson's new deal in foreign policy. He has admitted that the experience was highly instructive. But it is also true that he spent more energy defending the civil liberties that were sacrificed during the war than in aiding its prosecution. He indicated the reasons for his half-heartedness in a striking essay, "In a Time of National Hesitation," published while America was at war. Speaking of the conditions under which hesitation could be replaced by wholeheartedness, he wrote: "Not until the impossible happens, not until the Allies are fighting on our terms for our democracy and civilization, will that happen." In subsequent essays he made clear that by "our democracy and civilization" he meant not the entirety of existing practices in American life but those aspects which were in consonance with, or could be brought in consonance with, the ideals of freedom, and equality of opportunity for individual development. (Hook 1939, 228)

Hook also tackles the complaints common to Russell, Santayana, and Bourne that Dewey's pragmatism was the philosophic counterpart of an American capitalism and commercialism. Of this Hook says:

The judgment which identifies pragmatism as the philosophical expression of commercialism does concern us. For despite its currency, it is unscientific and superficial. It can sincerely be held only by those who understand pragmatism to mean that the truth of an idea depends upon the amount of money one can make by believing it, or by getting others

to believe it; which would make every successful confidence man a pragmatist instead of a candidate for a post in some European Foreign Office.
There is no way of meeting a criticism of this sort except by inviting those
who make it to give reasons for their statement, and, if they point to
James's metaphor about "the cash-value of ideas," inviting them to learn
the American language. (Hook 1939, 229)

Unfortunately, Hook's rhetoric would not persuade either critics of Bourne or
Karier's ilk. Bourne criticized Dewey on the basis of statements made after
Dewey had declared his intention that America should join the war. As well, it
does not address Dewey's seeming downplaying of the evils of such legislation
as the Sedition Act. Most unfortunately, Hook gives Dewey's critics the smok-
ing gun, so to speak: Dewey's strong allegiance to scientific method. "In Dewey's
philosophy we have a sustained and systematic attempt to take the pattern of
scientific inquiry as a model for knowledge and action in all fields. He does not
recognize any such thing as 'the bankruptcy of science' or even 'a crisis of science' except in the technical sense which marks a phase of rapid development"
(Hook 1939, 233). Hook continues: "Dewey's emphasis on science corrects,
purifies, and raises to the plane of a philosophy of life certain pervasive features
of everyday American experience" (Hook 1939, 233).

Part Two:
The Present-Day Debate on Democracy

As we might expect, there are strong affinities between Bourne and Karier's
readings of the failures of democracy, and J. P. Diggins's. In fact, Diggins uses
the Bourne-Dewey debate to segue into his particular concern with respect to
pragmatism: the failure of method owing to a lack of reverence for historical
authority. As Diggins puts it:

In 1917, the country's leading philosopher had no difficulty advising
Americans how to face the Kaiser. He rejected the warning of Bourne . . .
about the dangers of patriotism in times of war. Instead his defense of the
government's military efforts against Germany, and of conscription,
legitimated the power of the state and turned it into rightful authority
worthy of intellectual and moral support. Yet Dewey's reasoning points
up the difficulties in the pragmatic attempt to tie political authority to
the philosophical authority of scientific methodology, to the rule of efficiency and the criterion of consequences. . . . As a pragmatist more concerned with the outcome than with the origins of the war, with future
consequences rather than historical causes, Dewey could refer vaguely to

"forces" without specifying their political or economic nature and without analyzing the causal factors behind them. How, then, could he possibly conclude that the war could not be resisted? How could he grasp what was happening when he had no basis for knowing what had happened? (Diggins 1994, 256–57)

Even if we are to dispel these war-related criticisms, there remains another set, more subtle perhaps, but nevertheless as potentially damaging to the case for democracy. Thus far, I have discussed the importance of inquiry to democracy while begging the question of criticisms of inquiry's relevance to our contemporary political and social states of affairs. Prima facie, it may seem that establishing a strong relationship between inquiry and democracy through the interconnections with growth and community cements the case. But even this is presumptuous if we take seriously charges made by those inimical, not merely to Dewey's notion of inquiry, but to the very possibility of, or need for, inquiry in a postliberal or postmodern state.[3] The claim here is that, not only is inquiry not a requirement for such a state, but it gets in the way of further growth, generally considered to be the capacity for citizens of the state to construct their own meanings through either the build-up of new vocabularies or the expansion of pluralist identities. Inquiry represents a way of thinking no longer in vogue: one that still holds out for the possibility of growth to occur.

Two self-identifying pragmatists have raised the issue of whether or not pragmatism as a philosophy in the service of democracy has much to offer our postliberal state. Both have questioned Dewey and inquiry's role in the service of the postliberal state.[4] For John Stuhr, the question of relevance finds its corollary in the further question of what, as pragmatists, philosophers do when they claim the mantle for philosophy. Stuhr thinks that they become "philosophic assassins," proudly proclaiming to be the last philosophers, able to solve and/or dispose of all previous philosophical problems.[5] The attempt to get us to see that pragmatists cannot be the last philosophers, nor pragmatism the last philosophy, is to relinquish the notion that pragmatism is the future of philosophy. The consequences of this relinquishing are drastic changes in the way that philosophers see, describe, and understand social institutions such as education.

For Richard Rorty, the role for philosophy as we have come to understand it is abdicated entirely. Rorty famously thinks that philosophy has nothing to offer the liberal, bourgeois, postmodern state. This extends to philosophy's role in education and in other social institutions. I shall discuss Rorty's view of inquiry more fully here than in chapters 2 and 3, and suggest Rorty's statements on Dewey and inquiry are also those of Stuhr. For, whatever differences Stuhr and Rorty might have on their respective interpretations of Dewey and of pragmatism, they share at least this: a profound distrust of the capacity of pragmatism as a method to do anything special for contemporary postliberal social institutions.[6] This is the final challenge to Dewey's theory of inquiry that I take up.

Much of the criticism of those inimical to Dewey's project of social intelligence manifests as a disbelief in the capacity of schools to accomplish the task of socializing citizenry and democratizing inquiry. Of course, we see this in Clarence Karier's evaluation of Deweyan schools as the locus for social control. We see the converse claim as well—the claim that schools do not manifest enough social control. As discussed, a variant of this claim is put forth by J. P. Diggins. Yet another variant of this claim is to argue that the schools, as only one of many social institutions that interact on a daily basis with children, do not have the capacity to educate in the full sense of the word. That schools do educate is not what is in contention, here; rather it is that, as education cannot be confined to schooling, and as education takes place well before the onset of schooling and long afterward, schooling is neither the primary nor the preeminent means of educating. Critics who make a point of this are correct. John Stuhr is one of these, and in a recent work he puts the point forcefully: "The distinction between education and schooling is often erased, and it is overlooked even more often by 'educators' who are employed by, and primarily concerned with, schools. As such, educational problems and issues are often misinterpreted and viewed overly narrowly as schooling problems and school issues. Education, however, is a broader notion. School is one important means of forming the habits and dispositions of the immature members of a society, but it is only one means, and, compared to other, more powerful ones, a relatively superficial and ineffectual one" (Stuhr 2003, 12). Stuhr continues, "This view of education makes clear that major social institutions—the government, the economy, the family, the workplace, the legal system, volunteer organizations, the military, terrorist organizations, and religious groups, for example—have broader and deeper educational consequences than the schools" (Stuhr 2003, 13).

Stuhr's point is not that educators have confused schools with other institutions in the community, though it is a side concern. Rather, it is that educators,

> conflating education and schooling . . . are likely to believe that society has not recognized the liberal possibilities that Dewey outlined. They are likely to view this as an explanation for why too little time, too little attention, and too little money is put at the disposal of the schools, their schools. They are likely to feel that we have not yet realized the liberal values that Dewey championed, that he was a bit too hopeful, a bit too rosy, maybe a bit too American. They are likely to feel that Deweyan lib-

eralism, a liberalism committed to empowering freedom, communal individualism, and experimental intelligence, stands in front of us still. They are likely to feel that we are living *before liberalism*. (Stuhr 2003, 17)

In fact, argues Stuhr, we are living *after* liberalism. Our educators do educate. They are, quite simply put, not in the schools; rather, they are the "educational heavyweights such as: international businesses and global forces of production, marketing and consumption; media and entertainment giants; national governments and international legal groups; militaries, police, and organized crime and terror; systems of surveillance, information production, and information warfare; and religious organizations" (Stuhr 2003, 18).

But the larger point that Stuhr builds up to is not that education has been co-opted by institutions other than schools, though it, too, is telling; it is rather that, freed from schooling, education has been equally freed from growth. No longer holding growth (in its Deweyan sense) as an ideal, we as a community are living *after* liberalism. After liberalism, questions such as How do we fix our schools? cease to inspire. They become one of a piece with questions such as How can we fix the prisons? How can we make federal and international drug policies work? How can we make the health care and health insurance systems work? How can we deal with AIDS? (Stuhr 2003, 19). The lumping together of these sorts of questions is tantamount to proclaiming that the forces in practice in society are no longer interested in affirming the ideals of growth. To claim that society is post liberal is for Stuhr, to claim that it operates to satisfy desires other than growth.

> Why not say that the public schools and all these other institutions and practices are working just fine? They create desires and, at a societal level, they provide the means necessary for a sufficiently large number of persons to satisfy many of these desires. The desires, however, are not for growth. Perhaps they are desires for material wealth or comfort, a policed or medicalized or drugged existence, ready entertainment and amusement park lifestyle, consumer choices, or a gated community free from difference in practice as well as theory. (Stuhr 2003, 19)

Stuhr's point ought to be taken seriously. For as we have provided an education for children in areas not bounded by the four walls of the school that is largely authoritarian, piecemeal, and curiosity deadening, we have taught children that democratic ideals, including the ideal of growth, are ideals not worth valuing. That our schools are

> puny educational forces in comparison to other social institutions, now are swamped by a global business culture that produces habits of mind

inconsistent with the value of growth, is not new. What is new is the fact that schools themselves are now far along in internalizing this business culture, this anti-education-as-growth culture, and are becoming part of the production of habits of mind at odds with the ideal of growth. Schools now are taking on the structures and aims of business; schooling is becoming the education business, and students are becoming education consumers. (Stuhr 2003, 20)

Of course, none of this is new to school-based educators, who have been complaining, perhaps to their own self-satisfaction, of such a corporate takeover for years. But Stuhr does not congratulate the school-based educator for having spotted the problem earlier than most. School-based educators have largely been content to complain about the negative implications of the business culture in their schools, but have been silent elsewhere: education has been left largely to other educators. So it is no surprise that Stuhr is faint with his praise. "Dewey's radical conception of growth as a democratic way of life has never been included in the goals of the big educators, the big educational forces, in any society. Getting it on their agendas requires in part stepping outside the schools, academic organizations, and the largely intramural debates that go on there, and scholarly books like this one. . . . In the face of many constraints and difficulties for success, this remains the most important educational task, a genuinely Herculean labor, for anyone who professes anew pragmatism in the millennium after Dewey" (Stuhr 2003, 21).

Stuhr has a broader target than simply big business and educational institutions in mind. This target is none other than theory itself. And the theory under scrutiny, hinted at above, is pragmatism. Pragmatism has, to Stuhr's chagrin, been characterized throughout the twentieth century "as the future of philosophy, and they [pragmatists] proclaimed that the philosophers of the future will be, and/or should be, pragmatists" (Stuhr 2003, 168). Whereas many so-called pragmatic thinkers believe that the future of philosophy is pragmatic, Stuhr believes that "today pragmatists can successfully *stop* seeing pragmatism as the future of personal philosophy, and can successfully *stop* seeing pragmatism as the future of institutional, professionalized philosophy (or even see the future of pragmatism in this context at all)" (Stuhr 2003, 169). How so?

Stuhr does not turn to inquiry, fallibilism, social intelligence, pluralism, or any of the other pragmatic tools said to alleviate social concerns. Stuhr instead invokes Dewey as recognizing that pragmatism, as with any professionalized philosophy, can do very little about these states of affairs. Monoliths such as church and political organizations will have their day and pragmatism can do little to thwart them. Faced with the powerlessness of pragmatism to transform existing social institutions, Stuhr suggests that pragmatists drop their optimism and their proclamations of triumph. As he puts it: "Like any other philosophy, pragmatism at most satisfies its own criteria for the success of a philo-sophic theory; it does not satisfy the criteria of other theories (and indeed trans-forms and does violence to these criteria when it claims to have satisfied them). Pragmatism resolves the problems of other philosophies, but only if they adopt a pragmatic account of what counts as problems and their resolutions" (Stuhr 2003, 181). Stuhr claims that we (pragmatists) must take a long, hard, *genealog-ical* look at ourselves. Pragmatism's "own season of belief is local and transient. In the face of this recognition, it generates no need for consolation" (Stuhr 2003, 184).

What of pragmatism's violence? One of the least satisfying aspects of pragmatism is, for Stuhr, a history of the forced migration of spirituality and transcendence. Specifically, Stuhr comments on pragmatism's "forced reloca-tion, a long march, of traditional notions of transcendence and spirituality. It has located transcendence *within* immanence, relocated spirit *within* nature, re-located affirmation *within* negation, relocated salvation *within* a great commu-nity" (Stuhr 2003, 194). It has, in short,

> claimed to offer . . . spirituality without spirit and transcendence with-out transcendentalism. . . . From the beginning through its first century, pragmatism has offered its customers a two-for-one sale, a sale that is no doubt particularly appealing . . . to its American customers who want it all: radical empiricism and the will to believe, scientific fixation of our belief and God, experience and nature and the religious, philosophy as criticism and democratic faith, self-creation or, at least, private fulfill-ment and solidarity. (Stuhr 2003, 194–95)

Stuhr thinks that, simply by bringing spirituality and transcendence into the fold of radical empiricism and naturalistic philosophy, pragmatism "cannot win this rearguard battle—a battle against, or on behalf of, persons for whom prag-matism is not a live option from the start" (Stuhr 2003, 196). And pragmatists who claim that transcendence and spirituality are not somehow transformed in the process of envelopment must answer to the charges that not only does transformation take place but that spirit and transcendence, as they have come to be understood, are (à la Hegel) eliminated. Stuhr's recommendation for pragmatism is to get out of the business of reconciling opposites and bringing disparate notions and experiences into a satisfying through unifying, fold. It is, in short, to get out of the business of being airily theoretical. "Pragmatism's task is to deliberate about particular preferences on the way to different preferences and action on their behalf. Community designates no nonnatural fact or unity; it designates a practical agenda. As practical agenda, this deliberation does not have 'one foot in eternity.' Instead, it has both feet, temporarily, in embodi-ment and enactment; or rather, it is those two feet" (Stuhr 2003, 196).

Rorty makes little of the relation of method to democracy. To illustrate Rorty's position on this issue, I choose the debate that began in a collected volume of responses to Rorty's version of pragmatism; a volume edited by Herbert Saatkamp, Jr. In this work, two Dewey scholars, T. Z. Lavine and James Gouinlock, critique Rorty for his denigration of Dewey's championing of (scientific) method. Rorty then responds to their critiques. T. Z. Lavine and James Gouinlock have taken exception to Rorty's portrayal of John Dewey. Both of these authors castigate Rorty for supposedly jettisoning a large chunk of Dewey in the process of refashioning pragmatism. Specifically, Lavine and Gouinlock are troubled by Rorty's condemnation of Dewey's metaphysics of experience, his treatises on logic, and most of all, his passion for method as a solution to pressing human problems. Characteristically, Lavine and Gouinlock champion the very things that Rorty chides—especially Dewey's passion and insistence on method. Both Lavine and Gouinlock maintain that Dewey talked frequently and strongly about method. Therefore, they conclude, Dewey must have had something important to say about the topic. And indeed, according to both authors, he did. Lavine argues:

> Dewey meant by scientific method the pattern of inquiry finally formulated and elaborated in *Logic: the Theory of Inquiry*—the Hegelian working out of the conflictual problems of the problematic situation, most significantly in the testing of the proposed solution by its experiential outcomes. This pattern of inquiry is not only the method for all inquiry: it is also Dewey's procedure for scientific testing by valid prediction or by falsification: it is Dewey's realism: it is his form of the correspondence theory of knowledge; it is his form of the reality principle; it is Dewey's prescription for sanity against the flux of sensations, cosmic perspectives, or vocabularies. By seeing the method of inquiry as the reflective intervention by action into the problematic complex of events in which the intervention is tested by its outcomes, Dewey breaks out of traditional historicism and linguisticism. (Lavine in Saatkamp 1995, 44)

James Gouinlock, in similar fashion, contends that "Dewey's claim that art, science, and practical activity have significant subject matter and procedures in common is an instance of the position already documented: the perplexities of life require unified method. This is not the eradication of method, but its extension to all problems of conduct. It is not a denial of disciplined intelligence, but a demand for it" (Gouinlock in Saatkamp 1995, 78).

What is shared between these two thinkers is a sense of the strong and pervasive nature of scientific method. For Gouinlock, method means unity: unity that ties all of art, science, and practical activity together. It is the method of all sure future conduct. For Lavine, method represents Dewey's "epistemology." It is his characteristic appeal to claims of knowledge; his representation-alism; his correspondence theory of truth; his connection to reality. It is what lies outside the flux of the ordinary, the mundane, the historical, and the lin-guistic. What comes through clearly with these authors is the certainty that method provides; the surefooted consistency of its mechanism; the unifying tendency of its claims, and the imperviousness of its armor to chance.

It is just these claims that Rorty aims to refute. Contra Lavine, Rorty does not believe that method (or anything else) can get us closer to "the way things really are," or somehow stablize once and for all, the flux of sensation. This of course is a central motif in all of Rorty's writings, and it provides one of the clearest examples as to why it is that Lavine, Gouinlock, and Rorty, all avowed pragmatists, can differ so greatly on an issue of mutual concern. What Rorty is giving up when he claims that we cannot get closer to a thing's nature is just the idea of the correspondence theory of truth (Rorty 1998, 2). For Rorty, such thinking creeps into talk of method when method is made (as with Lavine) to be "the prescription for sanity against the flux of sensations," or with Gouin-lock's talk of singularity and uniformity of method. Such talk of method, Rorty argues, betrays a certain quest for certainty, for objectivity, that Rorty charac-teristically eschews. Such talk, Rorty argues, is a species of scientism (Rorty 1991, 27).

Rorty has little interest in talking about method because he thinks that it gets in the way of talk of democratic communities, science as solidarity, and other, better vocabularies that do not have the baggage of scientism along with them. Method detracts from the good that the scientific community has ac-complished. It replaces this notion of helpful communities with a view of the scientist as more objective, more logical, and thereby, closer to the truth. Such focus on method serves chiefly the function of hypostatization. The end result is that method becomes the one sure way to penetrate the inner workings of reality. What gets lost in all of this worship, Rorty fears, is the notion of science as an exemplary model of democratic, human solidarity. Scientists be-come quasi priests, while science becomes the one right way to truth.

As I discussed in chapter 3, Rorty is critical of what he says is Dewey's at-tempt to engage in metaphysical system building. It is Dewey's talk of "generic traits," of "experience," and above all, of "method," that worries Rorty so. The concern is that Dewey was so blinded by his own need to reconcile his thinking with the discipline of philosophy that he let go of what was most important to him—namely, his criticism of all past quests for certainty. Rorty self-consciously chooses to exaggerate and emulate this latter aspect of Dewey, at the cost of den-igrating the former.[7] The result is a Dewey that weighs in on the side of social and cultural criticism far more than philosophic system building. Certain things, of course, have to go if this view is to be maintained. And one of those things, argues Rorty, is Dewey's "strong" insistence on scientific method. In the introduction to *How We Think*, revised edition, Rorty puts this succinctly: "Dewey does not offer one [a method], and it seems evident that there can be no general procedure for deciding which of the beliefs one has picked up from "tradition, instruction, and imitation" to treat skeptically and which to leave alone (Rorty in Dewey 1986, xvi). Further, Rorty says of Dewey that "He was aware that no study of how we think can produce any formula or set of formulae, which would serve as such a panacea. But in *How We Think* and elsewhere he constantly talks as if he were offering such a strategy (Rorty in Dewey 1986, xvii).

Rorty's early criticisms of Dewey's "strong" insistence on method attempt the linkage of talk of scientific method to scientism. In terms of the affinity of method to scientism, Rorty argues that any talk of method necessitates equal talk of objectivity, which Rorty characteristically eschews. Once talk of objectivity is done away with, talk of method ceases to be very relevant (Rorty 1982, 203). In place of method, Rorty would rather see talk of "vocabulary," or as he would put it later, "conversation." As Rorty argues, talk of vocabularies replaces talk of objectivity in the neopragmatist conception of science. There is nothing very special about method because method has no insight into the "real" inner workings of nature or peoples. But Rorty adds some new arguments to his arsenal in responding to Lavine and Gouinlock. In challenging Lavine's insistence on Dewey as somehow having something privileged and special, Rorty responds by arguing that "as I see it, all Dewey had in mind when he talked about 'scientific method' was the familiar social practices of democratic communities when they are at their best—when they exemplify the moral virtues that Lavine lists" (Rorty in Saatkamp 1995, 51). And when confronting Gouinlock, Rorty adds the following two explanations of why Dewey was so insistent regarding method.

> As I see it, the main reason Dewey constantly attached the term "method of" to "critical intelligence" was to provide a contrast to "the a priori, deductive method"—the method supposedly followed by intellectuals in the bad old days before the New Science came along. But no such method was in fact followed. . . . The only other reason I can think of why Dewey, early and late, insisted on using the vacuous notion of "method" is that he wanted philosophy to stop offering a body of knowledge, while still offering something. "Method" was the name he chose for what he thought it might still provide. But it was not a fortunate choice. It promised more than he could offer—something positive, rather than the merely negative admonition not to get trapped in the past. (Rorty in Saatkamp 1995, 51)

In point of fact, Rorty never actually retreats from the early position he stakes out in his essay on Dewey's metaphysics. He remains confident that talk of sci-

entific method is something that Dewey should have let go of. In his final statement to Gouinlock on this subject, Rorty offers us this summary assessment of
the situation.

> Granted that Dewey never stopped talking about "scientific method," I
> submit that he never had anything very useful to say about it. Those who
> think I am overstating my case here, should, I think, tell us what this
> thing called "method"—which is neither a set of rules nor a character
> trait nor a collection of techniques—is supposed to be. Unless some rea-
> sonably definite third element can be specified, and chapter and verse
> cited from Dewey showing that this is what he had in mind, I shall stick
> by my claim that Dewey could have said everything he needed to say if
> he dropped the term "scientific method. (Rorty in Saatkamp 1995, 94)

Rorty's own brand of pragmatism, antinaturalistic in the extreme, yet
thoroughly nominalist and historicist, eschews talk of method. Offered in its
place are the context-bound rules and attitudes of discourse. "If one takes the
core of pragmatism to be its attempt to replace the notion of true beliefs as representations of 'the nature of things' and instead to think of them as successful rules for action, then it becomes easy to recommend an experimental, fallibilist attitude, but hard to isolate a 'method' that will embody this attitude"
(Rorty 1991, 65–66). Our duties as pragmatists are not methodological: they
are conversational. "We do have a duty to talk to each other, to converse about
our views of the world, to use persuasion rather than force, to be tolerant of diversity, to be contritely fallibilist. But this is not the same thing as a duty to
have methodological principles" (Rorty 1991, 67).

Rorty presents his contrite fallibilism as an attitude in much the same
manner as Dewey discussed attitudes and tempers in *How We Think*. But
whereas Dewey thought attitudes and tempers necessary for problem solving,
he did not think them sufficient. Rorty seems to. Rorty does not discuss how
attitudes hook up to other scientific practices, such as logic, experimentation,
and observation. One might assume that these practices, as important as they
are for scientific investigation and problem solving, are so highly contextual-
ized that to say there is anything methodological about them is to claim, un-
interestingly, that anything involving practical know-how and use of ready-
made, internal logics for the solution of a specific problem in a specific context
(or language game) is already methodical. To do so is to defang method, so to
speak. It is to remove any vestige of privilege that method has accumulated,
and to separate science and what scientists do, from priestly activity and honor.

Rorty of course has a more forceful criticism of method. As Rorty is suspicious of philosophy's pretense to be the queen of the sciences, the criticism
of all criticisms, or one of another of many possible self-congratulatory epithets,

he is anxious to see philosophy humble itself. What this means for Rorty is that philosophy limit itself to providing edification of an entirely private sort; that is, to limit itself to aesthetic self-creation. His criticism of the adoption of the thinking of Heidegger, Nietzsche, and Derrida for anything like a public philosophy as useless at best and dangerous at worst is equally a call for theorists to note the motivation behind such a criticism: philosophies are ill-suited for public consumption and use, owing to their metaphysical and epistemological agendas, which are private, aesthetic, and as such, unshareable. In much the same manner as Rawls, Rorty exhorts us to avoid making our primary conceptions of the Good a public affair.

Rorty thinks that he has spotted in some of Dewey's writings a tendency to put a primary conception of the Good into public service. Dewey's talk of generic traits, as I discuss in chapter 3, was said to lead Dewey to think of philosophy as illuminating some universal aspect of our experience. And this in turn led Dewey to think of philosophy as the "criticism of criticisms," a Kantian throwback to an avowedly anti-Kantian philosophy. Rorty's task is avowedly therapeutic—to rid ourselves of the traces of epistemology, methodologism, certainty, universalism, positivism, and ontology.

Rorty's pragmatism without method is unlike Dewey's in that it is disposable. Once shorn of its academic and philosophical pretensions, it is left with even less theoretical work to do than is Stuhr's. Not needed any longer, owing to the earlier work of Dewey and other pragmatic thinkers in debunking any pretenses we might have to certain knowledge, pragmatism itself is no longer a viable option. What is needed for Rorty is conversation. And this is a manifestly political undertaking. Philosophy dissolves into politics on the one hand, and (for those inclined to private, aesthetic, self-edification) poetry on the other. But nothing viable of pragmatism or a fortiori Dewey's inquiry remains.

Part Three:
Rereading Inquiry and Democracy

There are two sets of criticisms to be dispelled here. The first is that common to Bourne, Diggins, and Karier: in Dewey's pragmatism there is a failure to provide sufficient strength to resist the capacity to engage in a war raged, in Bourne and Karier's estimation, for bureaucratic and expert class interests, and in Diggins's, with complete disregard of historical precedent. For both Dewey's strong talk of scientific inquiry in the service of democratic interests betrays the weakness of both an altogether too heavy reliance on science and technique, and on present and future ends and means: a weakness that lends inquiry to support nondemocratic practices and thereby betrays the democratic spirit Dewey ostensibly sets for inquiry. As correct as these critics may be regarding Dewey as having erred in the debates about participating in the war, nevertheless, the conclusion that they each draw—that there is something fundamentally wrong with a pragmatism that would suggest such participation—is fallacious. And to suggest, as Bourne does, that education emerges as a willing participant in this failure, is, as I shall now claim, equally mistaken.[8] The second set of criticisms has to do with the very possibility of pragmatism as a helpful social and democratic tool. In fact, there is evidenced in these criticisms a profound distrust of the capacity of pragmatism as a method to do anything special for contemporary postliberal social institutions. These criticisms are less easily dispelled and require a more thoughtful approach than many have offered thus far. I shall deal with the first set of criticisms and follow with the second. But I wish to begin by turning to statements of Dewey's that seem in conflict with each other. These statements of Dewey's come from his contributions to the magazine *The New Republic*, as well as various bulletins, all published in 1917 and 1918 and related to the war effort.

> Just because the circumstances of the war have brought the idea of the nation and the national to the foreground of everyone's thoughts, the most important thing is to bear in mind that there are nations and nations, this kind of nationalism and that. Unless I am mistaken there are some now using the cry of an American nationalism, of an intensified national patriotism, to further ideas which characterize the European nations, especially those most active in the war, but which are treasonable to the ideal of *our* nation. . . . Since as a nation we are composed of representatives of all nations who have come here to live in peace with one another and to escape the enmities and jealousies which characterize old-world nations, to nationalize our education means to make it an instrument in the active and constant suppression of the war spirit, and in the positive cultivation of sentiments of respect and friendship for all men and women wherever they live. (Dewey 1916 [1980] 209)

> Certain commonplaces must be reiterated until their import is acknowledged. The industrial revolution was born of the new science of nature. Any democracy which is more than an imitation of some archaic republican government must issue from the womb of our chaotic industrialism. Science makes democracy possible because it brings relief from depending upon massed human labor, because of the substitution it makes possible of inanimate forces for human muscular energy, and because of the resources for excess production and easy distribution which it effects. The old culture [of Europe] is doomed for us because it was built up on an alliance of political and spiritual powers, an equilibrium of governing and leisure classes, which no longer exists. (Dewey 1916 [1980] 199–200)

It is for education to bring the light of science and the power of work to the aid of every soul that it may discover its quality. For in a spiritually democratic society every individual would realize distinction. Culture would then be for the first time in human history an individual achievement and not a class possession. An education fit for our ideal uses is a matter of actual forces, not of opinions. (Dewey [1916] 1980, 200)

That the gallant fight for democracy and civilization fought on the soil of France is not our fight is a thing not to be realized without pangs and qualms. But it is a fact which has slowly disclosed itself as these last long years have disclosed us to ourselves. It was not ours, because for better or for worse we are committed to a fight for another democracy and another civilization. Their nature is not clear to us: all that is sure is that they are different. This is the fact of a New World. The Declaration of Independence is no longer a merely dynastic and political declaration. (Dewey [1917] 1980, 258)

These statements, all written during the period encompassing World War I, share Dewey's optimism that American politics and democracy is far preferable to Europe's, with its violence-producing spiritual and cultural baggage.[9] Here, Dewey lauds the capacity for education to affect an industrial democracy in which class distinctions and disputes are obviated. Education is to be nationalized such that through it, the narrow and provincial interests that breed the war cry can be given over to unified and democratic ones. In 1916 and 1917, Dewey is of the opinion that the war is not America's fight. Now consider these passages:

And I believe—though it may be my hope is the source of my belief-that some of our intolerance at diversity [with the talk of passing the Sedition Act by the Wilsonian administration, which subsequently occurred the following year] of opinion and our willingness to suppress the civil liberties of democracy in the name of loyalty to democracy is merely a part of our haste to get into the war effectively, a part of the rush of mobilization, which, thank heaven, had to be improvised because of our historic and established unmilitarism. So far as such is the case, positive achievement will restore sanity because it will mean attainment of maturity and of the self-confidence and orderly discipline that mark the passage of youth into maturity. (Dewey [1917] 1980, 295)

In short, the war, by throwing into relief the public aspect of every social enterprise, has discovered the amount of sabotage which habitually goes on in manipulating property rights to take a private profit out of social needs. Otherwise, the wrench needed in order to bring privately controlled industries into line with public needs would not have had to be so great. The war has afforded an immense object lesson as to the absence of democracy in most important phases of our national life. Banking, finance, the supervision of floating of new corporate enterprises, the mechanism of credit, have been affected by it to various degrees. . . . Consequently the question of the control of land for use instead of for speculation has assumed an acute aspect, while a flood of light has been thrown upon the interruption of the flow of food and fuel to the consumer with a view to exacting private toll. . . . To dispose of such matters by labeling them state socialism is merely to conceal their deeper import: the creation of instrumentalities for enforcing the public interest in all the agencies of modern production and exchange. (Dewey [1918] 1982, 102)

The war looks like a war of physical resources, a war of material, a war of ammunition, munitions, with the factories behind them, a war of foods, a war of transportation, a war generally of the effective organizations and mobilizations of the physical and material resources of the various nations at war, a struggle of ships and railways, of farms and factories; but just in the degree in which the war has become more and more a war of the organization of materials, munitions, food and transportation, it has been made clear that effective production and mobilization of all these things is absolutely dependent upon the underlying human capacity, upon inventive, organizable, energetic human resources. (Dewey [1918] 1982, 59)

These statements evidence a somewhat different set of priorities: the United States had entered the war by the time that these were written, and there seems an atmosphere of complacency and acceptance present with respect to this. Dewey asks the public to weather the storm of the Sedition Act and downplays its passage and its effects as the product of overexuberance. Equally, Dewey seems concerned with trade, shipping, finances, and production and the positive effects that democratization has and will continue to have on these. Finally, there is the turn to analogizing human resources with material ones: resources built up through education and able, in turn, to produce more efficient "production and mobilization" of materials, suggesting that there may be a role for education to play in this design.

Here, I want to focus attention first on the issue of whether or not inquiry, as it is facilitated in and by schools, exists as a means to social control. For if Bourne and Karier are correct, and education is the means by which inquiry, as a set of value-neutral methods and techniques, is fostered, it seems right to say that potentially nondemocratic means are being pressed into service for ostensibly democratic ends. And this subverts democracy outright. To challenge this reading is not to challenge Bourne and Karier's first premise: that schooling is indeed about fostering inquiry. Rather, it is to challenge the second: that fostering inquiry in children is tantamount to inducing social control. I shall turn to inquiry as the method of pragmatism and then respond to the charge that theory and inquiry hold no value for postliberal, postmodern living. If, as I claim, theory cannot be so easily disconnected from practice, and inquiry cannot be completed until tested out in the solutions to problems-at-hand, then the charge that inquiry is of little or no use to postliberal society, though trenchant, can also be tempered.

The First Claim: Community, Democracy, and Social Control

Recall that growth is the transformation that occurs as one expands one's experiences. Expanding one's experiences connotes (at least) two separate but nevertheless interconnected activities. The first is the augmentation of the qualities and traits of an experience had. Individuality, continuity, relation, contingency, need, movement, and arrest all are connoted in the notion of growth. The second is the increase in the fund of meanings that one amasses. These meanings are bound to the augmentation of the qualities of an experience, as the qualities of an experience are circularly linked to the existing fund of meanings.

Community is both a means to and an end-in-view of growth. Communities supply the material for further growth. This happens as one increases one's human contacts and discovers that problems had are shared and that, through inquiry, shared solutions can arise. The satisfactory solution to problems had leads to enriched qualities of experience, which occasions growth. The realization that growth (in part) hinges on the shared experiences of others places community in the role of an end-in-view. Inquiry into the conditions that further growth reveals that one means to growth is the fostering of shared experiences. Inquiry sets as its goal the conditions required to have these shared experiences, and this begets community, defined as the nexus of people having and undergoing shared experiences, to the status of an end-in-view. The relation of means to ends with respect to growth and community is reciprocal: as community is the end-in-view of growth, a robust community leads to further growth and as such, growth is and becomes a further end-in-view of community.

In chapter 4, the results of the discussion on inquiry into community have shown that Dewey's theory of inquiry resists the criticism that inquiry portends an increase in top-down, bureaucratic management by an expert class beholden to capitalist and class interests. Presumably this obviates the charge that schools indoctrinate children into the ways and means of bureaucratic control, producing "docile bodies" responsive to the needs of the capitalist system, and subservient and respectful to it. This would be a hasty conclusion, for the charge still stands. This is not because Dewey thought the schools a factory for the production of complacent workers: far from it. Rather, the argument against the bureaucratic management of society has little force against the argument that the schools could conceivably exist as factories, though perhaps not for capitalist interests, but perhaps for other (collectivist or fascist or totalitarian) ones. The larger point is that schools, *by their very nature*, indoctrinate children into one or another system or way of life and that Dewey's rhetoric of community and democracy simply cloaks this uncomfortable fact. To see that this cannot be the case, it will do to discuss closely Dewey's notions of growth and community in conjunction with his statements on democracy. I shall follow up by briefly returning to Bourne's criticisms of pragmatism in the face of the war.

The most famous of Dewey's definitions of democracy comes from *Democracy and Education*.

> Since a democratic society repudiates the principle of external authority, it must find a substitute in voluntary disposition and interest; these can be created only by education. A democracy is more than a form of government; it is primarily a mode of associated living, of conjoint, communicated experience. The extension in space of the number of individuals who participate in an interest so that each has to refer his own action to that of others, and to consider the action of others to give point and direction to his own, is equivalent to the breaking down of those barriers of class, race, and national territory which kept men from perceiving the full import of their activity. (Dewey [1916] 1980, 87)

There is much going on in this passage, and it is worthwhile to dwell on certain significant claims. To begin with, Dewey tells us that democratic societies are obedient to no external authority: presumably this would include church authority and other supernatural or transcendental authorities. Further, education is the means by which "voluntary dispositions and interests" must be formed. I take it that this accords roughly with what I have been saying in regards to the noncoercive sharing of experiences and the resultant norms and interests arising thereby. Most importantly, democracies are associations of peoples. What keeps peoples together is "an interest" maintained only when one can "refer one's actions to that of others," and "consider the action of others to give point and direction to his own." It is in this way that the barriers to communication can be broken down.

There is also much here that is congruent with Dewey's (later) notion of community as set out in *The Public and Its Problems*. Communities too, are conjoint associations of peoples. What keeps peoples together in communities are also shared interests. And it is shared (conjoint communicated) experiences that denote associated living. And here, as with Dewey's position on the subject in this text, democracy is not simply a form of government. Prima facie, a democracy and a healthy, vibrant community seem coeval. There is some truth to this: for communities are the material out of which democracy is built. On this reading, democracy emerges from community: more specifically, it is *formalized* community. Though Dewey does not put the definition of democracy quite this way, nevertheless I believe that it is consistent with his overall intent. Democracy is the *formal* agreement of those within the community that the ways, means, and methods of settling disputes and solving problems are to be agreed upon such that each person's actions refer positively to (to the best of the community's ability) the community and other's actions in that community refer positively (to the best of their ability) to the person. This voluntary variation of what I see as a social contract takes the form of political institutions and laws designed to maintain the balance of actions.

Unlike some social contract theorists, though (notably Hobbes, Pufendorf, and Locke), Dewey is loath to locate the ground of subsequent political theory in natural law or nature. To do so, Dewey fears, is to give absolutist grounds (desire, reasonableness, and individualism, respectively) for maintaining the existing order. Subsequent transformation of institutions and laws in response to changing social and political conditions cannot under these circumstances occur. As Dewey puts it:

> The present predicament may be stated as follows: Democracy does involve a belief that political institutions and law be such as to take fundamental account of human nature. They must give it freer play than any non-democratic institutions. At the same time, the theory, legalistic and moralistic, about human nature that has been used to expound and justify this reliance on human nature has proved inadequate. . . . Because of lack of an adequate theory of human nature in its relations to democracy, attachment to democratic ends and methods has tended to become a matter of tradition and habit—an excellent thing as far as it goes, but when it becomes routine is easily undermined when change of conditions changes other habits. (Dewey [1938–1939] 1988, 150)

Dewey's concern about the reification of existing social structures and laws is sharpened in an ensuing paragraph.

> No matter how uniform and constant human nature is in the abstract, the conditions within which it operates have changed so greatly since political democracy was established among us, that democracy cannot

now depend upon or be expressed in political institutions alone. We cannot be certain that they and their legal accompaniments are actually democratic at the present time—for democracy is expressed in the attitudes of human beings and is measured by consequences produced in their lives. (Dewey [1938–1939] 1988, 151)

In place of a democracy predicated on previous notions of human nature, Dewey suggests that we conceive of democracy as a "humanist" enterprise. By this, Dewey means a democracy that is at once responsive to the needs and wants of the people who participate in it. Democracy is to also be a self-reflective enterprise: one that does not allow the means and procedures that function to maintain it, to become stagnant or fixed. To maintain the balance between too little political institutional involvement and too much requires vigilance on the part of the public. It requires in fine, inquiry into the problems of those members of the community with the goal of helping them to improve the conditions in which they live such that they are able to more fully participate in that community.

The fact that democracy ex hypothesi inhibits the possibility (or criticizes the reality) of political and social institutions as theoretically becoming reified, or what amounts to the same thing, as unresponsive to the needs of the community which they serve, forecloses the theoretic claim that a capitalistic, bureaucratic expert class could conceivably proffer social control under the cloak of inquiry. Inasmuch as schools are social institutions, they have the responsibility of keeping themselves flexible enough to meet the needs of the community and at the same time, solid enough to carry out this task. This seems to absolve Dewey of *consciously* placing education in the service of capitalist, fascist, or totalitarian interests, or the technical as opposed to political side of the war. It also provides a check on the capacity for overexuberance on the part of the nation: specifically a cultivated overexuberance that Dewey says is irrational, and a state of affairs that Bourne seems to want to celebrate and Dewey contain. In response to the criticism of Dewey as having little place for the irrational in his theory of inquiry, Dewey claims:

It is not the rise of the irrational as such, accordingly, that must give pause to those who would use intelligence as a director of instinct and passion. It is the deliberate cultivation of the irrational. For the cult is not spontaneous and natural; it is intentional and purposeful. . . . There are many ends, and the value of the deliberate cultivation of emotions depends upon what ends are held. Is rationality in the mass cultivated by a few in order that the attention of the many may be diverted from something which would otherwise arouse intelligent opposition? Is it being worked up to a boiling point in order that certain securities and guarantees which are hostile to the wishes of an influential class may be over-ridden, and that when the proper time comes certain schemes rendered invisible by the prevailing excitement, may be put over? Not the irrational itself, but the systematic cult of it, is, let it be repeated, the sinister thing. (Dewey [1918] 1982, 108)

But none of this quite yet absolves Dewey's talk of education as being an *unwilling* partner in this potential crime. Most educators would say, as I do, that education has been co-opted by less than democratic interests. And most educators would maintain that Dewey's talk of education has had some influence on the state of education today. The urge to draw the conclusion that, because these two claims sit in a relation to each other that therefore the relationship is a causal one (that Dewey's influence is complicit in this state of affairs) is a classic case of *post hoc ergo propter hoc*. As this argument is fallacious, the question becomes, Has this state of affairs occurred with or without the vast majority of teachers and researchers' presence? And if the answer is "without" (which I maintain), and to judge from Dewey's claims regarding community and democracy as potentially able to resist these incursions, what, specifically, of Dewey's talk of education can potentially resist? I shall take up this possibility in this next section.

The Second Claim: Inquiry, Education, and Social Control

Education is the means to growth, community, and democracy. But it must not be assumed that, because it is the means, it is therefore *merely* a means: in point of fact, according to Dewey it is both means and end. What I mean by this will be made clear at the end of this section. For now though, I wish to concentrate on the idea of education as means to these further goals. Notwithstanding his talk of growth, Dewey speaks of education in two related senses—as a means to intelligent action and as a means to the furtherance of democracy—and it will do to highlight these two senses with respect to the issue of education as in the service of capitalist (or fascist or totalitarian) interests. I shall begin with a discussion of education as a means to intelligent action. This will involve a rebuttal of the claim that intelligence is at once yoked to social control of the sort that critics suspect of Dewey: a control prompted by the interests of corporations, production facilities, financiers, and tradesmen. I follow by discussing Dewey's championing of education as democratic in the face of education as vocational. I do so because education as vocationalism is the chief means by which social control of the sort that critics are fearful of, is exerted upon children. To be democratic and to demonstrate freedom is, in Dewey's estimation, to resist just the sort of social control that Dewey's critics think he maintains.

Dewey's primary purpose of education is often said to be "growth" or "direction." While this is certainly true, what it implies is nevertheless the capacity and capability of the individual to inquire. Inquiry and intelligence are the chief attributes that education must develop. As Dewey puts it in *Democracy and Education*, "there is not adequate theoretical recognition that all which the school can or need do for pupils, so far as their minds are concerned . . . is to develop their ability to think" (Dewey [1916] 1980, 152). Inquiry is necessary because it functions as the chief instrument for the communication and decision making so important to conceiving and maintaining an efficient, democratic public. As such, the teacher's job is to provide an environment conducive to the formation and development of inquiry. She is saddled with the responsibility of directing and redirecting the child such that the child's own intellectual curiosity can take root and blossom into a fully fledged formalized and habituated inquiry. As Dewey puts it:

> While the customs and rules of adults furnish stimuli which direct as well as evoke the activities of the young, the young, after all, participate in the direction which their actions finally take. In the strict sense, nothing can be forced upon them or into them. To overlook this fact means to distort and pervert human nature. To take into account the contribution made by the existing instincts and habits of those directed is to direct them economically and wisely. Speaking accurately, all direction is but re-direction; it shifts the activities already going on into another channel. Unless one is cognizant of the energies which are already in operation, one's attempts at direction will almost surely go amiss. (Dewey [1916] 1980, 25–26)

In this manner, what counts for Dewey as social control in the classroom is assisting the child, through direction and redirection, to cultivate her own personal capacity for inquiry. This belies the possibility that Dewey thinks children are passive stores and reproducers of propaganda. In *The Sources of a Science of Education*, Dewey claims: "Control, in truth, means only an emphatic form of direction of powers, and covers the regulation gained by an individual through his own efforts quite as much as that brought about when others take the lead" (Dewey [1929–1930] 1984, 24). Social control is present in the educative process, but it is a means only, not an end. It serves to guide and direct the child's own process of inquiry such that she, once the inquiry is habitualized and developed, has the capacity to determine for herself whether or not to value or participate in certain social activities. It is a necessary means to what Dewey terms "freedom" in his last major educational work, *Experience and Edu-*

cation. Since freedom "resides in the operations of intelligent observation and judgment by which a purpose is developed, guidance given by the teacher . . . is an aid to freedom, not a restriction upon it" (Dewey [1938–1939] 1988, 46). The child participates in the direction that the teacher sets. Again, Dewey argues, "nothing can be forced upon them or into them." (Dewey [1916] 1980, 25)

In point of fact, the habits of inquiry that the child develops are her own. The experiences that help to cultivate those habits are also her own. True enough, the teacher provides opportunities for inquiry to be used, and in this way prods the inquiry to higher and more formalized operations. Nevertheless, any social control that is manifested by the teacher is that of direction and redirection. As Dewey eschews more direct means of authority in his insistence on the rejection of overt disciplinary maneuvers and the rejection of fixed dogmas, it falls to the teacher to exert some control in the name of the public interest. But again, the manner in which this control is exerted is via the assistance of the teacher in the development of the child's specific capacities of inquiry. The fundamental means of control ultimately becomes intellectual self-control through cultivation and application of inquiry. As Dewey puts it:

> The net outcome . . . is that the fundamental means of control is not personal but intellectual. It is not "moral" in the sense that a person is moved by direct personal appeal from others, important as is this method at critical junctures. It consists in the habits of *understanding*, which are set up in using objects in correspondence with others, whether by way of cooperation and assistance or rivalry and competition. (Dewey [1916] 1980, 33)

I have discussed the resistance of Dewey's notions of growth, community, and democracy to top-down, bureaucratic control by an expert class (such as legislators, administrators, policy crafters), in the previous sections. There, I suggested that education a fortiori would also be included in this resistance. I have just spoken of education as intelligent action negating the very (theoretical) possibility of the sort of social control that Dewey's critics think he proffers. Now I wish to discuss Dewey's talk of education in response to a prevailing concern of the early twentieth century: education for industry. Much is at stake in this debate. Not only is this the linchpin upon which much of the criticisms turns, but more so, education for industry is the chief mechanism for ensuring the availability of trained workers for private, commercial, or national interests. The concern is that if education remains yoked to prevailing business or state interests, the following, as Dewey maintains in *Individualism, Old and New*, results:

> Our public-school system merely turns out efficient industrial fodder and citizenship fodder in a state controlled by pecuniary industry . . . it is not

helping to solve the problem of building up a distinctive American culture; it is only aggravating the problem. That which prevents the schools
from doing their educational work freely is precisely the pressure—for
the most part indirect, to be sure—of domination by the money motif of
our economic regime. . . . Such an education is extremely one-sided; it
operates to create the specialized "business mind," and this, in turn, is
manifested in the cause of the tragic irrelevancy of prior schooling to the
controlling realities of social life. There is little preparation to induce
either hardy resistance, discriminating criticism, or the vision and desire
to direct economic forces in new channels. (Dewey [1929–1930] 1984,
102–03)

Dewey writes often about the effects of industry and corporate culture on
schooling. Many of these writings came as a result of the Smith-Hughes Act,
long discussed and ultimately passed in 1917, which declared that vocational
education receive federal support and funding.[10] Those in favor of some sort
of vocational education were saddled with the question of whether it should
be the public school system, or private schools, that undertook to train workers. Much was made of a dual system, whereby public schools would place students in one of two distinct tracks: the one academic, the other vocational.
Needless to say, businesses favored the dual system. And needless to say, Dewey
is a harsh critic of this.

Dewey's concern with the integration of industrial education into the
public schools is nowhere better represented than in his paper "Some Dangers
in the Present Movement for Industrial Education." Here, Dewey states:

Those who believe in the continued separate existence of what they are
pleased to call "the lower classes" or the "laboring classes" would natu-
rally rejoice to have schools in which these "classes" would be segregated.
And some employers of labor would doubtless rejoice to have schools
supported by public taxation supply them with additional food for their
mills. All others should be united against every proposition, in whatever
form advanced, to separate training of employees from training for citizenship, training of intelligence and character from training for narrow
industrial efficiency. (Dewey [1912–1914] 1979, 102)

The criticism of vocational education is the criticism of the creation (or
exacerbation) of class differences. Inasmuch as the exacerbation and creation
of class differences run counter to Dewey's goal of a democratic school and a
democratic community thereby, any tendency to enhance these differences is
doubtless challenged. In place of a vocational education that encourages class
divisions and tracking, Dewey recommends an education that fosters the de-

velopment of the habits of intelligence. It is in this way that children can learn to function as citizens in a democracy. Instead of emphasizing vocational education in schools, Dewey suggests that

> enthusiasm for vocational guidance should exhibit itself first in encouraging children to stay in school till they have an education which will fit them for work where there are genuine openings ahead; secondly, in guiding public opinion and activity to modify the regular school work so that it shall have a more genuine connection with social opportunities; thirdly, to provide supplementary agencies so that children when they do leave to go to work shall continue under some educational supervision that will counteract the tendency of almost any trade at the present time to arrest their further growth. (Dewey [1912–1914] 1979, 99)

The Third Claim: Democracy, Pragmatism, and Education

I now turn to the second set of criticisms: those that question the very possibility of pragmatism as being helpful to the concerns of democracy. The above subheading is suggestive of what John Stuhr might call an *ideal* version of growth in our postliberal times. That is to say, what should count as growth in our postliberal age is distinct from what counted as growth when Dewey wrote (as Dewey would no doubt have thought) and that growth is no longer tied to the conceptual play of the imagination or the dress rehearsal of ideas. Rather, it is come time to operationalize the imaginative results and heed the curtain call. Postliberal growth is the recognition that, to paraphrase Wittgenstein, we can and must, throw away our theoretical ladder. What this means for pragmatism, and indeed, the future of philosophy, is to place a moratorium on academic theorizing and get out in the streets and (so to speak), agitate for changes to our social and political institutions. Richard Rorty has in fact recommended just this in a recent publication.[11]

This seems to pose problems for Dewey's notion of inquiry. If inquiry is that aspect of experience which orders and controls our environments, as Dewey would have us believe, then inquiry is that aspect of experience which theorizes. And theory is just what is to be brought to a close in Stuhr and Rorty's estimation. If we are to take Stuhr and Rorty seriously, and abide by their conclusions, are we not placing great limits on, if not proposing an outright denial of, a role for inquiry in present and future talk of what to do with our social institutions? I answer no. For I believe that their conclusions regarding the role of inquiry, pragmatism and philosophy, now and in the future, accords well with the conclusions of this examination.

First of all, inquiry has been shown to be context bound and self-correcting. What drives inquiry is not some antecedently fixed standard, principle, or conception. Rather, it is the task at hand. And if the task at hand is to rebuild social institutions, then inquiry is to serve in that capacity. To say this is to say that the generic propositions that are developed in and through inquiry are suited for the task that inquiry undertakes. And the universal propositions, the conceptions developed through imaginative rehearsal, are universal only insofar as they yield suitable generic propositions, which can then be operationalized. A context-bound and self-correcting inquiry is not disconnected from the practical solutions that it ushers. To say so, though, may seem as if I am simply begging the question: how does the line get drawn between what is practical and what is theoretical?

Dewey of course, draws only a functional line. But it is nevertheless an important one for our purposes here. Universal conceptions or ideas, those used imaginatively to rehearse possible solutions to both real and anticipated problems, seem like the most likely candidates for the moniker "theoretical." Somewhat less likely for this moniker are generic propositions, as these must be actualized; tested out in their practical application to the problem at hand. What makes a neat distinction between theory and practice in Dewey's theory of inquiry impossible is that universal conceptions, too, are also, though indirectly, accountable to the problem at hand. For universal conceptions are only as helpful as their ability to drive generic propositions, and if generic propositions continuously fail to supply a working solution to the problem at hand, in Dewey's estimation, the universal conceptions themselves must be scrutinized and, if need be, replaced. There is no more telling account of this than in Dewey's repeated admonitions (as with Rorty) to dispense with the traditional problems of philosophy; the problems of subject and object, mind and matter or world, intellectual and sense-perceptive, and other various inhibiting dualisms. These universal conceptions of how the world and we are, are no longer useful; rather they limit the solutions of the problems of men, and, in Dewey's estimation, need to be discarded.

It would be absurd for philosophy to embrace a position free from theory. I don't believe that either Stuhr or Rorty, their rhetoric to the contrary, suggest such a path. I do think that it was unfortunate for Dewey to term philosophy "the criticism of criticisms," as he does in *Experience and Nature*. This aside, though, it is not unrealistic to say that philosophy is critical, or even to say that philosophy is a form of criticism. By this, I do not mean to exhaust all of the meanings of philosophy in its critical function, even though Dewey sometimes seems to have thought of philosophy in just this way. But I do mean to say that criticism, or what I would prefer to call inquiry, is a central function of philosophy. If I am right, philosophy-as-criticism-as-inquiry cannot do with-

out theory. Perhaps what Stuhr is advising, beyond the rejection of airy pretensions, is that pragmatism has generated enough theory, meaning conceptual
work, already, and that it is time to put the anticipated conclusions of these
thought experiments, to work. And I think that, if this is the case, then this is
absolutely correct. And by getting to work, I mean the broad distribution of its
(preliminary) findings to the general public. But I do not think that inquiry is
completed, because I do not think that inquiry can be complete until the universal and generic propositions are themselves evaluated according to both
imagined and real solutions to the problems at hand. Inquiry is unfinished even
if "theory" is tentatively completed.

Rorty advises that we stop talking about "method." But this seems an im-
possibly difficult order to fill. Rorty's contention that pragmatism can do without method can only hold if method looks something like the Cartesian quest
for certainty, something that Dewey was already at pains to do away with. Rorty
famously speaks of replacing "method" with "vocabulary," or "conversation."
But to have a conversation is to have rules for what counts as topics, the settlement of disputes, the appropriateness of speech and writing, and perhaps
most importantly, a way within the bounds of the discourse to justify, test, and
adjudicate claims: claims very often pertaining not to the rules of discourse but
to a connection between discourse and acts, behaviors, and (dare I say it)
things—what Wittgenstein would call "pointing."[12] Of course, it is possible for
inquiry to provide these without resorting to Cartesian certainties, as the last
fifty or so years of Anglo-American philosophy can attest to. So when Rorty
says that he wishes pragmatism without method, I take him to mean that he
wishes for pragmatism without Method.

What of education? Stuhr's admonition to replace talk of theory with talk
of agenda is appropriate. But it must be borne in mind that agendas do not come
ready-made. They are built up through shared experiences by conjoint, communicative, association. An agenda is agreed upon, not forced upon. While it
may be obvious to academics such as ourselves that education (and schooling)
is in dire straits and needs immediate care, it is not necessarily so with the general public. To present to the public an agenda for change as ready-made is to
substitute an imposed agenda for a real one. What hasn't taken place is the
shared experience that is the basis for any development of an agenda and this
not because of any lack of theory but of commonality. In a deeply pluralist country, such as the United States, it is extremely difficult to find a conversation that
carries across the divides of language, class, race, gender, age, geographic location, and so forth. But the conversation itself is where the work must begin.
Again, to propound or discuss practical solutions to problems that are of academic or legislative interest without engaging the public is to invite failure. If
it becomes too difficult to converse with the public on present or anticipated
problems; if it becomes too unwieldy to inquire into the many possible variables

involved in a social problem; if it becomes impossible to even *identify* a problem, owing to the lack of a shared, experienced, and conversational base, then so much the worse for democracy. Inquiry will proceed tribalistically, as it often has, and those who do not have the economic, political, linguistic, and cultural wherewithal to engage in the conversation will continue to be left out.

Ironically enough, the "problem" for education (as with all social institutions) is to foster a public that shares experiences *prior* to the identification and communication of specific problems. Inquiry too, has its limit, and this is nowhere more evident than in the Babel of conversations. Rorty notes this and advises just enough patriotism to keep conversations going.[13] But it is not evident to me that this is helpful. For, to keep patriotism going, there must be, in turn, a conversation that lasts long enough and registers enough of an impact that patriotism can take root. This is what is precisely in contention. This seems to imply an infinite regress of conversations and conditions. What must be in place before a conversation can go, what must occur before a shared experience can take root, is the will, on the part of the public, to make it so, and this is itself dependent upon prior experiences and conversations.

Another way to put this claim is that the public must volunteer to converse and be willing to share enough experiences such that a robust conversation can get underway. I say "volunteer" because, with Dewey and Rorty, I do not believe that any amount of lawful and democratic coercion beyond the usual persuasive force of reasoning will get the public to act. The sole opportunity that this reasoning has to operate fully is in the schools, at the day-care center, in family gatherings, on the television, at the movies, in the doctor's offices, on vacations—in short, in those settings where a more or less captive and impressionable audience of children is present. Schooling, if done well, has the advantage of providing opportunities for learning that cannot, whether from institutional inability or parent choice, be gotten elsewhere. Paradoxically, schools are the one area where (parent) preference is limited for the good of democratic citizenship. But this limit to preference in the schools is itself predicated upon a thriving voluntary democracy in society, and a public that freely chooses, on the basis of inquired-into problems and solutions, what is best for its members. And this is precisely what the public has been unable to manage.

The problem of social institutions, including education, is not, then, a manifestly theoretical one; it is practical. It is the question of engaging the public's attention long enough to help them to see a (real or potential) problem of others' note and design. Stripped of the heavy tools of indoctrination, fear, physical force and torture, reeducation camps, and murder, the communicative tools of those that theorize problems are extremely limited. The individuals and groups that constitute the public must voluntarily decide to, ceteris paribus, choose to see a problem of the theorists' making as a problem *simpliciter*. Aside from scrupulously conducted research and adherence to scientific community standards and ethics, the tools available to the concerned scholar and scientist are all of those found in democratic forms of inquiry: imagination, creativity, care and concern, a knack for communicating results in a nontechnical way, and perhaps most important, a good degree of circumspection and the patience to endure indifference, bewilderment, and skepticism.

Nevertheless, some indication as to which way for social institutions to go seems in order and further direction for inquiry warranted. Thus far, I have characterized the problem of inquiry's (and pragmatism's) value to democracy in theoretic terms and outcomes. One insists, rightly, that inquiry be actualized for a proper evaluation of its ability. To say this is to suggest that inquiry not only be investigated in and through real-world examples for its presence, but that impediments to inquiry be recognized and disassembled and environments, tools, and techniques favorable to inquiry be encouraged. I can frame this concern in the manner of a set of questions: Does it matter whether institutions privilege a scientistic inquiry over a nonscientistic one? Does a focus on inquiry as scientistic, or rigorously scientific, with attention to scientific objects, contexts, and problems, differ in practical consequences from an inquiry as context bound, self-correcting, and responsive to the aims of growth, community, and democracy? Indeed, does it matter whether inquiry is stressed at all? If, as I think Dewey maintains, inquiry is to be a means and a tool to solve the problems of men, and self-correcting and wedded to these three aims, then what is at stake in following inquiry down this path? And what is at stake in not doing so?

Dewey opposed any sort of education that would result in passivity, indoctrination, and dogma. These are foreclosed by Dewey's insistence that education equals growth, and that growth ex hypothesi cannot be yoked to any fixed agenda or belief. It will do to highlight again the role that education plays in fostering growth. In so doing, the stage is set for the further argument that it is (in part) inquiry that is being developed in growth, and that education, inasmuch as it implies growth, equally implies inquiry. Further, as inquiry is social, the education of the child as an individual and a social being implies equally the development of inquiry. Developing inquiry is the development of the individual such that she can participate fruitfully as a democratic being in a democratic community. Education thus becomes a necessary constituent of growth, community, and democracy, by fostering the habits of inquiry, which (again) fosters the movement of growth to community, to democracy, and back again.

Democracy is a formalized community: it is a self-determining, self-legislating, actualized community that agrees that the inquiry into social conditions and problems, and the results obtained, are to be shared. Education is (once again) the means to the development of democracy, through the fostering of inquiry by individuals, such that they can participate in the process of inquiring into the conditions and problems of the community with an eye to the formalization of solutions. Dewey nowhere makes the task of education-as-inquiry for community and for democracy more telling than in this passage from *Democracy and Education:*

> The emphasis [of the nation] must be put upon whatever binds people together in cooperative human pursuits and results, apart from geographical limitations. The secondary and provisional character of national sovereignty in respect to fuller, freer, and more fruitful association and intercourse of all human beings with one another must be instilled as a working disposition of mind. (Dewey [1916] 1980, 98)

Education results in growth, community, and democracy. Education implies growth, inasmuch as growth is the point and purpose of education and inquiry the chief tool in the service of growth. To say, with Dewey, that one is educated is to say that one is caught up in a (lifelong) process of growing. Growth requires community for its very sustenance. Community allows and provides for experiences to be shared, which in turn heightens the traits and meanings of, and satisfaction of having had, an experience. Democracy is the formalization of community, through the conscious decision to include all in, and to follow, inquiry in the ordering and controlling of community conditions and problems. This in turn results in heightened (individual) traits, meanings, and experiences. Inquiry plays a central role in all of these. It is inquiry that leads to heightened growth. And it is inquiry that leads to shared control and ordering of experiences that begets community, leading in turn to further (individual) heightened growth. And finally, it is the conscious use, on the part of the community, to formalize the mechanisms of inquiry that lead to democracy. This formalization strengthens the community, which in turn, strengthens growth. There is a strong linkage between growth, community, and democracy, whereby democracy begets community, which begets further growth, and growth leads to the desire for further growth, leading to community, leading to democracy. Driving the movement through the linkages is inquiry: inquiry provides us, through the tools of experimentation, ordering, direction, control, careful observation, and the construction of facts and objects, with the capacity to realize how to go about augmenting growth through community and democracy. It is inquiry into the conditions for further growth that leads to the notions of community and democracy. And it is education that provides for inquiry's development.

The criticism that inquiry leads to social control through the indoctrination of children is refuted by turning to Dewey's statements on growth and community on the one hand, and his statements on democracy, on the other. Far from indoctrinating children, the schools are the best social tools to pro-

mote the habits of free inquiry. How so? The development of the habits of inquiry ex hypothesi forecloses the possibility of indoctrination because inquiry
connotes the freedom of thought, on Dewey's account. When inquiry is fostered, the sort of freedom antithetical to indoctrination is equally fostered. To
educate the habits of inquiry is to educate for democracy. This is best seen in
Dewey's response to the challenge of the rank vocationalism of the schools.
Not only is class and race difference exaggerated in vocational education
(which may alone be enough to condemn it) but the habits of inquiry, so necessary for children to build up, are yoked to interests other than inquiry. And
to yoke inquiry to other interests is tantamount to indoctrination. This state
of affairs, properly speaking, is no longer inquiry. Indoctrination impedes
growth. Therefore, measures must be taken to ensure that growth can occur.
Democracy, the community as formalized, serves to maintain the possibility for
growth free (as much as possible) from conditions that would thwart it. Education is the means to the development of the habits of inquiry such that a person can learn not only how to manipulate and control the conditions that lead
to further growth, but equally share in the community of inquirers who can
help solve problems and improve conditions such that many can experience
heightened growth.

Part Four:
Educating Democracy

To say that growth, community, and democracy, together with the inquiry built
up through education that drives them, are bound up together, is to say that
these elements are indissolubly linked and that each is another's means and
end. Growth is said to be the ultimate concern of education and of inquiry.
And growth is none other than the increasing satisfaction of experience,
through the augmentation of the immediate qualities of that experience. Inquiry is the means and the tool to and for ordering and controlling the qualities of an experience such that further, satisfying experiences can arise. In part,
this is done by situating qualities in relation to each other and constructing
logical objects through these relations, temporally and causally, such that
worthwhile meanings develop. For Dewey, meanings are relations: real relations of logically constituted objects and events.[14] A fund of these objects and
events is built up. This fund serves in the present and future ordering of the
qualities of an experience. But equally, this fund of meanings is involved in the
having of present and future experiences. It is because meanings and objects
are built up such that the qualities of an experience had are attended to, selected, and result in increasingly satisfying experiences. Satisfying experiences
owing to immediate qualities therein, results in meanings built up, and mean-

ings built up help occasion further satisfying experiences. Satisfying experiences, leading to an increase in the fund of meanings, leading to further satisfying experiences, denotes growth.

In terms of the educational means that must be in place to satisfy the end that is growth, the most important is conscious, deliberate control of the child's environment (not the child) such that growth can occur. This can take many forms, from needed facilities, supplies, and other material resources, to climate control, adequate nutrition, and time for exercise and rest. The more environmental variables that are controlled, the more likely it is that the probability of a child to not be sidetracked by potential challenges to her attention, interest, and effort to the task at hand will be heightened. The more facilities and resources are available (and not necessarily state-of-the-art resources and facilities, rather the minimal facilities necessary to accomplish the task or experiment at hand), the more closely aligned will be the experiences that the student will have to those of others who have experimented before.[15] In short, the tools for the student to experiment must be in place. This seeming bit of common sense is of course endorsed by educators, Deweyan and otherwise. But to halt here, to say that these then, are the only requirement for the establishment of further and more satisfying experiences, is premature.

Growth cannot and does not occur in a vacuum. Inasmuch as human beings are social animals, and many of the conditions and problems encountered are shared, inquiry into problematic situations portends a sharing of inquiry. Equally, problems that seem insurmountable to one are readily manageable by many. By forming communities, peoples can contribute, through inquiry into problems and social conditions that heighten satisfying experiences, to growth. Growth and community are indissolubly linked. Inquiry into the conditions that foster growth leads to the conscious realization that community is the best means and tool to obtain increasingly satisfying experiences. As well, to grow implies a more fully capable human being who is able to return the results of her growth (her fund of meanings) back into the community, leading (hopefully) to the further growth of others.

Educational means that must be in place for the boundedness of growth and community include those that foster the togetherness of children representing wide variations in cultural background, race, gender, class, and geography. For one's experiences to expand, and for growth to occur, it is not enough to manipulate the natural environment with tools (though this is certainly necessary). One must also have face-to-face contact with others. The internet, mail, video conferencing, and other forms of communication with students not representative of those in the school, though they are certainly helpful, cannot replace close personal contact. The capacity for growth is stunted when classes and schoolmates resemble each other in most attributes and characteristics. For growth to occur, students must be placed together in such a way that

differences are made obvious and not minimized. This is a necessary precondition for growth: students must have at their disposal experiences and points of
view of others to see what it is that they can build in common. At a practical
level, policies that include school and classroom desegregation (including but
not limited to busing, the abandonment of tracking and ability grouping) encourage this precondition.

At some point in the history of the species, human beings began to realize that the best mechanism to ensure the continued growth of its members is
to formalize. This implies the creation of institutions and laws that support the
development of individuals to have increasingly satisfying experiences. This is
what is meant by democracy. To say that a community is democratic is to say
that it orders and controls the means and tools that lead to increasingly satisfying experiences of the individuals therein. These means and tools often take
the form of social institutions. Of course, one of these (and perhaps the most
important) is the school. The school supplies the means for the future citizen
to think. This is done by facilitating the habits of inquiry. To facilitate the
habits of inquiry is to give a student the capacity to realize his or her own
growth, as well as the growth of others in the community.

Certain means must be in place for schools to carry out this conscious
and deliberate path. Schools need to be more self-regulating: the capacity for
the individual school to develop and implement plans for the formalization of
codes of conduct that are inclusive of the varied members within—including
faculty, students, and ancillary personnel—must be promulgated. These codes,
together with curricular aims, administrative goals, and student-teacher interaction, must abide by the freedom demanded by inquiry: the freedom to pur-
sue imaginative ends and means, to try out novel scenarios and curricula, to
judge the results of inquiry with and through the participation of all parties that
have a stake in the implementation of the results.

But more is implied. Democracy within the school must mirror democracy without; that is, the school ought to attempt to resemble the community
and, indeed, the nation of which it is a part and to which its charges take their
bearings. Ours is a pluralistic (some say multicultural) nation: one that contains and even encourages differences of culture and opinion. To not recognize
this in the school and classroom setting is to establish a fundamental disconnect between society and school. Dewey's Laboratory School was at its weakest in this regard: it drew children from predominantly white, upper-middle-
class professorial families, and paid less than deserving attention to social
problems in the larger community. To ignore or downplay this disconnect is to
provide an environment that encourages the development of a truncated,
chauvinistic, and provincial view of one's community and one's self. It inhibits
the freedom that inquiry has set for itself: the freedom that is necessary to en-

sure that students can become citizens that can then turn toward the solution to the problems of men.

Inquiry functioning as such in the schools would appear (roughly) as follows: First, it would be context based, openended and self-correcting; that is, it would be amenable to transformation depending upon the context and circumstances in which it is used.[16] So for example, in the setting of a chemistry experiment, inquiry would have different aims, and different techniques and methods would be proffered than in a class on Shakespeare's sonnets. Experimentation, rather than denoting a rigidly scientific model applicable at all times and in all contexts, lends itself to the subject matter at hand.

The linkage between inquiry and growth will manifest itself in the conscious attention on the part of the teachers and administrators to the importance of increasingly satisfying experiences. What counts as a satisfying experience will not simply be the favorable stimulation of the senses—as some critics of Dewey have suggested he maintains. Rather, it will be the resolution of a problem undertaken: a closure of a situation that promotes emotional discharge and cognitive resettlement. That is, attention will be given to that inquiry which fosters the development of new meanings as well as heightening of an experience. As growth implies a bond between meanings already built up and satisfaction of an experience had, great attention to previously developed meanings of the child is paid. This entails familiarity with the child such that the teacher can become reasonably knowledgeable about the child's interests, capacities, and previous experiences—no doubt a tough requirement in today's understaffed, overstuffed classrooms. It also suggests that experimentation undergone by the child be closely scrutinized as to aims and effect. Lessons without much forethought as to their consequences are to be frowned upon.

The bond between inquiry, growth, and community insists that students having differing backgrounds and experiences be present in the school. This requires a conscious and determined effort on the part of school administrators to encourage means of bringing these children together on issues of (potentially) mutual concern. Some of these might include investigative reports by students on community issues; visitations to areas of a city or town previously not discussed or neglected; video conferencing; pen pals; internet communication, as well as others. Inventive uses of the curricula; uses that highlight that the concern of those different from ourselves as equally ours, is the best way to begin allowing students to share each other's experiences. The gold standard is of course, to have children face-to-face in the classroom when doing this. This no doubt will take a great deal of political maneuvering to accomplish, what with the trend to voluntarily resegregate schools, and the dislike of busing, particularly from those in suburban areas. Nevertheless, it must occur through community-wide consent and not legislative fiat.

Finally, for the school to resemble a democracy and for the future citizenry to develop the tools needed to construct and maintain this democracy, the schools require more self-governance than currently established. Rules from outside of the institution work to constrain the development of a formalized community—one that, by its very freedom, is able to adjust itself to the changes that take place therein. One end result of outside overgovernance is stagnation and stultification. But there is a more ominous threat to outside overgovernance, and this is the requirement that the school submit to arbitrary standards of conduct that serve to inhibit rather than promote the establishment of a diverse school body. Notwithstanding the concern of external overgovernance, undergovernance, too, must be avoided. This is particularly the case with respect to accessibility and entrance and exit requirements: in fine, legislation and oversight that maintains school segregation along the lines of race, class, gender, religious persuasion, geography, or emphasizes tests such that these become the sole or major route to entrance, promotion, or graduation, perpetuates the problem. Legislation and oversight need to be of the sort that inhibits segregation and promotes the sort of inquiry that is conducive to growth and to community: to wit, inquiry that is context based, self-correcting, and self-legislating. But (and this is the conundrum) this legislation should be formed by all community members actually and potentially involved in the changes to the community that this legislation will usher in, rather than by experts or special interests. Again, much (voluntary) political work needs to be done before these changes can occur.

I shall now list these main considerations in summary form.

1) Inquiry is to be context based and self-correcting. It requires, at a minimum, those technologies and facilities necessary to carry out the intended direction of the student's experience.

2) Growth is to be considered not only as the building-up of increasingly satisfying experiences, but also as the development of further and more robust meanings. This entails familiarity with previously developed meanings of the child, ascertained through the child's interests, capacities, and life events.

3) Community is to be fostered through the placing of students with differing socioeconomic and geographical backgrounds, races, religions, and gender, as much as possible in face-to-face proximity, or failing this, through other forms of communication with the help of technologies. This should be done with community consent rather than legislative fiat.

4) Democracy is to be fostered through increasing school self-governance, and legislation and regulation that are supportive, not prohibitive of, attempts to bring children of diverse backgrounds together and at the

same time minimize the harmful effects of an overreliance on testing, standards, and sorting as the means to judge entrance, promotion, and graduation. Again, this should be done with community consent rather than legislative fiat.

I am not claiming that these rather minimal preconditions for inquiry to flourish in the schools in such a manner that growth, community, and democracy will foment, is exhaustive: far from it. I readily concede that much, much more beyond these needs to be done. Nevertheless, the state of the schools and institutions that educate children today are such that many of these preconditions are not in place, and the capacity for inquiry to thereby take hold, and to develop the links of growth, community, and democracy, is rendered minimal. There are some schools though, that do follow, to varying degrees, Dewey's admonition that a broadly Deweyan notion of inquiry be in the service of the problems of men, and that this requires schools to reach out beyond themselves to the larger communities and society of which they are a part. These schools warrant close attention. Sadly though, this is beyond the scope of this work.

NOTES

Chapter 1. Introduction

1. Eames and Eames go on to claim that the way out of the impasse is to focus on Dewey's notion of continuity; one of Dewey's generic traits of existence as the binding force between the realism of scientific investigation and the idealism of the phenomenal turn to immediate qualities of experience. Unfortunately, as I shall show, this focus merely shifts the problem from the side of science to the side of experience. For continuity is a generic trait of existence, and therefore an immediate quality: thus the question of idealism is begged. I shall have a great deal more to say about the reading of Dewey as privileging immediate qualities in chapter 3.

2. Of course, not all readers of Dewey choose. For a number of them, there is no choice to be made, because, in their estimation, no choice is needed. Regrettably, I will only be able to allude briefly to these readers. Those that I consider strong and correct in their respective analyses of Dewey I do precisely for being able to either overcome, or better yet, sidestep completely the question of whether or not Dewey's inquiry is beholden to science or immediate experience. I count among these readers Larry Hickman, Richard Shusterman, Raymond Boisvert, and David Hildebrand.

3. Of course, most critics do not turn to the antifoundationalist arguments of Quine, Sellars, Wittgenstein, and like-minded thinkers. Certainly, the critics contemporary with Dewey had not the benefit of these later pronouncements, and very likely they would have been ignored if they did. For inasmuch as Dewey anticipates many of these later advances in empiricism, and the critics find fault with these, it is most likely that they, too, would find fault with the later advances. In one case though, the criticism of Morton White that Dewey holds to an analytic/synthetic distinction, Quine is directly invoked.

4. Dewey's notions of growth, community, and democracy, are defined somewhat differently here, than perhaps by other Dewey sympathizers and critics. I shall spend time supporting the argument as to why it is that Dewey's aims should be considered in the manner that I consider them in the chapters that follow.

5. I am thinking here of John Stuhr, particularly in his latest set of essays, entitled *Pragmatism, Postmodernism, and the Future of Philosophy*. I will have more to say about this in chapter 5.

6. No doubt, conscientious readers of Dewey are already aware of his use of the term "self-correcting" to describe a feature of inquiry. This trait has been acknowledged under the umbrella term of "experimentalism." In its broadest sense, self-correction is the willingness of the inquirer to adjust her methods to take into account the physical and behavioral changes of materials and peoples that occur as the result of inquiry into them. And this is correct, as far as it goes. What has been missing, however, is attention to the capacity for inquiry itself to "self-adjust," that is, to take the experimentalism privileged in the analysis and synthesis of material data and turn this back on itself. Though Dewey does not indulge in talk of this trait per se, it does arise. The most famous of these appearances occurs in the *Logic*. I will discuss this at more length in chapter 2. For now, I say only that this and other, invocations far from settles the matter. These do not emphasize this trait strongly enough. Nor do these dispel the many other and seemingly inconsistent statements Dewey makes on behalf of inquiry. Often, when these are invoked, they are done so only in passing.

Chapter 2. Inquiry and Science

1. Numerous Dewey scholars have taken Rorty to task for his pronouncements on Dewey's theory of inquiry and his metaphysics. A veritable cottage industry has developed out of these apologias and could easily fill several volumes. Two very recent ones come to mind. In terms of method, David Hildebrand's nicely sums up the prevailing sentiment. "Rorty's criticism—that Dewey searched for science's methodological secret, a unique 'set of rules' or 'collection of techniques'—fails to see the forest for the trees. Method is only a small part of inquiry in general. . . . What must be kept in mind, is that a 'subject matter' is not given, but taken—selected from experience. The selections that scientists make are determined by previously instituted habits, and more generally, purposes" (93). In David Hildebrand, *Beyond Realism and Antirealism: John Dewey and the Neopragmatists* (Nashville: Vanderbilt University Press, 2003). Another very recent polemic claims that "Rorty is so dismissive of metaphysics and epistemology that he hardly hides his penchant for misrepresenting Dewey's obvious connection that a pragmatic realism was both viable and worth constructing. You cannot really read Rorty for a reliable clue about Dewey's central labors" (109). Joseph Margolis, *Reinventing Pragmatism: American Philosophy at the End of the Twentieth Century* (Ithaca: Cornell University Press, 2002). I will discuss whether responses such as these pass muster further on in this and the following chapter.

2. John Shook discusses the development of Dewey's "realism" in detail

in his *Dewey's Empirical Theory of Knowledge and Reality* (Nashville: Vanderbilt University Press, 2000) See esp. 217–69. I shall return to the issue of Dewey's use of natural events in the following chapter. Suffice it to say, I do not think that the label of naive realism can be pressed too tightly onto Dewey's theory of inquiry. As I shall show, grounding the possibility of experience in "reals," whether qualitative wholes or natural events, while perhaps getting Dewey out of the representationalist trap, nevertheless still commits him to the very foundationalism that he wants to avoid. Beyond this, I avoid using the terms "realism" and "idealism" as much as possible: in my mind they make the unique contribution that Dewey provides to inquiry and to experience too dependent on older views and debates in the history of philosophy.

3. Dewey's response to Cohen will be considered here in part and as well in an upcoming chapter.

4. White specifically charges that Dewey's talk of method lent itself to political conservatism. This is so because, in privileging analytic statements or propositions, it sets itself up for (political) unchangeability.

5. White takes his bearings from Quine. In Quine's classic paper "Two Dogmas of Empiricism," Quine claims that empiricists (notably logical positivists) have separated the meaning of an object from its (extralinguistic) reference to the object. In this scenario, "Once the theory of meaning is sharply separated from the theory of reference, it is a short step to recognizing the primary business of the theory of meaning simply the synonymy of linguistic forms and the analyticity of statements: meanings themselves, as obscure intermediary entities, may well be abandoned" (14). Interestingly, Quine seems to think that Dewey is guilty of just this separation. At the end of the paper, after acknowledging Carnap's change of heart regarding the separation of meaning from extralinguistic fact, he notes that Morton White's paper of 1948 is an "effective expression of further misgivings over the distinction"(18). In W. V. O Quine, "Two Dogmas of Empiricism." In *From a Logical Point of View: Nine Logico-Philosophical Essays* (Cambridge: Harvard University Press, 1953).

6. White has not repudiated this position. In his most recent book *A Philosophy of Culture*, he claims (again) that "if the statement that connects the relation of interaction with the experience is 'ideational,' Dewey is involved in the dualism between the analytic and synthetic." Morton White, *A Philosophy of Culture: The Scope of Holistic Pragmatism* (Princeton: Princeton University Press, 2002), 40.

7. A forceful example of this concern, beyond that of Israel Scheffler, comes from R. S. Peters. He states, "Dewey actually grossly exaggerated the connection between scientific theories and everyday practical problems. But to represent scientific theories, which are some of the greatest products of the human imagination, just as aids to action, is to ignore a whole dimension of human life" R. S. Peters, *Essays on Educators* (London: George Allen and Unwin, 1981), 86.

8. Similar criticisms are made manifest by E. D. Hirsch in *The Schools We Need*. Hirsch speaks about the vast difference between Dewey and Kilpatrick and cites the Dewey biographer Robert Westbrook's statements on the subject as evidence. He also states that "the integrationist tradition, represented by Dewey . . . and others was the finest and soundest tradition of pedagogical thinking in the United States" (Hirsch 1996, 124). But the criticisms that Hirsch heaps upon certain research methods, combined with his aversion to the naturalistic, problem-solving method, betray his allegiance. Interestingly, Hirsch charges the naturalistic method with being easily pressed into service for rank utilitarian ends, and concludes that the naturalistic method is not beneficial for a democratic society. But the case can be turned against Hirsch. As Walter Feinberg has suggested, the "focused and guided learning" that Hirsch privileges has little place for the problems and concerns of the students. And the only discovery that can take place must do so within the context of the core content. The question becomes, Is this an antidemocratic means to a purportedly democratic end? See Walter Feinberg, "Educational Manifestos and the New Fundamentalism." *Educational Researcher* 26, 8 (November 1997): 33.

9. Though arguing against Dewey's theory of inquiry as being holist is not my intention, it is tempting to point out that the sort of circularity evidenced by holistic approaches to science could not happen with Dewey, as what are specifically manipulated are existential traits that are not "part of the knowledge-system." This I shall discuss more fully in the upcoming chapter.

10. No current interpreters of Dewey suspect him of swearing allegiance to *logical* positivism. Ernest Nagel recounts that, in 1931, John Dewey was approached by the philosopher Otto Neurath regarding a contribution to the *Encyclopedia of Unified Science*. Dewey did not want to contribute an article because he "did not subscrib[e] to the belief in atomic facts and propositions." Neurath had to raise his hand and swear that the logical positivists did not accept the doctrine of atomic propositions before Dewey would grant the request to write the monograph. In *Dialogue on John Dewey*, edited by Corliss Lamont (New York: Horizon, 1959), 11–12.

11. Of course, Denis Phillips also claims that Dewey and Comte shared affinities. But Phillips does not back up his claim with textual support, whereas Mounce does. Therefore, I shall concentrate on Mounce's claims only.

12. Dewey refers to this as "the common pattern of inquiry." Interestingly, John Stuhr finds this passage inimical to what he takes as the tenor of Dewey's *Logic*. As Stuhr puts it: "This general account of inquiry, this account of the general or common pattern of inquiry, readily appears to decontextualize inquiry and thus appears counter to much of the rest of the *Logic*. However, because of what Dewey does not say, it frequently is the result." (282). I would argue that, even though a general pattern of inquiry is set out in these pages,

it seems to be no more than a caution to follow an experimental approach to problem solving. The lack of attention to context in this and similar passages is not a denigration of context; rather, it is an admonition to say little else about inquiry beyond or outside of, the context in which it finds itself. As such, it seems rather meager in comparison to most other accounts of logic and of inquiry. John Stuhr, "Power/Inquiry: The Logic of Pragmatism." In *Dewey's Logical Theory: New Studies and Interpretations*, edited by E. Thomas Burke et al., 275–86. (Nashville: Vanderbilt University Press, 2002).

13. Tom Burke describes Dewey's theory of inquiry as a "corkscrew" that contrasts past and present "successful" inquiries. The general pattern that Burke acknowledges is "indeterminate situation (stimulus)—identification of problem—determination of solution—determinate situation (response)." It is the circular pattern of inquiry that secures judgment. We go back and forth through the general stages before settling on the sequence that works. In this way, Dewey's "stages of inquiry" can be said to be both general and specific: general because they are necessary for the further progress of inquiry; specific because they do not necessarily occur in the order presented, nor are they linear in the sense that one must complete the first in order to proceed to the second. This view shares affinities with Dewey's statements in the second edition of *How We Think:* that the formal steps involved in thinking (inquiring) are less important than the sequence that results in a solution to the specific problem. Tom Burke, *Dewey's New Logic: A Reply to Russell* (Chicago: University of Chicago Press, 1994), 158–59. The problem with the corkscrew description of Dewey's theory of inquiry is that it makes no allowances for the "response" to reinitiate the satisfaction of an experience had, without the corkscrew devolving into a circle. At some point, the corkscrew must return to its beginnings, even as these beginnings are themselves transformed, otherwise it becomes a species of Wilfred Sellars's "great Hegelian serpent of knowledge with its tail in its mouth" (Sellars [1956] 1997, 79).

14. Larry Hickman seems to be making a similar point when he claims, "Dewey's characterization of this overarching method—technology—is itself an idea, a complex hypothesis about the general features of inquiries that have proven successful. As an idea about the general pattern of inquiry, it has been elicited from data that include elements of the history of the technosciences, the histories of the arts, and even the histories of the protosciences that preceded the development of technoscience during the seventeenth century and the trial-and-error techniques that reach into the distant past of mankind." Larry Hickman, *Philosophical Tools for Technological Culture: Putting Pragmatism to Work* (Bloomington: Indiana University Press, 2001), 67.

15. I take it that this is David Hildebrand's argument against Richard Rorty, whom he accuses of misreading Dewey's allegiance to method. In response to Rorty's dim view of Dewey's talk of inquiry, Hildebrand says: "Dewey's

writings about science's use and refinement of intelligent methods never intended to imply that these methods were categorically unlike other methods of
inquiry. He spent a great deal more time expounding upon the source of intelligent methods, inquiry, which is generally present in human experience" David
Hildebrand, *Beyond Realism and Antirealism: John Dewey and the Neopragmatists*
(Nashville: Vanderbilt University Press, 2003), 94. When Hildebrand claims
that inquiry is the source of methods, I take him to say that specific methods are
born out of, and work within, the context of something larger and that something larger is inquiry. If this is a correct reading, then I concur.

    16. Dewey prefigures Quine in this respect: that no statement or propo-
sition, whether analytic or otherwise, is wholly a linguistic form. As Quine puts
it: "It is obvious that truth in general depends on both language and extralinguistic fact. The statement 'Brutus killed Caesar' would be false if the world
had been different in certain ways, but it would also be false if the word 'killed'
happened rather to have the sense of 'begat'. Thus one is tempted to suppose
in general that the truth of a statement is somehow analyzable into a linguistic component and a factual component. Given this supposition, it next seems
reasonable that in some statements the factual component should be null; and
these are the analytic statements. But, for all its a priori reasonableness, a
boundary between analytic and synthetic statements simply has not been
drawn. That there is such a distinction to be drawn at all is an unempirical
dogma of empiricists, a metaphysical article of faith" (38). In W. V. O Quine,
"Two Dogmas of Empiricism." In *From a Logical Point of View: Nine Logico-
Philosophical Essays* (Cambridge: Harvard University Press, 1953).

    17. In a letter to Arthur Bentley, Dewey clarifies further the nonanalytic
import of conceptions. He states, "If there is an over-use of 'conception and
conceptual,' it is probably due to what I have just indicated. I regret now that
I nowhere, as far as I recall . . . attempted a formal definition, stating just how
I was using the word. If the word 'idea' is permissible—in its idiomatic sense,
not of course, as a mental state—I think an observable meaning can be assigned
to "conception," along the line of an "idea" that has become first in use and
then in formulation a standardized rule of operations for ordering perceived
materials. . . . However, as far as usage is concerned, I realize that the word is
likely to be understood by many readers in the objectionable sense that has become traditional, so that it would have been better to have used the word much
less frequently, and then with qualifying explanations." In John Dewey, *The
Dewey-Bentley Correspondence*, edited by Sydney Ratner et al. (New York: Columbia University Press, 1964), 63.

    18. In passages such as this, Dewey (anachronistically) comes to look a
lot like W. V. O. Quine, who argued that the distinction between analytic and
synthetic statements was an empirical and pragmatic one. That is, that the
methods whereby analytic and synthetic statements are validated are not sep-

arate, rather co-eval. Quine proposes a methodology that operates to validate both sorts of statements: a pragmatic methodology that is experimental and logical. Where Dewey and Quine part ways is in the applicability of the scientific methodology for differing contexts. While Dewey believes that the experimental method is helpful in the solutions to the problems of men, Quine thinks that ethical claims cannot be validated on the basis of any scientific methodology. Also, Quine seems to think that all method devolves into the method of the physical sciences. Dewey, as I am claiming, did not share this physicalist and reductive view of method. See further, W. V. O. Quine, "Two Dogmas of Empricism," in *From a Logical Point of View: Nine Logico-Philosophical Essays* (Cambridge: Harvard University Press, 1953), 20–46. Interestingly, while White thinks Quine an improvement over Dewey's "half-rationalistic" theory of inquiry, he chides Quine for distinguishing between logical and ethical statements. See further, Morton White, A *Philosophy of Culture: The Scope of Holistic Pragmatism* (Princeton: Princeton University Press, 2002), 53.

19. This is of course, a central theme of Dewey's. As he argues in many works, the reification of existing customs and norms by virtue of their being clothed in absolute ideas contributes to the problems of men. Dewey, of course, labels the mistaking of existing social conditions for universal, natural laws the "philosophic fallacy."

20. Dewey is not averse to the benefit of the circle metaphor in detailing logic. For example, he says of propositions that "since existence is existence and facts about it are stubborn, ascertained facts serve to test the hypothesis employed: so that when there is reconception (hypothesis or theory), the material ground is provided for modification of the hypothesis. Here also is a circular movement, but it is a movement within inquiry, controlled by the operations by means of which problematic situations are resolved" (265). But Dewey also places limits on the capacity of the circle to represent all inference. Speaking of the nature of "inclusion," Dewey states: "The sense in which 'inclusion' applies to definitions and conceptions determines a different logical form. It cannot be symbolized by circles but may be symbolized appropriately by brackets or parentheses." (306), (Dewey [1938] 1986). But the problem of applying the circle metaphor to Dewey's theory of inquiry is the parallel to applying the corkscrew metaphor: in this case, there is no room for expansion of experiences or meanings because the circle admits of no openings.

21. The claim that inquiry functions in a bounded manner may seem to suggest to the reader that I am claiming Dewey an idealist. Dewey's express belief and claims regarding the existence of the external world via the presence of natural events seem to foreclose the possibility that he maintained any sort of *subjective* idealism. Nevertheless, the claim of something like Hegel's "absolute idealism" might remain. Is constituting Dewey's theory of inquiry as inextricably bound tantamount to claiming that Dewey thought of logic (or that

Dewey's logic should be thought of) as Hegel did? I answer no, because Dewey does not (and cannot) accept Hegel's thesis that structure (logic) determines content. Consider Hegel's "Inverted World" thesis in the *Phenomenology of Spirit*. "According to the rule of this inverted world what is named similarly (*das Gleichnamige*) in the first world is the not-same (*das Ungleiche*) of itself, and the not-same of the first is similarly not-same itself, or it becomes the same with itself. In determinate matters, this portends that what in the rule of the first world is sweet is sour in this inverted self-same (*Ansich*), what in the first is black is white in the latter. What, in the law of the first world, is the north pole of the magnet is, in its other, supersensible self-same" (122). There are many different interpretations of Hegel's thesis here, but what seems obvious is that, if the world was inverted, the self-same would become its opposite and its opposite the self-same. There would be no discernable difference in the *structure* of the world. This is because the logic of the world is, at the stage of imagining such a scenario, sufficiently robust to realize the strength of its own (self-conscious) structural capabilities. Now Dewey would certainly disagree with this, because for Dewey it is qualities had, and not relations, that (in part) determine what is inquired into. As Sellars nicely puts it, the self-corrective enterprise avoids the trap of "the picture of a great Hegelian serpent of knowledge with its tail in its mouth (where does it begin?)" (Sellars [1956] 1997, 79). Qualities provide the ever-changing material that is classified and related and not the converse. Inasmuch as Dewey does think that there is a real, content-full world of qualities, he cannot go all the way with Hegel and his brand of idealism. Interestingly, many if not most present-day apologists of Dewey play up his supposed realism and downplay any vestiges of his idealism. This is, in my opinion, to be lamented. His connection with Hegel and German Idealism generally, is one of his best and lasting characteristics. G. W. F. Hegel, *Phänomenologie des Geistes*. In *Werke*, edited by E. Moldenhauer and K. M. Michel (Frankfurt: Suhrkamp Verlag, 1970–1971). Translation mine.

22. Williams put the claim more forcefully further on in the book. "Purely reliabilist accounts of knowledge are attractive to many philosophers because they seem to advance the project of naturalizing epistemology. But in my view, epistemological concepts are irreducibly normative: justification involves entitlement, responsibility, and adequate grounding. Standards of responsibility and adequacy are not fixed by nature: they are fixed by us in the light of our interests, projects, and assessment of our situation. Even judgements of reliability reflect tacit presuppositions of this sort and are thus covertly normative. If naturalizing epistemology means eliminating normative content from epistemic concepts, or reducing that element to non-normative vocabulary, then epistemology cannot be naturalized." Here, Williams has in mind W. V. O. Quine and the Rorty of *The Philosophy of Nature*. In Michael Williams,

Problems of Knowledge: A Critical Introduction to Epistemology (Oxford: Oxford University Press, 2001), 255.

23. Presumably, it would be evidence of the same kind or sort that led to the original justification.

24. I use the terms "self-correcting" and "self-adjusting" over "adapting" or "self-adapting" not only because Dewey privileges the first in his own writings, but also because I believe that the latter terms underdetermine what happens in inquiry. Of adaptation, Dewey writes: "While the words 'accommodation', 'adaptation', and 'adjustment' are frequently employed as synonyms, attitudes exist that are so different that for the sake of clear thought they should be discriminated. . . . Instead of accommodating ourselves to conditions, we modify conditions so that they will be accommodated to our wants and purposes. This process may be called adapation." Now this is what inquiry does to material objects and traits, but it underdetermines the state of affairs with respect to inquiry transforming itself. For this, Dewey's notion of "adjustment" better fits the bill. Here, Dewey states: "But there are also changes to ourselves in relation to the world in which we live that are much more inclusive and deep seated. . . . Because of their scope, this modification of ourselves is enduring. It lasts through any amount of vicissitude of circumstances, internal and external. There is a composing and harmonizing of the various elements of our being such that, in spite of changes in the special conditions that surround us, these conditions are also arranged, settled, in relation to us" (Dewey [1933–1934] 1986, 11–12). For a different use of these passages, see Hans Joas, *Die Entstehung der Werte* (Frankfurt: Surkamp Verlag, 1997).

Chapter 3. Inquiry, Experience, and Growth

1. Interestingly, the focus on Dewey has been to play up the realist strains in Dewey, at the expense of the idealist ones. For example, John Shook, Joseph Margolis, and David Hildebrand have all published works claiming that Dewey was one or another variant of a realist: that Dewey not only believed that the world/objects existed outside of our knowledge of it/them, but that the source for these lay in ontological primitives, such as generic traits. The converse, on all three of these accounts, would be to admit solipsism—self-referentiality—and invite vicious circularity, thereby. The idealist menace has frightened them into claiming that traits, quales, immediate wholes, and the like are somehow more defensible than "knowns," and that this is all the proof that is needed for there to be an external world. I dispute this approach. Neither of these seems acceptable. While one clearly must object to the notion that the external world, whatever that is, outside of one's experience of it has no impact or influence on us, one must be very careful to say that there are

traits or quales of experience that are just primordial without immediately rais-ing the question of how it is that we know that, leading to the very idea of generic traits being a result of a (settled?) inquiry. To claim the first without ac-knowledging the second invites a vicious circularity; to claim the second with-out acknowledging the first is to occasion an infinite regress. It seems clear to me that Dewey is neither a "realist," nor an "idealist" in the historical sense of these terms—though I do think that naive or direct realism is suggestive of what he in part, maintains. Though Dewey attempted to defend himself from the attacks of both sides during his long struggle to get his ideas across, he suc-cumbed to the temptation to label himself on more than one occasion (usually as a realist). This got Dewey into more trouble than the labels were worth. I see no reason to place what Dewey has accomplished in one camp or another: in point of fact, Dewey's thought belongs at once to both and neither.

2. Russell argues for this position in various texts. A succinct example of his argument can be found in his response to Ernest Nagel in the Library of Liv-ing Philosophers series devoted to Russell. Here he claims: "Imagine a number of concentric spheres, all of which contain my body. Let one of these spheres be called S. Then in two worlds in which events inside S are the same, all the events in my body will be the same. Therefore, there can only be a valid infer-ence from events inside my body to events outside S, insofar as events inside S uniquely determine events outside S" (Russell [1944] in Schilpp 1971, 713).

3. Russell and Dewey had a tortuous relationship. Frequently testy to-ward each other, they could also be amazingly sympathetic and helpful. When Dewey was in Beijing in 1920, Russell was also present, stricken with pneu-monia. Dewey was at his bedside and it has been claimed that he took down Russell's will. Though the claim cannot be substantiated the presence of Dewey at Russell's bedside can. Further, Dewey lobbied on behalf of Russell in the lat-ter's attempt to secure a faculty position at the City College of New York in June 1940, though his interventions were ultimately unsuccessful owing to strong Catholic pressures in the face of Russell's *Why I Am Not a Christian*. See further, Alan Ryan, *John Dewey and the High Tide of American Liberalism* (New York: Norton, 1997).

4. Dewey responded to Russell's concerns in the final chapter of the Li-brary of Living Philosophers volume on Dewey, entitled "Experience, Knowl-edge and Value: A Rejoinder." Speaking of Russell's complaint that Dewey says little about the nature of things before they are inquired into, Dewey states: "If I have said or tried to say the tiniest bit about the 'nature of things' prior to in-quiry into them, I have not only done something completely contradictory to my own position but something that seems to me inherently flawed" (Dewey [1939–1941] 1988, 31). Dewey is clearly irritated at Russell for continuing to misunderstand him. At one point Dewey remarks of Russell's comment on Dewey's Hegelianism, that since Hegel left a permanent deposit on Dewey's

thinking, and Hegel was a holist, therefore Dewey must have used the term "situation" in a holistic sense. Dewey then suggests that Russell, logician that he is, try this little bit of logic out in another context and see if it passes muster! Dewey was not a holist in Russell's sense—he did not think that the structures of experience grounded their content. This was his express criticism of Hegel's view of knowledge.

5. This criticism has found its way into contemporary educational literature. For example, Julie Webber, writing of Dewey's theory of community, makes a similar claim when she states: "Our bad conscience is always present to make sure that we react to events in devitalizing ways. Dewey has a sort of naïveté concerning this point in the judgmental process, assuming that we are open to deciding in many ways, he argues that sense qualities are more important for determining the outcome of an event than is any psychological predisposition." Julie Webber, "Why Can't We Be Deweyan Citizens?" *Educational Theory* 51 2 (2001): 171–90, 178.

6. Rorty here follows George Santayana's complaint of *Experience and Nature*. I shall provide Dewey's response to these charges in a further chapter. Almost all Dewey scholars are dissatisfied with Rorty's seemingly cavalier approach to Dewey. In addition to T. Z. Lavine and James Gouinlock, discussed earlier, James Campbell and John Stuhr have weighed in on Rorty's reading of Dewey's metaphysics. Campbell chides Rorty for not paying attention to Dewey's statements on education and accuses Rorty of missing the central feature of Dewey's metaphysics: to wit, that philosophy is based not on aesthetics, rather ethics (181). In Campbell, "Rorty's Use of Dewey," *The Southern Journal of Philosophy* 22 (1984): 175–87. John Stuhr criticizes Rorty's approach to Dewey for misconstruing the latter's' metaphysics of experience. Stuhr argues: "Whatever else it is, Dewey's 'metaphysical' description of the generic features of experience definitely is not 'an attempt to attain an end beyond life, an escape from freedom into the atemporal.' Any careful reader must realize that this runs counter to the word and the spirit of Dewey's philosophy. Amazingly, Rorty, the self-styled philosopher of contingency, fails to recognize that Dewey's description of experience is a theory of that contingency—and anything but its denial. As a result, Rorty repeatedly announces his discovery of a condition that Dewey long ago not only recognized but described in depth. It is no surprise that Rorty's 'discovery' and conquest of a contingent philosophical New World is hardly news to its pragmatic native inhabitants" John Stuhr, "Dewey's Reconstruction of Metaphysics." *Transactions of the Charles S. Peirce Society* 28, 2 (1992): 161–76.

7. Interestingly, at the very time Rorty's essay "Dewey's Metaphysics" was published, Robert Dewey (no relation to John Dewey) came out with a book that pressed similar charges. Robert Dewey saw a contradiction between what he called John Dewey's "realism" and his "empiricism." John Dewey's realism is

encapsulated in his talk of "antecedents," meaning for John Dewey, prior experiences. John Dewey's empiricism is encapsulated in his talk of "consequents," meaning for John Dewey, future ones. Robert Dewey suggests that John Dewey "runs these two together" and that this seems a "fundamental contradiction." John Dewey is caught on the horns of a dilemma. He either emphasizes antecedents, which makes the prospect of inquiry into current problems unlikely, or consequents, which does away with historical memory. Robert Dewey's suggestion is to reject the dualism John Dewey sets up, saying that "to admit a retrospective reference in these matters does not preclude our taking a forward look to consequences when choices and predictions must be made." In *The Philosophy of John Dewey: A Critical Exposition of His Method, Metaphysics, and Theory of Knowledge* (The Hague: Martinus Nijhoff, 1977), 172–74.

8. Richard Shusterman has recently addressed the problem of generic traits. For Shusterman, Rorty's claim that Dewey used generic traits in the foundational sense of grounding all experience is faulty. Shusterman argues instead that "he [Dewey] was wrong to think that an unconscious, nondiscursive immediate quality was the necessary grounding guide or regulatory criterion of all our thinking, though he was right to insist that nondiscursive background experience influences our conscious thought. . . . Dewey's mistake is not in emphasizing the unifying quality of experience, but only in positing it as an antecedent foundational fact rather than regarding it as an end and means of reconstruction" (138). Shusterman claims that Dewey attempted to ground experience in generic traits because of the importance he attached to aesthetic satisfaction. "Why then does Dewey affirm non-discursive experience as an epistemological foundation? His real aim, I believe, was not to provide such foundations but to celebrate the importance of non-discursive immediacy. Its importance was first of all aesthetic, central to the realm of experienced value. . . . For Dewey, aesthetic satisfaction takes privilege over science, which is simply 'a handmaiden' providing the conditions for achieving such satisfaction more frequently, stably, and fully" (135–36). For Shusterman, it is not that generic traits are foundational: it is rather that their importance lies in our attention to "non-discursive immediacy" over and above control and reflection. I shall return to this claim in a further chapter. Shusterman, Richard. "Dewey on Experience: Foundation or Reconstruction?" *The Philosophical Forum* 26, 2 (Winter 1994): 127–48.

9. A section of the quote that Hirsch provides is as follows: "But [Dewey] insisted that projects must have as one of their goals the child's mastery of organized subjects. . . . [M]uch of what critics then (and now) attacked as aimless, contentless 'Deweyism' was in fact aimless, contentless 'Kilpatrickism.'" Robert Westbrook, *John Dewey and American Democracy* (Ithaca: Cornell University Press, 1991), 504f. In Hirsch, *The Schools We Need*, 122.

10. In *The Revisionists Revised: A Critique of the Radical Attack on the*

Schools, a work arising out of a publication of the national Academy of Education, Ravitch is quite eager to defend Dewey against Clarence Karier and
others, whom she believes have committed the thinker to positions that he did
not endorse. This exuberance for Dewey, though, was short-lived. Shortly
thereafter, she began what would be an increasingly critical take on the
thinker. See further Diane Ravitch, *The Revisionists Revised: A Critique of the
Radical Attack on the Schools* (New York: Basic, 1978).

11. Thomas Alexander is the most recent thinker responsible for the reading of Dewey as privileging generic traits and qualitatively immediate wholes as
primordial, and particularly the trait of continuity. Continuity is an amalgam of
rhythm and regularity, the traits added to experience by Dewey in his *Art as Experience*. Though Alexander is quick to point out that these generic traits do not
demonstrate the actuality of nonexperiential *substances*, their presence in any and
all experiences suggests that as *qualities*, they do. It is not simply that they arise
out of the interaction of a person with the world. In the case of continuity,
Alexander claims that it is "both metaphysical and regulative" (116). The claim
is that continuity exists as something both "had" and "known." But to say that
one "has" continuity seems suspiciously like claiming that continuity is there to
be 'had.' This is a claim that I shall address more fully in a further chapter. See
Thomas Alexander, *John Dewey's Theory of Art, Experience, and Nature: The Horizons of Feeling* (Albany: State University of New York Press, 1987), esp. 116–17.

12. This is also John Shook's claim. Shook claims Dewey as a "naive
realist"—a label Dewey took on for himself around 1911. For Shook, this
means that "something objectively exists independently of the mental" (245).
He claims that for Dewey "many of our ordinary noncognitive experiences of
things have never been inquired into, and hence have never received any mental reworking of their meanings. . . . Second, simply because in one context we
do experience a thing as known does not mean that in all contexts we must experience a thing as known. . . . Naïve realism rejects the ubiquity of the knowledge relation. We have many relations with things apart from knowing them"
(245–46). I shall take up this claim of Shook's further on in the chapter. John
Shook, *Dewey's Empirical Theory of Knowledge and Reality* (Nashville: Vanderbilt University Press, 2000).

13. Commenting on the relation of common sense to science, Hickman
claims: "Science grows out of common sense as its tools of inquiry become more
refined. But science is not 'final' in the sense of being the end or point of inquiry. It does not tell us how the world 'really' is in any final sense, and it is not
the paradigm for all other forms of inquiry." Larry Hickman, "Dewey's Theory
of Inquiry." In *Reading Dewey: Interpretations for a Postmodern Generation*, edited by Larry Hickman (Bloomington: Indiana University Press, 1995), 171.
This is a statement that I wholeheartedly agree with, and it will be my task in
this chapter to substantiate this claim.

14. Boisvert is alluding to an earlier criticism of Dewey by Richard Rorty. In Rorty's paper "Dewey's Metaphsyics," it is claimed that Dewey's turn to generic traits as the foundation for any experience reproduces a dualism and an ontology that Dewey, in his more sanguine moments, would want to avoid. I shall speak more of this in the upcoming section.

15. Jackson cites an older commentator of Dewey's, John E. Smith, as an example of a "scientistic" reader of Dewey (123). Jackson does not cite any of the newer literature on the subject, such as, e.g., H. O. Mounce. The full citation is John Smith, *The Spirit of American Philosophy* (New York: Oxford University Press, 1963).

16. Garrison is suspicious of any attempt to hunt for "the one right method." This is evident in Garrison's response to Barbara Stengel's *Philosophy of Education 1998* article entitled "Dewey on Method/s." Stengel argues that "the pre-eminence of method over methods finds clear expression. . . . Dewey suggests that without the method of intelligence, effective teaching is impossible; with it, even apparently inappropriate action is transformed by it" (Stengel 1999, 348). Commenting on this distinction between methods and Method, Garrison states: "Superficially, it sounds as if Stengel and Dewey are methodological monists. I have heard many otherwise competent educators accuse Dewey of methodological scientism, so I would like Stengel to restate the method of Deweyan inquiry and then distinguish it from the individual teacher's selection of particular methods of instruction" (Garrison 1999, 354). See further, Jim Garrison, "Dewey on the Virtues of Method/s." In Stengel, *Philosophy of Education 1998*, edited by Steven Tozer, 356–58. (Urbana: Philosophy of Education Society, 1999), 354.

17. Richard Shusterman is largely successful in his attempt at the quandary. Shusterman uses the language of habit, as opposed to meaning, but the effect, I think, is the same. For example, in *Pragmatist Aesthetics*, commenting on Dewey, Shusterman says of the relation of intelligence to perception that "for most of the selection involved in our ordinary acts of perception and understanding is done automatically and unconsciously (yet still intelligently and not mechanically) on the basis of intelligent habits, without any reflection or deliberation at all" (PA, 124). Shusterman, Richard. *Pragmatist Aesthetics: Living Beauty. Re-thinking Art*, 2nd edition. (Boston: Rowan and Littlefield, 2000). Raymond Boisvert's response is to choose "events" over traits. Events have what Boisvert calls the "dimensions of the real." These are interaction, complexity, temporality, and irreducibility. But this seems also to simply push the problem up a level. For instead of having generic traits that are primordial, we now have events with these qualities that are primordial. Shusterman's is the better solution by far.

18. In *Experience and Nature*, Dewey defines meanings as relations inhering between (cognized) objects and events. He also calls these "ideas."

Meanings, as Dewey puts it, are always "meanings of" (Dewey [1925] 1981, 219). Here, Dewey claims that objects do not have meaning on the face of them: meanings may become aesthetic, or moral, or intellectual. "The idea that meanings are originally floating and esthetic and become intellectual, or practical and cognitive, by a conjunction of happy accidents, puts the cart before the horse. Its element of truth is that there is a genuine distinction between having a meaning and using it; the element of falsity is in supposing that meanings, ideas, are first had and afterwards used" (Dewey [1925] 1981, 220).

19. This reading of experience and meaning is analogous to the reading of habit that Dewey provides in *Human Nature and Conduct*. Habits do not transform unless some situation, some problem, occurs that cannot be solved or dealt with by the organism's existing stock of habits. When this situation occurs, the habit is reconstructed and a new habit emerges out of the old. The suggestion here is that meanings act in a manner akin to habits: they are brought to bear on experiences in such a way that experiences are given meaning. When a consummatory experience occurs, new meanings are formed. But these new meanings do not exist ab initio. Rather, they rely (much like reconstructed habits) on older meanings for their very meaning.

20. The reader will no doubt note the seeming affinity that this reading of Dewey shares with the empiricist reading of "sense-qualia" as primordial in a reflective act. To say that qualities are real and are "sensed" is to say that these are "had" irrespective of cognition, reflection, language, or one or another second-order activity. Phenomenalists, though they posit sense perceptions as known, unlike Dewey, quite happily claim that sense qualia exist only within our perception of them. Direct realists think somewhat differently with respect to the traits or quales of an experience. Direct realists claim that there are immediate qualities that are had. The problematic claim arises when cognition is said to supervene upon these already had qualities. This is to disconnect cognition from the qualities as such. It is, to use a familiar Deweyan notion, creating a dualism where one does not exist, and, if Dewey is read this way, would seem to saddle him to a strange variant of Wilfred Sellars's "myth of the given"; in this case, the given as traits, quales, wholes, and the like. The myth of the given has been heavily criticized since the time of Kant and Hegel, and is most notably present in such works as Sellars's *Empiricism and the Philosophy of Mind* and John McDowell's great modern-day criticism of sense empiricism, *Mind and World* (Cambridge: Harvard University Press, 1994), esp. lecture 2, "The Unboundedness of the Conceptual."

Needless to say, those apologists that play up the immediacy of experience at the expense of inquiry serve as well to play up the realist reading of Dewey. For example, David Hildebrand, a cautious reader of Dewey, supports this reading of Dewey, as he rescues Dewey from Rorty's misreadings of Dewey's generic traits. "Dewey's pragmatism can make that distinction [between language and nonlanguage] in part because he has not deligitimated all meta-physical enterprises but has instead devised one in which notions like 'experi-ence,' 'generic traits,' and 'antecedent objects' may be invoked and used with-out necessarily being hypostatized in the process." Unfortunately, as I have shown, Dewey does at times make generic traits and quales of experience seem primordial. Without due attention to this, Hildebrand comes close to begging the question. Hildebrand, however, is on to something. An earlier statement in regard to the charge that nothing but the immediate is real has Hildebrand responding: "As a brief illustration, consider the opening melody of Beethoven's Fifth Symphony. If one isolates a single interval, that interval still has a tex-ture, a grain. But re-place that interval in a sequence with different antecedents and consequents, and qualitative elements of that interval change. What this shows is that our experience of the 'immediate' qualities of the interval depends heavily on something which is never instantaneous, the context" (85). This is Hildebrand's best statement on the subject, and fully in line with what Dewey has to say in response to Santayana. Unfortunately, in responding to Rorty's charges, Hildebrand's defense is to claim that "Though generic traits of exis-tence may be irreducible and ubiquitous, they are not intuited or deduced and do not provide the foundations of certainty long sought after by epistemology. They are discovered by empirical inquiry as generic and irreducible, and be-yond that we cannot go" (117). This gets Dewey out of the trap of phenome-nalism (which never seemed a problem for Dewey): But even if this is the case, are we not back to the dualism of immediacy and inquiry, and the question of foundationalism that is so disconcerting? Does it matter whether traits are in-tuited or deduced, or whether they just are real? Is this not foundationalism by other means? Hildebrand's first instinct—to bind generic traits in a larger con-text of which inquiry plays a decided part—seems best, and avoids the dualism trap. David Hildebrand, *Beyond Realism and Antirealism: John Dewey and the Neopragmatists* (Nashville: Vanderbilt University Press, 2003).

21. Hildebrand quite rightly points out that it is Dewey's seeming alle-giance to industrialism and capitalism that weighs most heavily in Santayana's claim of what foreground it is that dominates in Dewey's talk of experience. Regardless of Santayana's political allusions, it is also the case that he is charg-ing Dewey with placing immediate experience in the position of fundamental. David Hildebrand, *Beyond Realism and Antirealism: John Dewey and the Neo-pragmatists* (Nashville: Vanderbilt University Press, 2003), esp. 77–80.

22. Hildebrand comes close to this view when he states: "Inquiry drives metaphysics because through inquiry metaphysics is furnished with its initial objects, and inquiry permanently retains the right of revision. Metaphysics' challenge is to depict "life experience" without lionizing it, that is, without se-lectively emphasizing only those aspects we value, such as stability or certainty, and then positing them as the veritas entis. If life contains both the precarious

and the stable, our metaphysical accounts must reflect that. Theoretically driven starting points yield metaphysical accounts that misrepresent experience, and while such speculative results are expected of idealisms, realists are supposed to be empirical, about the existences we encounter." David Hildebrand, *Beyond Realism and Antirealism: John Dewey and the Neopragmatists* (Nashville: Vanderbilt University Press, 2003), 74.

23. John Shook nicely encapsulates the difference between Russell and Dewey on this matter. He says: "Similarly, the sense-data epistemology of Bertrand Russell, by taking perceptions to be instances of knowledge and making them the logical ground for all other kinds of knowledge, was untenable for Dewey. . . . Dewey responds to Russell by arguing that the category of internal mental states cannot possess meaning except where contrasted with a category of external things. There is no logical way to establish the existence of momentary knowing perceptions without assuming the existence of external things standing in various natural relations to the perception." John Shook, *Dewey's Empirical Theory of Knowledge and Reality* (Nashville: Vanderbilt University Press, 2000), 244.

24. Dewey is making a point that Hegel once made. Hegel, in his 1804–1805 "Logic," treats of syllogisms similarly. For example, Hegel tackles the problem of the invalidity of the syllogism, "Socrates is white, white is a color, therefore Socrates is a color." The suggestion is that what counts as a valid syllogism cannot rely solely on the structure internal to the logic of the syllogism. It must also depend on the material conditions of the concept. Interestingly, by the time Hegel writes the *Phenomenology*, this position is all but abandoned and structure is made to surpass matter. G. W. F. Hegel, *Jenaer Systementwürfe II Logik, Metaphysik, Naturphilosophie*. In *Werke*, edited by E. Moldenhauer and K. M. Michel (Frankfurt: Suhrkamp Verlag, 1970–1971), 371.

25. As I understand it, this would apply equally to what Dewey called between 1911 and 1917 "naïve realism," the view that "perceptions of things are natural events on an ontological par with all of nature. As natural events they in themselves are not cases of knowledge, although they have a central role to play in the knowledge process" (230–31). John Shook, *Dewey's Empirical Theory of Knowledge and Reality* (Nashville: Vanderbilt University Press, 2000). Though Dewey dropped the label "naïve realism," his stance on experience throughout the later years of his writing leaves little doubt that he clung to the notion that natural events are immediately "had," and that this "having" is fundamental for further knowledge. This view of realism, it seems, Williams would be comfortable with, providing that it avoids the foundationalist trap of having the immediate whole of an experience as an ultimate source of further inquiry.

26. One might be tempted to conclude, on the basis of this statement, that Dewey's talk of growth is too individualistic: little seems to be said here

about the role of others, of communities, of society, in the formation of growth. I urge the reader to turn to chapter 4 for a comprehensive response to this seeming problem. For, as I shall soon claim, growth depends upon the community of others.

Chapter 4. Inquiry, Growth, and Community

1. Karier is not the only reader of Dewey that takes the position that Dewey was right about pedagogy, while his followers were wrong. A number of other readers read the situation this way. Diane Ravitch and E. D. Hirsch also make this claim.

2. The sea change in Karier's estimation of Dewey is remarkable. The circumstances surrounding it are fuzzy; nevertheless, several pivotal events happened in the ensuing years. In Vietnam, Operations Rolling Thunder and Linebacker, two of the most extensive bombings ever conducted in the history of battle, had occurred. As well, the Mai Lai massacre, in which hundreds of Vietnamese peasants were slaughtered, was broadcast to the nation's horror. Finally, the crushing of the student uprisings across campuses and the Kent State shootings, together with the Democratic National Convention protest and subsequent riots, had taken place. The suggestion here is that a confluence of unsavory events in which bureaucratic and corporate America participated, helped Karier to form an opinion that progressivism, and particularly Dewey's leadership in it, was of a piece with the regulative state of the following generation. As well, certain of Dewey's students, while maintaining the pragmatist label, took part in the CIA-sponsored Committee for Cultural Freedom. Sidney Hook was in fact the first president of this organization. Though he was critical of Sen. Joseph McCarthy for the Senate Subcommittee's raucous investigations, this was not because he thought the cause unjust; rather because he felt that these sorts of investigations should best be left to experts to judge. See further, Christopher Lasch, "The Cultural Cold War." In *Towards a New Past*, edited by Barton J. Bernstein (New York: Pantheon, 1968).

3. Hogan and Karier's criticisms of Dewey involve his response to a grievance, filed by representatives of the Local 5 teachers union over the potential splintering of two left-wing segments. The committee convened to address the potential split and to form guidelines for the behavior of members. Dewey was the chairman of the committee. The committee voted to enact an elected assembly of officials from the union to "moderate the use of disruptive tactics and bickering procedures that tend to disgust large numbers of members" (342). More ominously, the committee voted to create a statute that gave the chair of the committee "the power to suspend from any meeting any member guilty of improper conduct at that meeting" (343). Further, "Any member or group of members spreading false or libelous statements or charges against

any other member or group of members, using obstructive tactics, or showing repeated insubordination to the Chairman at meetings, may be suspended, after a hearing, by the Executive board for a period not exceeding six months" (343). But suspension orders were somehow not communicated to the president of the teachers union. As a consequence, the left-wing segments were not successfully quashed and several more years of conflict ensued. (Dewey [1933–1934] 1986). Alan Ryan calls this episode "a depressing and ultimately unsuccessful business." Alan Ryan, *John Dewey and the High Tide of American Liberalism* (New York: Norton, 1997), 297. I shall not address this issue further, as it seems an interminable debate is underway between the protractors and detractors of Dewey. But it seems to me that no theory of (public) inquiry can determine all of the applications to which inquiry is put without being itself authoritarian. Dewey's theory of inquiry may have failed in this situation. But it can self-transform, whereas other theories of inquiry cannot. This is the benefit of a self-correcting theory of inquiry. Alan Ryan makes this point nicely. He says: "Connecting philosophy and democracy is no small task. Democracy and Education spelled out its case with Plato's defence of rule by Guardians and Rousseau's insistence that we must protect young Emile from a society that has been corrupted by the growth of the arts and sciences firmly in view. The entire book was a response to them." Alan Ryan, "Deweyan Pragmatism and American Education." In *Philosophers on Education: New Historical Perspectives*, edited by Amelie Oksenberg Rorty (London: Routledge, 1998), 407.

4. John Patrick Diggins is professor of history at the City University of New York. His writing covers a wide range of subjects, though all of it is rooted in the question of the viability of democracy. He shares Henry Adams and Max Weber's cynicism regarding the impossibility of dismantling social institutions and political patronage and he is critical of what he sees as pragmatist attempts at community building and consensus formation. Though he certainly maintains that he is a democrat, he does not think that democracy can exist without a strong foundation that is itself rooted in knowledge derived from the past. He does believe that the public can only come together if the precondition of a normative "firmament" that lends authority to community choices is present.

5. Walter Feinberg has an early variation of Diggins's chief theme. Feinberg has this to say about Dewey's method. "It is more than obvious that Dewey did not desire that his method be interpreted in a narrow way, he did not see it as merely a means to already pre-established ends, but rather as a way to re-evaluate old ends and to create new ones. Yet even if we do accept this interpretation, the question remains whether the method, as Dewey sees it, might not rest upon certain value assumptions which are themselves unquestioned and absolute. What evidence could intelligence possibly yield which would lead Dewey to give up democracy and community as values?" (240). Feinberg argues that Dewey must have a metaphysical concept behind his talk of method

to ground the possibility of justification. As Feinberg puts it: "As much as Dewey would have preferred to escape metaphysical concepts and thereby maintain a completely biological model of man and values, his affirmation of community must rest upon those concepts. Although intelligence 'properly directed' does aid community, it does not justify it. . . . Intelligence alone . . . guarantees nothing except a keen assessment will be made towards any particular goal or for any particular association of human beings and if such a direction is desired, then it requires a leap beyond biology into metaphysics." Walter Feinberg, "The Conflict between Intelligence and Community in Dewey's Educational Philosophy." *Educational Theory* 19, 4 (1969): 236–48, 240. I suspect that the metaphysics that Feinberg suggests Dewey has is similar to the metaphysics of generic traits that Garrison, Alexander, and Boisvert make much of, and Rorty laments.

6. David Fott has a variant of Diggins's charge. Speaking of Dewey's seemingly dogmatic adherence to scientific method and the perils that this causes for Dewey's liberalism—the perils of refusing to consider a religious or metaphysical notion of truth—Fott says: "Dewey's claims that science is no longer desirous of finding ultimate causes and that the human mind has a mechanism seem to drift forward or even reflect an unintentional metaphysical materialism. He [Dewey] wants to subscribe to a scientific method without adopting the philosophical positions that often accompany it; but it appears he is unable to do so. Perhaps he is simply slipping into unwarranted speculation; or perhaps something in him sees a need to consider those ultimate questions that he claims we can and should leave behind. If I am correct here, this teaches us that ultimate questions are not so easily avoided as Dewey believes or as we often think." David Fott, *John Dewey: America's Philosopher of Democracy* (London: Rowman and Littlefield, 1998), 140.

7. Stuhr goes on to say, "These problems are avoided if one sees the impact of cultural conditions on inquiry in a different way—not as distorting or blocking inquiry, but as constituting and determining it in specific and different ways in specific and different contexts" (Stuhr in Burke et al. 2002, 281).

8. The history of debate regarding the place of the public in choosing and effecting change goes back to an earlier work, written in 1922 by Walter Lippmann, entitled *The Phantom Public*. In this work, Lippmann pushed for an expert society predicated upon the impossibility of the public to organize in a fashion capable of addressing its very own problems. To the extent that Dewey thinks the public splintered and uncommunicative, he agrees with Lipmann. However, he disputes that experts should have the lion's share of the role in leading the public. Rather, he feels that the public should, with the tools of inquiry, lead itself, using experts to gather factual data that can then be judged as to consequences for associated living. See Walter Lipmann, *The Phantom Public* (New York: Macmillan, 1925). For further discussion, see Robert West-

brook, *John Dewey and American Democracy* (Ithaca: Cornell University Press, 1991), 300–18. Alan Ryan, *John Dewey and the High Tide of American Liberalism* (New York: Norton, 1997), 216–17. Michael Eldridge, *Transforming Experience: John Dewey's Cultural Instrumentalism* (Nashville: Vanderbilt University Press, 1998), 76–78.

9. This does not preclude the possibility (indeed, the likelihood) that some problems will remain unsolvable. One can only surmise that inquiry can perform the impossible on the mistaken view that Dewey thought as well. But he does not. He simply (re)affirms that the experimental method is the best tool that we have.

10. The concern is also Aaron Schutz and John Stuhr's. See chapter 1 for the details of these concerns. For Schutz, the only solution to the dilemma of the failure of progressivism to manage this problem (Schutz deals with the institution of education) is the abandonment of the Progressivist ideal that we can enlighten peoples sufficiently such that they can enact through the public, their freedoms. For Stuhr, (as with myself) the way inquiry is to be looked upon, contra certain statements of Dewey's, is to be self-correcting.

11. Alphonso D'amico says of Dewey's notion of growth that "if there is some difficulty with Dewey's theory, the most sensible charge would be that his criteria for distinguishing between educative and miseducative experiences are either wrong or too ambiguous" (37). He goes on to claim that growth be tied to individuality, which in turn, is "basically the development of one's ability to relate means and ends, to see the interconnections among social forces, and to foresee the consequences of some course of action" (38). This is true, as it goes, but it underdetermines growth. The notion of growth as increasingly satisfying experiences through heightened qualities of generic traits, cannot, as the experientialist interpreters of Dewey have shown, be glossed over. Any "educational" growth seems to require both Damico's and the experientialists's sense of growth to be complete. Alphonso D'amico, *Individuality and Community: The Social and Political Thought of John Dewey* (Gainsville: University of Florida Press, 1978).

12. Dewey's pronouncements on the shortcomings of monopoly capitalism and laissez-faire economics are famous. The question is often asked: What sort of political theory does Dewey thereby, embrace? Alan Ryan considers Dewey closely allied with "guild socialism." Alan Ryan, *John Dewey and the High Tide of American Liberalism* (New York: Norton, 1997), 312. Robert Westbrook considers Dewey a "social democrat." Robert Westbrook, *John Dewey and American Democracy* (Ithaca: Cornell University Press, 1991), 431. Longtime acquaintances and friends of Dewey's also had trouble pigeonholing him. For example, Sidney Hook, longtime proponent and expositor of Dewey, claimed, "it requires no exegesis whatsoever to show that Dewey's present position is one that differs from democratic socialism only in name." Sidney

Hook, *John Dewey: An Intellectual Portrait* (New York: John Day, 1939), 161. Perhaps Dewey himself was uncertain. Nevertheless, there are clues to guide the interpreter. As Dewey became increasingly concerned with the plight of the less fortunate with his advancing age, it will do to quote Dewey from a later text. In *Individualism Old and New,* Dewey says: "In a society so rapidly becoming corporate, there is need of associated thought to take account of the realities of the situation and to frame policies in the social interest. Only then can organized action in behalf of the social interest be made a reality. We are in for some kind of socialism, cal it by whatever name we please, and no matter what it will be called when it is realized" (Dewey [1929–1930] 1984, 98). It is interesting to speculate on what Dewey's opinion of late capitalism would be, but certainly he would dislike the neoliberal return to a prewelfare-state America, and he would be most unhappy, I think, with the tendency toward preemptive strikes on other nations.

13. It would be very interesting to see how Dewey would respond to the demands of individuals and groups for exit strategies from mandatory public schooling, property taxation, and other so-called essential citizenship requirements, as well as attendance and financial support of private schools, vouchers, etc. My guess is that Dewey, inasmuch as he did not criticize the presence of private schools during his many years of commenting on the state of education, would not be inherently critical of them. As to the desire to "opt out" of public schooling, my sense is that Dewey would have qualms with this. He would particularly lament the lack of future experiences so necessary for the child to become a citizen that he would feel a consequence of being removed from the public school setting. In the case of vouchers, I cannot see Dewey agreeing with thus unless the funds were to come from other than those set aside for public schooling. I can't conceive of this happening, though.

14. In fact, Dewey asked William Rainey Harper, the president of the University of Chicago, for the Department of Pedagogy to be separate, with its own faculty, budget, and course listings. See Robert Westbrook, *John Dewey and American Democracy* (Ithaca: Cornell University Press, 1991), 95.

15. Mayhew and Edwards document several cases in which this was necessary. One example of this concerns the eleven-year-olds' discussion of European history and specifically, their inability to "express in written form what they talked about with such evident pleasure." "Time was given daily for each child to develop skill in formulating clearly and correctly and in written form their knowledge of the English village community. There were drill lessons in spelling, writing, and those language forms which they were unable to use because they were unfamiliar." Anna Camp Edwards and Katherine Camp Mayhew, *The Dewey School* (New York: Atherton, 1938, 189). Contrary to popular belief, the Laboratory School did use "rote" methods to instruct the children. But these were used judiciously and as a means to get the students to

appreciate the material studied, and not for the simple sake of learning a pre-determined skill.

16. The rest of this bibliographic material comes from George Dyk-huizen, *The Life and Mind of John Dewey* (Carbondale: Southern Illinois University Press, 1973), 99–115.

17. Mayhew and Edwards also report that further integration of social oc-cupations into the curriculum was put forth in the second year of the school's existence. Commenting on this, Lauren Tanner says: "The portrayal of Dewey's pedagogical theory as virtually complete and unchanged not only is inaccurate but ignores the significant contributions made by teachers, supervisors, and graduate students to its development. Dewy owed them a debt that he would continue to acknowledge. . . . Theory development in education is—or should be—a collaborative affair" (41). Tanner is surely correct. Laurel Tanner, *Dewey's Laboratory School: Lessons for Today* (New York: Teacher's College Press, 1997).

18. Lauren Tanner devotes a number of pages to discussing Dewey's de-velopmental stages in her book *The Dewey School: Lessons for Today*. She does a fine job of pointing out the intrinsic corelation of physiologic development and intellectual development. However, nothing is said of what counts as a sat-isfying experience. Presumably, this would be just the acquisition of skills and habits leading to further and better doings and undergoings. But this is not made clear. Laurel Tanner, *Dewey's Laboratory School: Lessons for Today* (New York: Teacher's College Press, 1997), 138–46. Arthur Wirth fares no better, here. Though he has a complete chapter on growth in his book, very little is mentioned about the relationship between growth and experience: the em-phasis is rather on physiology and intellect. Arthur Wirth, *John Dewey as Ed-ucator: His Design for Work in Education (1894–1904)* (New York: Wiley, 1966), 102–18.

19. Dewey makes a great number of rhetorically laden statements on the importance of the school to social life in his early works. Perhaps the greatest of these is found in his famous "My Pedagogic Creed." Here he claims, "I be-lieve it is the business of every one interested in education to insist upon the school as the primary and most effective interest of social progress and reform in order that society may be awakened to realize what the school stands for, and aroused to the necessity of endowing the educator with sufficient equip-ment properly to perform his task." John Dewey, "My Pedagogic Creed." In *John Dewey: The Early Works, 1882–1898*. Vol. 5: 1895–1898, 84–95, edited by Jo Ann Boydston (Carbondale: Southern Illinois University Press, 1972), 94.

20. Any celebration of the success of the Laboratory School must be tem-pered by a qualification: the Laboratory School, though able to briefly engage all of the students in the activity of construction, nevertheless did not engage directly in the social problems of the urban poor in Chicago. That the Labora-tory School chose not to bridge the gap between the principles of inquiry,

growth, and society, and the society of which it was a part, though, is not a sufficient criticism of its worth. In addition to the claims of Diggins and Schutz, other, more sympathetic readers of Dewey have drawn conclusions that suggest that the school somehow failed in this capacity. Mayhew and Edwards first broach the subject of the shortcomings of the Laboratory School. As they put it: "One reason for the measurable success of the experiment lay in the choice of subject matter which was genuine and important—the activities fundamental to the art of living. However, thirty years ago as now, the implications of such a social philosophy meant isolation and conflict with the larger society for those who went out of its doors. In such a school intelligent choices had come to mean social choices which were also moral choices. Attitudes had been cooperative in spirit; individual ideals and interests had tended largely toward alignment with those of the school society. Now as then, society brings both shock and conflict to a young person thus trained, even if he be forewarned. His attempts to use intelligent action for social purposes are thwarted and balked by the competitive antisocial spirit and dominant selfishness in society as it is." Anna Camp Edwards and Katherine Camp Mayhew, *The Dewey School* (New York: Atherton, 1965), 189. Robert Westbrook makes a similar claim in *John Dewey and American Democracy* (Ithaca: Cornell University Press, 1991), 108–109. The authors overstate the case: the young person in question would certainly have a difficult time approaching the public at large with a predetermined set of principles to expound: but this is not how Dewey envisioned inquiry as transpiring. In Dewey's (later?) estimation, it is shared problems that occasion inquiries, which occasion solutions, which bring people further together. Inquiry is a ground-up affair. It is only by one person, one group, and one problem at a time, that inquiry can address, and that people can come together over. The Laboratory School's greatest achievement is to show that there is a means to obtain further, satisfying experiences and that these experiences can be, and often are, shared. The sharing of experiences leads to community formation, which leads back to further growth. The answers to the questions of how growth and community can be fostered, arising from the Laboratory School, do not indicate how it is that the solution (the development of the tools of experimentation, of inquiry) is to be disseminated beyond the general advocating of other schools to take up this task. But this advocacy is nothing beyond an urging to investigate what would happen if inquiry were to be developed along the lines that Dewey imagines, since Dewey characteristically rules out the imposition of the principles arising from one context and one school, on another. Ultimately, the deliberation and subsequent acceptance of any particular method or means does not rest with Dewey, and he would say so: This is a matter to be inquired into and decided upon by the public.

21. I am thinking here of the many instances when the students had to pause to learn by rote in order to progress in the activity. One example con-

cerns the need for the older students to have an appreciation of French, German, and Latin for the purposes of reading and contextualizing medieval and renaissance poetry. Problems of syntax and grammar were stressed. Anna Camp Edwards and Katherine Camp Mayhew, *The Dewey School* (New York: Atherton, 1965), 354.

Chapter 5. Inquiry, Growth, Community, and Democracy

1. This school was lauded as a result of a visit that Bourne made in 1915. Interestingly, John Dewey and his daughter Evelyn visited the Gary School and were to write about it at length in their shared *Schools of Tomorrow*. Unfortunately for Bourne, rumors began to circulate that Wirt was misleading scholars and journalists about the achievements of his students and the adminstration of the school. Things came to a head in 1916: Wirt was under fire for attempting to "vocationalize" immigrant students in his newly opened public school in Brooklyn, New York. Labor unions and others called for an investigation, which was undertaken by Abraham Flexner in 1918. Flexner, in recalling the investigation, concluded that "it was pointed out that the school system consisted not only of a few modern buildings but of a great many unsatisfactory makeshifts; that administration was hopelessly confused and inadequate; that the so-called duplicate scheme, by which school facilities could be kept in constant use, was far from being either universal in the town or effective where it was in use; that supervision was so crude that it was impossible to speak of the system in general terms; that there was practically no bookkeeping, so that it was absurd to claim that the system was inexpensive." Abraham Flexner, *I Remember: The Autobiography of Abraham Flexner* (New York: Simon and Schuster, 1940), 255.

2. This historical detail comes from Robert Westbrook, *John Dewey and American Democracy* (Ithaca: Cornell University Press, 1991), 202–12, and Thomas Dalton, *Becoming John Dewey: Dilemmas of a Philosopher and Naturalist* (Bloomington: Indiana University Press, 2002), 106–13). Westbrook takes Dewey to task for trivializing the stakes of the debate. As he puts it: "Faced with the facts of domestic repression, Dewey reached for very wistful explanations and dismissed out of hand any suggestion of an 'organic' connection between war and intolerance. . . . None of Dewey's reservations led him to give Bourne's criticism the serious attention it demanded" (212). Nevertheless, Westbrook has little truck with many of Dewey's left-leaning critics of his war talk. "The consistent ideological elements in Dewey's thinking about issues of war and peace are slighted in the substantial literature on his activism in these years, a literature that focuses on the merits of the shifting political commitments he made in the service of this world view. . . . Dewey's less sympathetic critics on the left have echoed Bourne's attack on him, but have often over-

looked the in-house, Deweyan nature of much of Bourne's critique and the extent to which Dewey's postwar writings and activism constituted, in effect, a concession to Bourne's arguments. Focusing on Dewey's most short sighted efforts to find the means of action appropriate to the creation of a democratic world, they have ignored the radicalism that animated these efforts" (196). Westbrook then goes on to mention directly Karier's article "Making the World Safe for Democracy: An Historical Critique of John Dewey's Pragmatic Liberal Philosophy in the Welfare State," *Educational Theory* 27, 1 (1977): 12–47.

3. The term "postliberal" is John Stuhr's, and it refers to the present political state of affairs. Stuhr claims that we are postliberal because we no longer have a unified notion such as "growth" in mind.

4. Joseph Margolis has also questioned the role and scope of recent Anglo-American philosophy. Unlike Stuhr and Rorty though, he is more sanguine about the prospects of philosophy having something useful to say or do. He is particularly critical of Rorty's reading of Dewey and generally critical of Rorty and Putnam's attempts to carve out a new pragmatism from the old. For Margolis, whatever defects classic pragmatism had, it was far superior (philosophically) to what passes for pragmatism today. Equally, it is superior to much analytic and postanalytic philosophy. What Margolis wants is for Anglo-American philosophy to get beyond the false issues that drive the new pragmatism, review and rethink classic pragmatism's achievements through non-neopragmatic lenses, and resist the urge to remain in the grip of Cartesian thought. "I foresee that a good part of our century will spend itself in the old *agon*, though among new champions. . . . The pragmatists have little more than their original intuition to rely on, namely, that whatever is paradigmatic of the human in thought and action remains *sui generis*, however continuous it must be with the biological world from which (we concede) it must have emerged" (160). Margolis is not as skeptical as either Stuhr or Rorty: he believes that if we get past our fetish for the debates that have entranced both Rorty and Putnam, we can recast ourselves and still have a philosophically valuable role to play in society. But this will take time. Joseph Margolis, *Reinventing Pragmatism: American Philosophy at the End of the Twentieth Century* (Ithaca: Cornell University Press, 2002).

5. Stuhr borrows the term "philosophic assassins" from Wallace Stevens's 1942 poem *Parts of a World*. See John Stuhr, *Pragmatism, Postmodernism, and the Future of Philosophy* (New York: Routledge, 2003), 167–68.

6. It is interesting to note the change in Stuhr's estimation of both Dewey and inquiry in his most recent work. Whereas Stuhr was content to criticize Rorty in 1992 for having misread Dewey, and equally content to laud Dewey's talk of philosophy-as-criticism in response to this misreading, he seems no longer willing to do so. Consider Stuhr's comments on Rorty's criticism of Dewey's *Experience and Nature*. "To ask liberals why we shouldn't be cruel need

not be to ask for any transcendental proof. It is a request for liberals to support intelligently their commitments. It is a request for criticism—what Dewey calls 'criticism of criticism.' This request may not be important to like-minded liberal professors who converse principally with one another, but it has been and continues to be important in real struggles and larger cultures. Moreover, to investigate how to avoid cruelty need not be to mouth timeless transcendental principles. It is inquiry into the conditions upon which concrete social relations depend at given times and places" (169). It is unclear to me whether or not, in asking us to leave theory behind, Stuhr is repudiating this earlier position. John Stuhr, "Dewey's Reconstruction of Metaphysics," *Transactions of the Charles Pierce Society* 28, 2, (Spring 1992): 161–76.

7. Daniel Conway has, in an interesting article, called Rorty's preferred way of reading the philosophical past "peritropaic criticism." This is "a turning back upon a dominant tradition of philosophy," and thereby subjects "Dewey himself to the critical scrutiny that he applied to others" (194). In a passage reminiscent of John Stuhr, Conway claims: "Pragmatists, who pride themselves on conducting an unsentimental appraisal of the historical resources arrayed before them, have typically exempted themselves and their charger from this interrogation. Arrogating themselves to an evaluative prerogative that smacks of priestly privilege, pragmatists have been quick to separate themselves and their efforts from the tools and implements they mobilize on behalf of the epoch they represent" (202). Elsewhere, Conway describes what Rorty does as "the self-cancellation of pragmatism" (203). I think that this is correct, and I think that John Stuhr has called for something similar of late. I do not think, however, that this places either theory as it has been worked out here, or inquiry for that matter, in jeopardy. Daniel Conway, "Of Depth and Loss: The Peritropaic Legacy of Dewey's Pragmatism." In *Richard Rorty Vol. II: Sage Masters of Social Thought*, edited by Alan Malachowski, (193–214) (London: Sage, 2002). Joseph Margolis is much less sanguine about Rorty's reading of Dewey, classic pragmatism, and philosophy. Margolis charges Rorty with the attempt "to displace completely the grand canon of Western metaphysics and epistemology, which (as it turns out) cannot find a rhetoric more fundamental or more convincing than Dewey's, in order to turn against Dewey's own acceptance of the continued pertinence of the questions postmodernism would dismiss." Joseph Margolis, *Reinventing Pragmatism: American Philosophy at the End of the Twentieth Century* (Ithaca: Cornell University Press, 2002), 12.

8. Dewey scholars and biographers have dealt with Dewey's reaction to both world wars extensively. Many of these admit that Randolph Bourne was correct: Dewey misread the causes behind the intervention of the United States, and he mistakenly assumed that Germany's military propensities arose from the philosophy of German idealism. Chief among these is Robert Westbrook and Alan Ryan. See further, Robert Westbrook, *John Dewey and Ameri-*

can Democracy (Ithaca: Cornell University Press, 1991), 202–12. See also Alan Ryan, *John Dewey and the High Tide of American Liberalism* (New York: Norton, 1997), 169–73). Westbrook and Ryan do not see Dewey's failure in reconciling his pragmatism with the two wars as evidence of a failure of pragmatism, whereas Bourne does. In what follows, I defend pragmatism from the conclusion that, because Dewey erred in certain of his prescriptions and beliefs, therefore Dewey's version of pragmatism is a failure.

9. In 1915, Dewey wrote a scathing critique of German Idealism, entitled *German Philosophy and Politics*. In this work, Dewey tied the German proclivity for war to Germany's past history of Idealism, and Kant, Fichte, and Hegel, specifically. This book caused a great deal of controversy. At the time, the loudest critic was Ernest Hocking, in an article entitled "Political Philosophy in Germany." Subsequent criticisms have come from Sidney Hook, Robert Westbrook, and Alan Ryan. See further, "German Philosophy and Politics." In *John Dewey: The Middle Works, 1899–1924*, vol. 9, 1915, edited by Jo Ann Boydston, 135–204 (Carbondale: Southern Illinois University Press, 1979). Ernest Hocking, "Political Philosophy in Germany." In *John Dewey: The Middle Works, 1899–1924*, vol. 9, 1915, edited by Jo Ann Boydston, 473–77. (Carbondale: Southern Illinois University Press, 1979). Sidney Hook, "Introduction." In *John Dewey: The Middle Works, 1899–1924*, vol. 9, 1915, edited by Jo Ann Boydston, XI–XXXVI (Carbondale: Southern Illinois University Press, 1979). Robert Westbrook, *John Dewey and American Democracy* (Ithaca: Cornell University Press, 1991), 202–12). Alan Ryan, *John Dewey and the High Tide of American Liberalism*. (New York: Norton, 1997), 169–73).

10. This historical detail comes from Robert Westbrook, who deals extensively with this event. Robert Westbrook, *John Dewey and American Democracy* (Ithaca: Cornell University Press, 1991), 173–82.

11. Richard Rorty has (now famously) castigated the "new left" for theorizing difference rather than attempting to join forces with historically marginalized groups—such as laborers—and has admonished the former for not being willing to engage in deliberate democratic practices. He recommends that scholars get out of the theory business and join forces with those who have a great deal to lose. See Richard Rorty. *Achieving Our Country: Leftist Thought in Twentieth-Century America*. (Cambridge: Harvard University Press, 1998). See esp. 73–110.

12. David Hall suggests that, far from being nonmethodical in his own readings of philosophy and literature, Rorty "provides some significant new content for the term 'inquiry' (213). According to Hall, Rorty "parallel[s] the old distinctions of habit and inquiry" with two sorts of contexts. "One set of contexts is constituted by a new set of attitudes toward sentences already in one's vocabulary, the other by the acquisition of attitudes towards sentences

towards which no attitudes previously existed. Hall labels this 'recontextual-ization'." See David Hall. *Richard Rorty: Prophet and Poet of the New Pragmatism* (Albany: State University of New York Press, 1994).

13. Patriotism for Rorty has nothing to do with nationalism. It is perhaps closest to Dewey's notion of a common faith in humanity, in democracy, though not in inquiry, rather the solidarity that arises from conversing. But the conversation itself is predicated upon a set of shared experiences, which is precisely what seems to be lacking. I think Rorty recognizes this paradox when he says, pessimistically, of participatory democracy that "the cultural left offers no answers to such demands for further information, but until it confronts them it will not be able to be a political Left. The public, sensibly, has no interest in getting rid of capitalism until it is offered details about the alternatives. Nor should it be interested in participatory democracy—the liberation of the people from the power of the technocrats—until it is told how deliberative assemblies will acquire the same know-how which only the technocrats presently possess. Even someone like myself, whose admiration for John Dewey is almost unlimited, cannot take seriously his defense of participatory democracy against Walter Lippmann's insistence on the need for expertise" (104). Rorty, sensibly, comments in an endnote that perhaps he is mistaken about his pessimism. See Richard Rorty, *Achieving Our Country: Leftist Thought in Twentieth-Century America* (Cambridge: Harvard University Press, 1998).

14. Dewey's response to Hans Reichenbach in the *Library of Living Philosophers* volume is instructive here. In commenting on the position that Reichenbach attributes to Dewey, the position that Dewey somehow maintains the "nonreality" of scientific objects, Dewey replies: "I certainly have never intended to say anything which could lead directly or indirectly to a belief that I hold a "non-realistic interpretation of scientific concepts.' On the contrary . . . the actual operative presence of *connections* (which when formulated are *relational*) in the subject-matter of direct experience is an intrinsic part of my experience" (Dewey [1939–1941] 1988, 20). In this way Dewey does support a "realist" position: the relations inhering among logical objects are real.

15. Dewey advocates a variant of "recapitulation theory," originated with Ernst Haeckel, a German embryologist famous for noting that the development of the fetus (allegedly) parallels the development of the (cultural) species. In the 1890s and on into the 1900s, Dewey believed that children learned in part from passing through stages of previous knowledge. At the time, this was a fashionable counter to the "imitation theory," which held that children build up habits through the observation of others. Dewey of course, found this latter theory too facile and underdetermining of children's behavior, which in his estimation, was far more complex and drew on many more sources than simply the imitation of others. Dewey thought there was a biological disposi-

tion to carry out learning, and that this manifested in recapitulating that learn-ing gone on previous.

16. Much of what I have to say is not novel: indeed, most educators who give more than a passing glance at Dewey come to similar conclusions. I sim-ply reinforce these and in so doing, hope to make evident the connection be-tween these and the linkage of growth, community, and democracy.

A Note on the Sources

The author wishes to acknowledge the following sources for permission to in-clude previously published material:

Selections from *The Collected Works of John Dewey*, copyright held by the Board of Trustees, Southern Illinois University, publisher Southern Illinois University Press.

"John Dewey and the Role of Scientific Method in Aesthetic Experi-ence," in *Studies in Philosophy and Education*, Kluwer Academic Publishers, The Netherlands, Vol. 21, No. 1, January 2002, pp. 1–15.

"Authority, Inquiry, and Education: A Response to Dewey's Critics," in *Educational Studies*, Vol. 35, No. 3, June 2004, pp. 230–247.

"Reflections on Richard Shusterman's Dewey," in *Journal of Aesthetic Education*, University of Illinois, Vol. 38, No. 4, Winter 2004, pp. 99–109.

REFERENCES

Alexander, Thomas. *John Dewey's Theory of Art, Experience, and Nature: The Horizons of Feeling*. Albany: State University of New York Press, 1987.
———. "The Aesthetics of Reality: The Development of Dewey's Ecological Theory of Experience." In *Dewey's Logical Theory: New Studies and Interpretations*, 3–26, edited by E. Thomas Burke et al. Nashville: Vanderbilt University Press, 2002.
Ayer, A. J. *Language, Truth, and Logic*. New York: Dover, 1936.
Battacharaya, Nikhil. "John Dewey's Philosophy of Science." *The Philosophical Forum* vii (1976): 106–25.
———. "The Concept of 'Intelligence' in John Dewey's Philosophy and Educational Theory." *Educational Theory* 19, 2 (1969): 185–95.
Bernstein, Richard. *The New Constellation: The Ethico-political Horizons of Modernity/Postmodernity*. Cambridge: MIT Press, 1992.
Boisvert, Raymond. *Dewey's Metaphysics*. New York: Fordham University Press, 1988.
———. "Dewey's Metaphysics: Groundmap of the Prototypically Real." In *Reading Dewey: Interpretations for a Postmodern Generation*, 149–65, edited by Larry Hickman. Bloomington: Indiana University Press, 1995.
———. *John Dewey: Rethinking Our Time*. Albany: State University of New York Press, 1998.
Bourne, Randolph. *War and the Intellectuals: Collected Essays 1915–1919*, edited by Carl Resek. New York: Harper Torchbooks, 1964.
Burke, Tom. *Dewey's New Logic: A Reply to Russell*. Chicago: University of Chicago Press. 1994.
Campbell, James. "Rorty's Use of Dewey." *The Southern Journal of Philosophy* 22 (1984): 175–87.
Cohen, Morris. "Reason, Nature and Professor Dewey." In *John Dewey: The Later Works, 1925–1952*. Vol. 6, 1931–1932, 488–91, edited by Jo Ann Boydston. Carbondale: Southern Illinois University Press, 1985.
———. "Some Difficulties in Dewey's Anthropocentric Naturalism." In *John Dewey: The Later Works, 1925–1952*. Vol. 14, 1939–1941, 379–410, edited by Jo Ann Boydston. Carbondale: Southern Illinois University Press, 1988.
Comte, Auguste. *Philosophie Premiere: Cours De Philosophie Positive, Lecons 1 a 45*. Paris: Hermann, 1975.

Conway, Daniel. "Of Depth and Loss: The Peritropaic Legacy of Dewey's Pragmatism." In *Richard Rorty Vol. II: Sage Masters of Social Thought*, 193–214, edited by Alan Malachowski. London: Sage, 2002.

Dalton, Thomas. *Becoming John Dewey: Dilemmas of a Philosopher and Naturalist*. Bloomington: Indiana University Press, 2002.

D'amico, Alfonso J. *Individuality and Community: The Social and Political Thought of John Dewey*. Gainsville: University of Florida Press, 1978.

Dewey, John. *Lectures on Philosophy of Education, 1899*, edited by Reginald Archambault. New York: Random House, 1966.

———. "My Pedagogic Creed." In *John Dewey: The Early Works, 1882–1898*. Vol. 5, 1895–1898, 84–95, edited by Jo Ann Boydston. Carbondale: Southern Illinois University Press, 1972.

———. "The Reflex-Arc Concept in Psychology." In *John Dewey: The Early Works, 1882–1898*. Vol. 5, 1895–1898, 96–110, edited by Jo Ann Boydston. Carbondale: Southern Illinois University Press, 1972.

———. "Interest in Relation to Training of the Will." In *John Dewey: The Early Works, 1882–1898*. Vol. 5, 1895–1898, 111–50, edited by Jo Ann Boydston. Carbondale: Southern Illinois University Press, 1972.

———. "Plan of Organization of the University Primary School." In *John Dewey: The Early Works, 1882–1898*. Vol. 5, 1895–1898, 223–43, edited by Jo Ann Boydston. Carbondale: Southern Illinois University Press, 1972.

———. "A Pedagogical Experiment." In *John Dewey: The Early Works, 1882–1898*. Vol. 5, 1895–1898, 224–46, edited by Jo Ann Boydston. Carbondale: Southern Illinois University Press, 1972.

———. "The University School." In *John Dewey: The Early Works, 1882–1898*. Vol. 5, 1895–1898, 436–41, edited by Jo Ann Boydston. Carbondale: Southern Illinois University Press, 1972.

———. "The School and Society." In *John Dewey: The Middle Works, 1899–1924*. Vol. 1, 1899–1901, 1–112, edited by Jo Ann Boydston. Carbondale: Southern Illinois University Press, 1976.

———. "The School as Social Centre." In *John Dewey: The Middle Works, 1899–1924*. Vol. 2, 1902–1903, 80–96, edited by Jo Ann Boydston. Carbondale: Southern Illinois University Press, 1976.

———. "The Child and the Curriculum." In *John Dewey: The Middle Works, 1899–1924*. Vol. 2, 1902–1903, 271–92, edited by Jo Ann Boydston. Carbondale: Southern Illinois University Press, 1976.

———. Studies in Logical Theory. In *John Dewey: The Middle Works, 1899–1924*. Vol. 2, 1902–1903, 293–378, edited by Jo Ann Boydston. Carbondale: Southern Illinois University Press, 1976.

———. "The Postulate of Immediate Empiricism." In *John Dewey: The Middle Works, 1899–1924*. Vol. 3, 1903–1906, 158–67, edited by Jo Ann Boydston. Carbondale: Southern Illinois University Press, 1977.

———. "Democracy in Education." In *John Dewey: The Middle Works, 1899–1924.* Vol. 3, 1903–1906, 229–39, edited by Jo Ann Boydston. Carbondale: Southern Illinois University Press, 1977.

———. "How We Think." In *John Dewey: The Middle Works, 1899–1924.* Vol. 6, 1910, 177–356, edited by Jo Ann Boydston. Carbondale: Southern Illinois University Press, 1978.

———. "The Logic of Judgments of Practice." In *John Dewey: The Middle Works, 1899–1924.* Vol. 8, 1912–1914, 14–82, edited by Jo Ann Boydston. Carbondale: Southern Illinois University Press, 1979.

———. "Some Dangers in the Present Movement for Industrial Education." In *John Dewey: The Middle Works, 1899–1924.* Vol. 8, 1912–1914, 98–105, edited by Jo Ann Boydston. Carbondale: Southern Illinois University Press, 1979.

———. "Democracy and Education." In *John Dewey: The Middle Works, 1899–1924.* Vol. 9, 1916, edited by Jo Ann Boydston. Carbondale: Southern Illinois University Press, 1980.

———. "The Need for a Recovery of Philosophy." In *John Dewey: The Middle Works, 1899–1924.* Vol. 10, 1916–1917, 3–48, edited by Jo Ann Boydston. Carbondale: Southern Illinois University Press, 1980.

———. "American Education and Culture." In *John Dewey: The Middle Works, 1899–1924.* Vol. 10, 1916–1917, 196–201, edited by Jo Ann Boydston. Carbondale: Southern Illinois University Press, 1980.

———. "Nationalizing Education." In *John Dewey: The Middle Works, 1899–1924.* Vol. 10, 1916–1917, 202–10, edited by Jo Ann Boydston. Carbondale: Southern Illinois University Press, 1980.

———. "In a Time of National Hesitation." In *John Dewey: The Middle Works, 1899–1924.* Vol. 10, 1916–1917, 256–59, edited by Jo Ann Boydston. Carbondale: Southern Illinois University Press, 1980.

———. "Introduction to Essays in Experimental Logic." In *John Dewey: The Middle Works, 1899–1924.* Vol. 10, 1916–1917, 310–65, edited by Jo Ann Boydston. Carbondale: Southern Illinois University Press, 1980.

———. "What Are We Fighting For?" In *John Dewey: The Middle Works, 1899–1924.* Vol. 11, 1918–1919, 98–106, edited by Jo Ann Boydston. Carbondale: Southern Illinois University Press, 1982.

———. "The Cult of Irrationality." In *John Dewey: The Middle Works, 1899–1924.* Vol. 11, 1918–1919, 107–10, edited by Jo Ann Boydston. Carbondale: Southern Illinois University Press, 1982.

———. "Human Nature and Conduct." In *John Dewey: The Middle Works, 1899–1924.* Vol. 14, 1922, edited by Jo Ann Boydston. Carbondale: Southern Illinois University Press, 1983.

———. "Experience and Nature." In *John Dewey: The Later Works, 1925–*

1952. Vol. 1, 1925, edited by Jo Ann Boydston. Carbondale: Southern Illinois University Press, 1981.

————. "The Public and Its Problems." In *John Dewey: The Later Works, 1925–1952.* Vol. 2, 1925–1927, 235–72, edited by Jo Ann Boydston. Carbondale: Southern Illinois University Press, 1982.

————. "Half-Hearted Naturalism." In *John Dewey: The Later Works, 1925–1952.* Vol. 3, 1927–1928, 73–81, edited by Jo Ann Boydston. Carbondale: Southern Illinois University Press, 1984.

————. "Meaning and Existence." In *John Dewey: The Later Works, 1925–1952.* Vol. 3, 1927–1928, 82–91, edited by Jo Ann Boydston. Carbondale: Southern Illinois University Press, 1984.

————. "The Quest for Certainty." In *John Dewey: The Later Works, 1925–1952.* Vol. 4, 1929, edited by Jo Ann Boydston, Carbondale: Southern Illinois University Press, 1984.

————. "Qualitative Thought." In *John Dewey: The Later Works, 1925–1952.* Vol. 5, 1929–1930, 243–62, edited by Jo Ann Boydston. Carbondale: Southern Illinois University Press, 1984.

————. "The Sources of a Science of Education." In *John Dewey: The Later Works, 1925–1952.* Vol. 5, 1929–1930, 1–40, edited by Jo Ann Boydston. Carbondale: Southern Illinois University Press, 1984.

————. Individualism, Old and New. In *John Dewey: The Later Works, 1925–1952.* Vol. 5, 1929–1930, 41–144, edited by Jo Ann Boydston. Carbondale: Southern Illinois University Press, 1984.

————. "Context and Thought." In *John Dewey: The Later Works, 1925–1952.* Vol. 6, 1931–1932, 3–21, edited by Jo Ann Boydston. Carbondale: Southern Illinois University Press, 1985.

————. "A Philosophy of Scientific Method: Review of Morris R. Cohen's *Reason and Nature: An Essay on the Meaning of Scientific Method.*" In *John Dewey: The Later Works, 1925–1952.* Vol. 6, 1931–1932, 299–303, edited by Jo Ann Boydston. Carbondale: Southern Illinois University Press, 1985.

————. "How We Think." In *John Dewey: The Later Works, 1925–1952.* Vol. 8, 1933, 105–352, edited by Jo Ann Boydston. Carbondale: Southern Illinois University Press, 1986.

————. "The Report of the Special Grievance Committee of the Teachers Union." In *John Dewey: The Later Works, 1925–1952.* Vol. 9, 1933–1934, 320–46, edited by Jo Ann Boydston. Carbondale: Southern Illinois University Press, 1986.

————. "A Common Faith." In *John Dewey: The Later Works, 1925–1952.* Vol. 9, 1933–1934, 1–58, edited by Jo Ann Boydston. Carbondale: Southern Illinois University Press, 1986.

————. "Logic: The Theory of Inquiry." In *John Dewey: The Later Works, 1925–*

1952. Vol. 12, 1938, edited by Jo Ann Boydston. Carbondale: Southern Illinois University Press, 1986.

————. "Art as Experience." In *John Dewey: The Later Works, 1925–1952*. Vol. 10, 1934, edited by Jo Ann Boydston. Carbondale: Southern Illinois University Press, 1987.

————. "Liberalism and Social Action." In *John Dewey: The Later Works, 1925–1952*. Vol. 11, 1935–1937, 3–66, edited by Jo Ann Boydston.Carbondale: Southern Illinois University Press, 1987.

————. "The Dewey School: Appendix 2." In *John Dewey: The Later Works, 1925–1952*. Vol. 11, 1935–1937, 202–16, edited by Jo Ann Boydston. Carbondale: Southern Illinois University Press, 1987.

————. Experience and Education. " In *John Dewey: The Later Works, 1925–1952*. Vol. 13, 1938–1939, 1–62, edited by Jo Ann Boydston. Carbondale: Southern Illinois University Press, 1987.

————. "Freedom and Culture." In *John Dewey: The Later Works, 1925–1952*. Vol. 13, 1938–1939, 63–188, edited by Jo Ann Boydston. Carbondale: Southern Illinois University Press, 1987.

————. "Theory of Valuation." In *John Dewey: The Later Works, 1925–1952*. Vol. 13, 1938–1939, 189–252, edited by Jo Ann Boydston. Carbondale: Southern Illinois University Press, 1987.

————. "Experience, Knowledge and Value: A Rejoinder." In *John Dewey: The Later Works, 1925–1952*. Vol. 14, 1939–1941, 3–90, edited by Jo Ann Boydston. Carbondale: Southern Illinois University Press, 1988.

————. "Philosophy's Future in Our Scientific Age." In *John Dewey: The Later Works, 1925–1952*. Vol. 16, 1946–1948, 369–82, edited by Jo Ann Boydston. Carbondale: Southern Illinois University Press, 1989.

Dewey, John, and Arthur Bentley. "Knowing and the Known." In *John Dewey: The Later Works, 1925–1952*. Vol. 16, 1946–1948, 1–294, edited by Jo Ann Boydston. Carbondale: Southern Illinois University Press, 1989.

Dewey, Robert. *The Philosophy of John Dewey: A Critical Exposition of His Method, Metaphysics, and Theory of Knowledge*. The Hague: Martinus Nijhoff, 1977.

Diggins, John Patrick. *The Promise of Pragmatism: Modernism and the Crisis of Knowledge and Authority*. Chicago: University of Chicago Press, 1994.

————. "Pragmatism and Its Limits." *The Revival of Pragmatism: New Essays on Social Thought, Law, and Culture*, 206–31, edited by Morris Dickstein. Durham: Duke University Press, 1998.

Dykhuizen, George. *The Life and Mind of John Dewey*. Carbondale: Southern Illinois University Press, 1973.

Eames, Morris. "Primary Experience in the Philosophy of John Dewey." *The Monist* 48, 3 (1964): 407–18.

Eames, Morris, and Elizabeth Eames. "The Leading Principles of Pragmatic Naturalism." *The Personalist* 43 (Summer 1962): 322–37.

Edwards, Anna Camp, and Katherine Camp Mayhew. *The Dewey School.* New York: Atherton, 1938.

Eldridge, Michael. *Transforming Experience: John Dewey's Cultural Instrumentalism.* Nashville: Vanderbilt University Press, 1998.

———. "The Teachers Union Fight and the Scope of Dewey's Logic." In *Dewey's Logical Theory: New Studies and Interpretations,* 262–74, edited by T. Burke et al. Nashville: Vanderbilt University Press, 2002.

Feinberg, Walter. "The Conflict between Intelligence and Community in Dewey's Educational Philosophy." *Educational Theory* 19, 4 (1969): 236–48.

———. "Educational Manifestos and the New Fundamentalism." *Educational Researcher* 26, 8 (November 1997): 27–36.

Festenstein, Matthew. *Pragmatism and Political Theory: From Dewey to Rorty.* Chicago: University of Chicago Press, 1995.

Flexner, Abraham. *I Remember: The Autobiography of Abraham Flexner.* New York: Simon and Schuster, 1940.

Garrison, Jim. "Realism, Deweyan Pragmatism, and Educational Research." *Educational Researcher* 23 (January–February 1994): 5–14.

———. *Dewey and Eros: Wisdom and Desire in the Art of Teaching.* New York: Teacher's College Press, 1997.

———. "Dewey on the Virtues of Method/s." In *Philosophy of Education 1998,* 356–358, edited by Steven Tozer, Urbana: Philosophy of Education Society, 1999.

Garrison, Jim, and Immaneul Shargel. "Dewey's Experience and Nature and Husserl's Crisis: A Surprising Convergence of Themes." In *Philosophy of Education 1986,* 256–64, edited by Nicholas Burbules. Urbana: Philosophy of Education Society, 1987.

Gouinlock, J. "Rorty's Interpretation of Dewey." In *Rorty and Pragmatism: The Philosopher Responds to His Critics,* 71–90, edited by Herman Saatkamp, Jr. Nashville: Vanderbilt University Press, 1995.

Hegel, G. W. F. "Phanomenologie des Geistes." In *Werke,* edited by E. Moldenhauer and K. M. Michel. Frankfurt: Suhrkamp Verlag, 1970–1971.

———. "Wissenschaft Der Logik I." In *Werke,* edited by E. Moldenhauer and K. M. Michel. Frankfurt: Suhrkamp Verlag, 1970–1971.

———. "Grundlinien der Philosophie des Rechts." In *Werke,* edited by E. Moldenhauer and K. M. Michel. Frankfurt: Suhrkamp Verlag, 1970–1971.

Hickman, Larry. *Philosophical Tools for Technological Culture: Putting Pragmatism to Work.* Bloomington: Indiana University Press, 2001.

Hildebrand, David. *Beyond Realism and Antirealism: John Dewey and the Neopragmatists.* Nashville: Vanderbilt University Press, 2003.

Hirsch, E. D. *Cultural Literacy: What Every American Needs to Know*. New York: Vintage, 1987.

———. *The Schools We Need and Why We Don't Have Them*. New York: Doubleday, 1996.

Hofstadter, Richard. *Anti-intellectualism in American Life*. New York: Knopf, 1963.

Hook, Sydney. *John Dewey: An Intellectual Portrait*. New York: John Day, 1939.

Jackson, Phillip. *The Practice of Teaching*. New York: Teacher's College Press, 1986.

———. *John Dewey and the Lessons of Art*. New Haven: Yale University Press, 1998.

———. *John Dewey and Philosophic Method*. New York: Teacher's College Press, 2001.

Joas, Hans. *Die Entstehung der Werte*. Frankfurt: Surkamp Verlag, 1997.

Karier, Clarence. *Man, Society, and Education*. New York: Free Press, 1968.

———. "Introduction." In *Roots of Crisis: American Education in the Twentieth Century*, 1–30, edited by Clarence Karier et al. New York: Rand McNally, 1973.

———. "Liberal Ideology and the Quest for Social Change." In *Roots of Crisis: American Education in the Twentieth Century*, 84–110, edited by Clarence Karier et al. New York: Rand McNally, 1973.

———. "Making the World Safe for Democracy: An Historical Critique of John Dewey's Pragmatic Liberal Philosophy in the Welfare State." *Educational Theory* 27, 1 (1977): 2–45.

———. *The Individual, Society, and Education*, 2d ed. New York: Free Press, 1986.

Kaufmann, Felix. "John Dewey's Theory of Inquiry." In *John Dewey: Philosopher of Science and Freedom*, 217–29, edited by Sidney Hook. Westport: Greenwood, 1950.

Kincaid, Herbert. "Positivism in Social Science." In *Routledge Encyclopedia of Philosophy*, Vol. 7, 558–61, edited by Edward Craig. London: Routledge, 1998.

Lamont, Corliss. *Dialogue on John Dewey*. New York: Horizon, 1959.

Lasch, Christopher. "The Cultural Cold War." In *Towards a New Past*, edited by Barton J. Bernstein. New York: Pantheon, 1968.

Lavine, T. Z. "America and the Constestations of Modernity: Dewey, Bentley, Rorty." In *Rorty and Pragmatism: The Philosopher Responds to His Critics*, edited by Herman Saatkamp, Jr. Nashville: Vanderbilt University Press, 1995.

Manicas, Peter. "Pragmatic Philosophy of Science and the Charge of Scientism." *Transactions of the Charles S. Peirce Society* 24, 2 (1988): 179–222.

Margolis, Joseph. *Reinventing Pragmatism: American Philosophy at the End of the Twentieth Century*. Ithaca: Cornell University Press, 2002.

McCarthy, Christine. "Why Be Critical? (or Rational, or Moral?): On the Justification of Critical Thinking." In *Philosophy of Education 1992*, 59–69, edited by H. A. Alexander. Urbana: Philosophy of Education Society, 1993.

———. "Probabilistic Reasoning and Teaching for Critical Thinking." In *Philosophy of Education 1993*, 225–34, edited by Audrey Thompson. Urbana: Philosophy of Education Society, 1994.

———. "When You Know It and I Know It, What Is It We Know? Pragmatic Realism and the Epistemologically Absolute." In *Philosophy of Education Society 1996*, 21–29, edited by Frank Margonis. Urbana: Philosophy of Education Society, 1997.

———. "Dewey's Ethics: Philosophy or Science?" *Educational Theory* 49, 3 (1999): 339–59.

McCarthy, Christine, and Evelyn Sears. "Science Education: Constructing a True View of the Real World?" In *Philosophy of Education 2000*, 369–77, edited by Lynda Stone. Urbana: Philosophy of Education Society, 2001.

———. "Deweyan Pragmatism and the Quest for True Belief." *Educational Theory* 50, 2 (2000): 213–28.

Meier, Deborah. *The Power of Their Ideas: Lessons for America from a Small School in Harlem*. Boston: Beacon, 1995.

Meier, Deborah, and Paul Schwartz. "Central Park East Secondary School: The Hard Part Is Making It Happen." In *Democratic Schools: Lessons from the Chalk Face*, edited by Michael W. Apple and James E. Beane. Buckingham: Open University Press, 1999.

Moore, Harold. "Dewey and the Philosophy of Science." In *Man and World Vol. 5*, 158–68. The Hague: Martinus Nijhoff. 1972.

Mounce, H. O. *The Two Pragmatisms: From Peirce to Rorty*. London: Routledge, 1997.

Nagel, Ernest. *On the Logic of Measurement*. New York: Columbia University Press, 1930.

———. "Can Logic Be Divorced from Ontology?" In *John Dewey: The Later Works, 1925–1953*, Vol. 5, 1929–1930, 453–60, edited by Jo Ann Boydston. Carbondale: Southern Illinois University Press, 1984.

———. *Sovereign Reason and Other Studies in the Philosophy of Science*. Glencoe: Free Press, 1954.

———. *The Structure of Science: Problems in the Logic of Scientific Explanation*. New York: Harcourt, Brace and World, 1961.

———. "Introduction." In *John Dewey: The Later Works, 1925–1953*, Vol. 12, 1938, vii–xxv, edited by Jo Ann Boydston. Carbondale: Southern Illinois University Press, 1986.

Noddings, Nel. *Philosophy of Education*. Boulder: Westview, 1995.

Paringer, William Andrew. *John Dewey and the Paradox of Liberal Reform*. Albany: SUNY Press, 1990.

Peters, R. S. *Essays on Educators*. London: George Unwin and Allen, 1981.

Phillips, Alan. *Dewey and Scheffler on the Relationship of Learning and Inquiry*. UMI Dissertation Services: Ann Arbor, 1999.

Phillips, D. C. *Holistic Thought in Social Science*. Stanford: Stanford University Press, 1976.

————. *Philosophy, Science, and Social Inquiry: Contemporary Methodological Controversies in Social Science and Related Applied Fields of Research*. Oxford: Pergamon, 1987.

Phillips. D. C. and, Nicholas C. Burbules. *Postpositivism and Educational Research*. Lanham: Rowman and Littlefield, 2000.

Quine, W. V. O. *From a Logical Point of View: Nine Logico-Philosophical Essays*, 2d ed. Cambridge: Harvard University Press, 1980.

Quinton, Anthony. "Inquiry, Thought and Action: John Dewey's Theory of Knowledge and Inquiry." In *John Dewey as Educator*, 1–17, edited by R. S. Peters. London: Routledge, 1971.

Ravitch, Diane. *The Revisionists Revised: A Critique of the Radical Attack on the Schools*. New York: Basic, 1978.

————. *The Troubled Crusade: American Education 1945–1980*. New York: Basic, 1983.

————. *The Schools We Deserve: Reflections on the Educational Crises of Our Time*. New York: Basic, 1985.

————. *Left Back: A Century of Battles over School Reform*. New York: Touchstone, 2000.

Reichenbach, Hans. "The Verifiability Theory of Meaning." In *Readings in the Philosophy of Science*, 93–102, edited by Herbert Feigl and May Brodbeck. New York: Appleton-Century Crofts, 1953.

Rorty, Richard. *Consequences of Pragmatism*. Minneapolis: University of Minnesota Press, 1982.

————. "Introduction." In *John Dewey: The Later Works, 1899–1924*. Vol. 8, 1933, ix–xxxi, edited by Jo Ann Boydston. Carbondale: Southern Illinois University Press, 1986.

————. *Contingency, Irony, Solidarity*. Cambridge: Cambridge University Press, 1989.

————. *Objectivity, Relativism, and Truth: Philosophical Papers Vol. 1*. Cambridge: Cambridge University Press, 1991.

————. "Response to Gouinlock." In *Rorty and Pragmatism: The Philosopher Responds to His Critics*, 91–99, edited by Herman Saatkamp, Jr. Nashville: Vanderbilt University Press, 1995.

————. *Truth and Progress: Philosophical Papers Vol. 3*. Cambridge: Cambridge University Press, 1998.

———. *Achieving Our Country: Leftist Thought in Twentieth-Century America*. Cambridge: Harvard University Press, 1998.

———. *Philosophy and Social Hope*. London: Penguin, 1999.

Rosenthal. Sandra. "John Dewey: Scientific Method and Lived Immediacy. In *Transactions of the Charles S. Peirce Society* 17, 4. (1981): 148–56.

Russell, Bertrand. *The Analysis of Matter*. New York: Dover, 1955.

———. "Reply to Criticisms." In *The Philosophy of Bertrand Russell*. 2d ed. 679–42, edited by Paul Schilpp. New York: Open Court, 1971.

———. "Professor Dewey's 'Essays in Experimental Logic.'" In *Dewey and His Critics: Essays from The Journal of Philosophy*, 231–52, edited by Sidney Morgenbesser. New York: Journal of Philosophy, Inc. 1977.

———. *The History of Western Philosophy*. London: Unwin. 1979.

———. "Dewey's New Logic." In *The Philosophy of John Dewey*. 3d ed., 137–56, edited by Paul Schilpp and Louis Hahn. New York: Open Court, 1989.

Ryan, Alan. *John Dewey and the High Tide of American Liberalism*. New York: Norton, 1997.

———. "Deweyan Pragmatism and American Education." *Philosophers on Education: New Historical Perspectives*, 394–410, edited by Amelie Oksenberg Rorty. London: Routledge, 1998.

Savage, Daniel. *John Dewey's Liberalism: Individual, Community, and Self-Development*. Carbondale: Southern Illinois University Press, 2001.

Scheffler, Israel. *Reason and Teaching*. New York: Bobbs-Merrill, 1973.

———. *Four Pragmatists*. New York: Routledge and Kegan Paul, 1974.

———. "Making and Understanding," In *Philosophy of Education 1987*, 65–78, edited by Barbara Arnstine and Donald Arnstine. Urbana: Philosophy of Education Society, 1988.

Schutz, Aaron. "John Dewey's Conundrum: Can Democratic Schools Empower?" In *Teachers College Record* 103, 2 (2001): 267–302.

Sellars, Wilfred. *Empiricism and the Philosophy of Mind*. Cambridge: Harvard University Press, 1997.

Shlick, Moritz. "Positivism and Realism." In *Logical Positivism*, 83–107, edited by A. J. Ayer. New York: Free Press, 1946.

Shook, John. *Dewey's Emprical Theory of Knowledge and Reality*. Nashville: Vanderbilt University Press, 2000.

Sleeper, Ralph. *The Necessity of Pragmatism*. Ithaca: Cornell University Press, 1986.

Stengel, Barbara. "Dewey on Method/s." *Philosophy of Education 1998*, 346–52, edited by Steven Tozer. Urbana: Philosophy of Education Society, 1999.

Stuhr, John. "Dewey's Reconstruction of Metaphysics." *Transactions of the Charles S. Peirce Society* 28, 2 (Spring 1992): 161–76.

———. "Power/Inquiry: The Logic of Pragmatism." In *Dewey's Logical Theory: New Studies and Interpretations*, 275–86, edited by E. Thomas Burke et al. Nashville: Vanderbilt University Press, 2002.

———. *Pragmatism, Postmodernism, and the Future of Philosophy*. New York: Routledge, 2003.

Tanner, Laurel. *Dewey Laboratory School: Lessons for Today*. New York: Teacher's College Press, 1997.

Tiles, J. E. *Dewey*. London: Routledge, 1990.

———. "Dewey's Realism: Applying the Term 'Mental' in a World without Withins." In *Transactions of the Charles S. Peirce Society* 31, 1 (1995): 137–66.

Villemain, F., and N. Champlin. "Frontiers for an Experimentalist Philosophy of Education." In *Art Education*, 445–53, edited by Elliot Eisner and David Ecker. Stanford: Stanford University Press, 1967.

Waks, Leonard. "Experimentalism and the Flow of Experience," *Educational Theory* 26, 2 (1998): 1–19.

———."Postexperimentalist Pragmatism," *Studies in Philosophy of Education* 29, 1 (1998): 7–28.

Webber, Julie. "Why Can't We Be Deweyan Citizens?" *Educational Theory* 51, 2 (2001): 71–90.

Westbrook, Robert. *John Dewey and American Democracy*. Ithaca: Cornell University Press, 1991.

———. "Schools for Industrial Democrats: The Social Origins of John Dewey's Philosophy of Education." *American Journal of Education* 100 (August 1992): 401–18.

White, Morton. *The Revolt against Formalism*. Boston: Beacon, 1957.

———. *Science and Sentiment in America: Philosophical Thought from Jonathan Edwards to John Dewey*. New York: Oxford University Press, 1972.

———. *Pragmatism and the American Mind: Essays and Reviews in Philosophy and Intellectual History*. New York: Oxford University Press, 1973.

———. *A Philosophy of Culture: The Scope of Holistic Pragmatism*. Princeton: Princeton University Press, 2002.

Williams, Michael. *Problems of Knowledge: A Critical Introduction to Epistemology*. Oxford: Oxford University Press, 2001.

Wirth, Arthur. *John Dewey as Educator: His Design for Work in Education (1894–1904)*. New York: Wiley, 1966.

INDEX